GPS Mapping

GPS Mapping
Make Your Own Maps

Rich Owings
TEN MILE PRESS
FORT BRAGG, CALIFORNIA

Although the author and publisher have made every effort to ensure the accuracy and completeness of information contained in this book, they assume no responsibility for errors, inaccuracies, omissions, or any inconsistency herein. Any slights of people, places, or companies are unintentional.

Outdoor/recreation organizations and corporations: Take 40% off and use our books as fundraisers, premiums, or gifts. Please contact the publisher:

Ten Mile Press
633 North Harrison Street
Fort Bragg, CA 95437
707.972.8082
info@TenMilePress.com
www.TenMilePress.com

Library of Congress Control Number: 2005900914
ISBN: 0-9760926-3-8

Cover by Elizabeth Petersen
Interior design by Meg Coughlin, megcoughlindesign.com
Edited by Lisa Gluskin Stonestreet, ampedit.com

Acknowledgements

Digital mapping is a complex and diverse subject, and I depended upon a number of individual reviewers to ensure the technical accuracy of this book. Thanks go to Doug Adomatis, Scott Alexander, Shane Burrows, Kris Nosack, and Richard Smith for their help in this regard. Especially helpful was John Galvin, who took the time to review and comment on an early draft of each and every chapter. This book would not be what it is without their valuable input and insights.

I also want to thank the online mapping community for teaching me so much, especially the Yahoo Ozi Users and Map Authors discussion groups. And thanks to the companies that provided hardware and software for testing—DeLorme, Fugawi, Garmin, Global Mapper, Lowrance, Magellan, Maptech, National Geographic, TopoFusion, and TopoGrafix.

My wife Lisa was incredibly supportive throughout the entire process, and took on several major roles related to production of this book. Without her encouragement and support, this project would never have been realized. More important, though, is how grateful I am to have her as my partner in outdoor adventure. Whether climbing steep abandoned logging roads on mountain bikes, rappelling into slimy potholes in slot canyons, or backpacking at high elevations, she is always there, exploring with me all that this world has to offer.

I want to thank a few others who have inspired my love of maps and quest for adventure. Sparrel Wood was my partner on my first mountain bike rides, joining me in the quest to explore new terrain (which we'd highlight on topo maps as "blue line"). Scott Philyaw first piqued my interest in cartography with his map of the Great Smoky Mountains National Park. Ron Lance, a consummate outdoorsman, led me on my first expeditions into truly wild and remote areas such as the Horsepasture River gorge. I also want to thank Gary Spry, who, with a family geocaching trip, helped me get over my initial bias against GPS. Last, but certainly not least, I want to thank my mom, Ruth Owings, for passing along her love of exploring the outdoors.

Table of Contents

Section One Getting Started
Chapter 1 Making Your Own Maps

It's hard to believe my initial resistance to getting a global positioning system (GPS) receiver. After all, I thoroughly enjoyed paper maps, and I rarely used a compass. Instead, I was fascinated with reading the land. It felt great to take a topographic map and translate what I saw on paper into the landscape before me. I felt a kind of snobbery toward the techies who relied on GPS, imagining they would get lost if their batteries died. Don't get me wrong; I was no Luddite—not at work, where I knew as much as anyone about computers, nor at home, where computers and high-tech toys seemed to appear faster than our checkbook could handle them.

My anti-GPS bias changed one Christmas when I traveled east to visit family. My nephew gave his wife a GPS, though I think he was the one who really wanted it. I love the outdoors, so when they asked, "Want to go geocaching?" they didn't have to ask twice. After that trip, I was hooked on GPS. My wife, who is also my outdoor adventure partner, had just as much fun.

I then bought a fairly basic GPS, a Garmin Etrex Venture. Deciding which GPS to buy wasn't difficult. But figuring out if and how I could connect it to my computer was another matter. The GPS came with a cable for this purpose, but the documentation didn't specify what kind of software I would need. Buying the GPS was costly enough, and since I couldn't afford an expensive software package right away, I made do with shareware. The first shareware I tried was USAPhotoMaps, which offered GPS interface capabilities and free topographical maps and aerial photos of the entire United States. When I wanted to do more waypoint and route management, I downloaded EasyGPS. Both of these free software packages are covered in subsequent chapters.

The first big trip my wife and I took with our new GPS was to Utah's San Rafael Swell, a maze of slot canyons that, though portions were proposed as a national park in the mid-1930s, remains unprotected and in the hands of the Bureau of Land Management. The trip was pretty much a washout: The threat of rain kept us out of the canyons for the most part, and gale-force winds sandblasted us with red rock dust. We did manage to get in a technical descent of Music Canyon and a nice mountain bike ride before being driven from the desert. During our exit up Music Canyon, my wife commandeered the GPS to keep watch on our position, upcoming landmarks, and our estimated time of return. It seemed we had both caught the GPS bug.

Back home, I was ready to put the GPS to use on our weekly mountain bike rides. I wanted software that included maps of our area, but was once again confronted with a confusing array of choices: Would it have to be Garmin software since that was my GPS brand? What could I do with the software once I bought it?

I ultimately decided to go with National Geographic's TOPO!, spending $100 for the software for our state. I immediately started having fun with it, using it to guide us to locations and, when we returned, overlaying onto a map the GPS's "track" showing where we'd been. It was a real kick the first time I was able to pinpoint a trail location more accurately than the U.S. Geological Survey!

Before long, I had graduated to more sophisticated software. I live near extensive timberlands. Some of the corporations that own the land tacitly allow public access to hundreds of miles of old logging roads, which makes for ideal mountain biking. Soon I was using various electronic and paper sources to transfer roads to my maps, creating a highly accurate base map for our area. I even managed to add land ownership boundaries, first sketching them into TOPO! and later transferring them to other programs from geographic information system (GIS) data I found online.

Before long I was downloading free USGS maps and aerial photos. This kept me from having to pay for another set of state CDs for our next trip to Utah. I could also use recent aerial photos to find and place roads that weren't on maps. I could even generate 3-D images from topographic maps and aerial photos. I was having a blast.

Why Use Mapping Software?

It's fun to create your own maps to use with your GPS—but there are also plenty of practical reasons to do so.

Improved waypoint and route management top the list of reasons for making your own maps. Keying waypoint coordinates into the tiny screen on your GPS is a pain in the rear, and it's fraught with opportunities for error. Typing them into your computer is much easier and faster. Often you can bypass this step entirely by simply clicking on the map where you want to establish a waypoint.

Another reason for creating your own maps is that many GPS units limit you to 500 waypoints. What happens when you exceed that number? With most mapping software, this is no longer a problem. The extra waypoints are stored on your computer until you need them. There you can easily organize them, creating files for your favorite river basin or for that upcoming vacation.

Route management is another task that mapping software makes easy. Instead of having to use your GPS's onscreen keyboard or scroll through a long list of waypoints, you just click a waypoint on a map or drag and drop a waypoint into a list. What is painful with your GPS becomes a breeze on your computer. Waypoint and route management are covered in more detail in the chapters on specific software and in Chapter 6.

With the exception of mouse-type GPS units made to connect to PDAs, all handheld GPS units record tracks, those breadcrumb-like trails that mark where you have traveled. Although they have some use in the field, allowing your GPS to direct you back over the route you took, these tracks become powerful tools when downloaded from your GPS to your PC. Perhaps the road you jogged today isn't even on a USGS map (they're updated only every twenty years or so). Download your track from your GPS when you get home and you instantly have a current map, along with a record of your trip. Want to see how many miles you covered or how much elevation you gained? Find out quickly and easily when you connect your GPS to a computer.

Almost all of the programs discussed in this book support the two-way transfer of waypoints, routes, and tracks between your GPS and computer. They're great aids for trip planning and map preparation, and for creating records and analyzing trips after you return.

Deciding What Type of Software You Need

It would be nice if cost and features were the only things to consider when deciding which mapping software to use. Unfortunately, this is not the case.

Some of the more user-friendly mapping packages provide you with all the USGS 1:24,000-scale topographical maps for your state or region for around $100. Other software lets you download those same maps for free. The key word here is "download." If you have broadband, such programs—which include everything from the simple and straightforward USAPhotoMaps to the more complex and complete OziExplorer—can be an attractive option. Though they can be used with dialup connections, downloads take much more time.

Many users who don't have broadband access turn to maps on CD. If you want simplicity, rarely travel far, and don't mind spending $100, a package that includes all the maps for your state may be an excellent choice.

Another factor to consider is moving maps. Do you want to be able to track your position in real time with a laptop or personal digital assistant (PDA)? While it won't really help you on the trail (without a Sherpa toting a lot of extra batteries), it may help you find that isolated trailhead on a poorly marked national forest road—not to mention that cool Vietnamese restaurant in the city. And speaking of cool, there's nothing like having your PDA or laptop audibly tell you where and when to turn. Programs with moving-map capabilities are discussed in the individual software chapters, and PDA-based programs are covered in Chapter 22.

Table 1.
Feature comparison chart. Please note that some features not present in the tested version are planned for upcoming releases. See specific software chapters for details.

	Cost	Demo	Entire US	3-D	Aerial Photos	Moving Map	PDA Module[d]	Printing	Shape File Import
USA PhotoMaps	Free	Yes	Yes	No	Yes	Yes	No	Minimal	No
National Geographic TOPO!	$99.95[a]	No	No	Yes[e]	No	Yes	Yes	Yes	No
Terrain Navigator	$99.95[a]	Yes	No	Yes	No	Yes	Yes	Yes	No
Terrain Navigator Pro	$299.95[a]	Yes	No	Yes	$[c]	Yes	Yes	Yes	No
3-D Topo Quads	$99.95[a]	No	No	Yes	$ (satellite)[c]	Yes	Yes	Yes	No
Topo USA	$99.95	No	Yes	Yes	$[c]	Yes	Yes	Yes	No
TopoFusion	$40.00	Yes	Yes	Yes	Yes	Yes	No	No	No
Expert GPS	$59.95	Yes	Yes	No	Yes	Yes	No	Yes	No
OziExplorer	$85.00	Yes	Download[b]	Yes	Download[b]	Yes	Yes	Yes	Yes
Fugawi	$99.00	Yes	Download[b]	No	Download[b]	Yes	Yes	Yes	No
Garmin MapSource	$116.65	No	Yes	No	No	Yes	Yes	Yes	No
Magellan MapSend	$149.99	No	Yes	No	No	Yes	No	Yes	No
Lowrance MapCreate	$99.95	No	Yes	No	No	No	No	Yes	No

a – These costs are per state or region. Some packages are available at lower cost for limited areas, such as when several national parks are grouped together.

b – Maps and aerial photos must be downloaded online, typically for free. They can also be purchased on CD.

c – Aerial photos are available at extra cost. There is no charge with Terrain Navigator Pro until year two.

d – Costs and capabilities in this area vary dramatically. Refer to Chapter 22 for more information.

e – An expansion pack is required, at a cost of $19.95.

Finally, how much fun do you want to have on rainy days when you aren't in the backcountry? Some software programs offer 3-D capabilities that, when combined with aerial photos, offer the next best thing to actually being there. And don't get hung up on making a single choice. Until the perfect software comes along, you may find that a combination of several programs best serves your needs. Table 1 offers a comparison of features, but don't rely on it alone. As they say, the devil is in the details. A program may have a feature you want, but that doesn't mean it's simple and intuitive.

In summary: A GPS alone is nice, but a GPS in combination with a desktop computer and free or low-cost mapping software extends your capabilities dramatically. You may never need to buy a map again.

Using This Book

You are about to embark on a grand adventure. On this journey you'll learn about mapping software that lets you locate waypoints before a trip and generate maps to help you pinpoint your location in the field. And when you come back home, you'll be able to download all the information you collected and see the actual route you took. The chapters ahead will focus on what you can do with your GPS and computer. If you need more basic information on how to use your GPS, take a look at the books listed in the bibliography. This book, unlike those listed in the bibliography, assumes you have a working knowledge of using waypoints, routes, and tracks. Even so, most people who have just purchased a GPS will find a wealth of useful information here.

Even though many of the software packages discussed here focus on the U.S., readers of other nations will also find useful information. International mapping enthusiasts frequently turn to OziExplorer and Fugawi, the subjects of Section Four, which accept a wide range of map file formats from around the globe. You can also construct maps for other countries from GIS files, as discussed in Chapter 23, and create international maps for your GPS, using the methods found in Chapter 24.

Another thing to keep in mind: This book focuses on PC applications, simply because there are so many PC-based mapping programs on the market and so few for the Macintosh. There is, however, a brief section on mapping resources for Mac users at the end of Chapter 3.

In addition, as GPS technology becomes more commonplace, all sorts of uses and models have been showing up in the marketplace. Marine GPS units, dedicated automotive navigation devices, and the like are beyond the scope of this book.

Finally, please note that all prices and descriptions listed here are as of the time of printing; please check company Web sites for any changes.

Following a few introductory chapters, we'll look at several free mapping and waypoint-management software packages that are so useful they should be in almost everyone's mapping arsenal. These are discussed in Chapters 5 and 6. The next section of the book, Maps on CDs, deals with user-friendly consumer software that, in general, covers a single state or region. Section Three, Downloading Maps: More Microsoft TerraServer-Based Programs, investigates two programs that allow you to download maps and aerial photos for the entire United States. Section Four, Downloading Maps: Free Maps from USGS and Other Sources, delves into a more involved process that gives you access to powerful mapmaking tools. Section Five, GPS-Based Maps, looks at the latest generation of hand-held mapping tools that put detailed topographic maps on your GPS screen. Finally, Section Six, Power Mapping, explores aerial photos, satellite imagery, 3-D applications, Palm- and Pocket PC-based moving maps, geographic information systems (GIS), making your own GPS-based maps, and moving data between programs.

Like most readers, you may be more interested in some chapters than others. But I encourage you to carefully read the introductory remarks at the start of each section. Even if you'll primarily use a single mapping program, the tools covered elsewhere may be of interest.

The software chapters provide the following information:

- **Basic Information.** This covers software costs, system requirements, GPS compatibility, contact information, additional options that may be available, and Internet resources such as online discussion groups focused on a particular brand of software.

- **Advantages** and **Disadvantages.** This covers unique features found in each program, or common features missing from it, that make it stand out from the competition. Many features common to a software group are covered in the introduction to each section, so don't rely solely on the advantages and disadvantages discussed in the individual chapters.

  Remember, most of the software in this book is updated frequently, and any disadvantages are sure to be on the radar screen of the designers. Be sure to check the software companies' Web sites for information about new releases and upgrades before basing a purchase decision on any information you read here.

- **Tutorial/Manual.** This section lets you know if the software you're considering includes a tutorial, where to find the help files, and just how useful those components are.

- **Installation and Configuration.** Here you will learn where to change coordinate formats, set up your brand of GPS, and, in some cases, do much more.

- **Getting Started.** Here's where the fun begins. You'll learn how to move around a map and zoom in and out.

- **File Structure.** As you get more involved with computerized mapping, you'll probably want to know where the software stores information on your computer. You'll find that information here, along with tips for organizing map data.

- **Waypoints and Waypoint Management, Routes**, and **Tracks.** Here you will learn each program's unique way of placing, editing, and managing these critical items.

- **Printing.** These pages give you tips and tricks for creating the most useful field maps.

- **Moving Map.** Here we explore the capabilities of programs that provide real-time location tracking on a laptop. Similar PDA-based applications are covered in Chapter 22.

- **3-D.** Where a program offers 3-D capabilities, these features are discussed in detail. Look for more information on 3-D in Chapter 21.

- **Working With Other Programs.** This is where you can learn how to import and export data such as waypoint files.

- **More Tips.** Here you'll find tips and tricks that will make you a power user.

The order of some of these items may vary, depending upon the design of the application discussed.

Finally, be sure to visit **www.MakeYourOwnMaps.com** regularly, for updates to the information presented in this book.

Disclaimer!
Computers and people are both fragile and prone to damage. Use good sense when you're out in the wilderness and when you make changes to your computer. I wish both you and your computer a long and healthy life!

Updates to this book will be posted at www.MakeYourOwnMaps.com.
Bookmark and visit often to see what's new in the world of digital mapping.

Chapter 2 GPS: A Short Course

A wide array of GPS units, designed for ever-expanding purposes, appears continually in today's marketplace. Though an exhaustive review of this quickly evolving hardware is not possible here, we should look at a few of the choices you face.

The entry point is a basic GPS unit, which may be all you ever need. Review the capabilities as you shop, though. A bottom-of-the-line $100 unit may allow you to store only one route, while spending another $50 may allow you to store 20 routes.

If cost is not a critical factor, you may prefer a more advanced unit that can display the type of detailed maps we review in Sections Five and Six.

If you're an outdoor recreation type, you'll typically use a conventional handheld GPS, though new models (such as the Garmin ForeRunner) are designed to be worn while running.

There are also GPS units for PDAs. These units come in various forms: They can be built in, they can be mouse-type receivers, or they can slide into a Compact Flash (CF) expansion slot. But PDAs tend to go through batteries more quickly than stand-alone GPS units do, and they aren't built for rugged outdoor use. PDA/GPS combinations are better used in vehicles for moving maps, where an alternative power source is available. An advantage of a stand-alone GPS unit is that you always have the option of connecting it to a PDA or laptop, giving you a moving map that tracks your position as you drive.

Safety First

Never rely on your GPS alone for navigation; always carry a compass and waterproof map. GPS units don't work under dense canopy, in canyons, or in other locations without a clear view of the sky.

When you first get your GPS, try it out under real-life conditions. Before depending on it in the wilderness, learn to use it at night in the rain in your own neighborhood.

Always carry spare batteries. (I like to carry my spares in the plastic clamshell cases many lithium batteries come in; they snap shut and secure the batteries nicely.)

Remember Murphy's Law... anything that can go wrong will go wrong. The corollary is that it will go wrong at the worst possible time. Also keep in mind the Boy Scout motto, and be prepared!

Waypoints, Routes, and Tracks

This book assumes you have a working knowledge of navigating with your GPS. If you haven't learned your way around your GPS, I urge you to pick up one or more of the excellent references listed in the Bibliography.

Let's review some basic GPS terminology:

- **Waypoints.** A waypoint is a location, in the form of coordinates, that is stored in your GPS. Each waypoint has a name or number associated with it.

- **Routes.** Routes are used for navigation; they are about where you are going. A route is a series of waypoints you select and then follow to your chosen destination. The distance between two waypoints along a route is called a leg.

Autorouting

Autorouting is more typically found in automotive navigation software. Autorouting software automatically creates a route for you, using a starting point, a destination, and perhaps some stops along the way that you select. The only autorouting program discussed in this book is DeLorme's TopoUSA, the subject of Chapter 11. If you think you might purchase automotive navigation software with autorouting, make sure your GPS supports this feature.

- **Tracks.** Tracks are about where you've been. People often use the term "breadcrumb trail," a la Hansel and Gretel, to describe tracks. Your GPS collects these points as you go, allowing you to follow the breadcrumbs back to your starting point. Once you return, you can download the track to your computer and superimpose where you've been on a map or aerial photo. Many of the mapping programs we'll discuss also allow you to draw tracks on a map and to place trails, roads, and other features.

Active Track Logs vs. Saved Tracks

Garmin GPS units handle tracks a little differently than other brands do. When you use your Garmin GPS in the field, it stores your data as the active track log. To create a new track log, you must first clear the active track log. (You can save the existing track before creating a new log.)

Typically, an active track log holds more track points than a saved track does. The active log also retains the exact time for each track point; this data is lost when a track is saved.

I try to download my active track log to my computer as soon as I return from a trip, so that I can clear the track log for my next outing without losing data.

Internet Resources

- Jack Yeazel, Dale DePriest, and Joe Mehaffey's Web site, www.**gpsinformation.net** is a great resource. It's full of information about GPS, PDAs, cables, software, and nearly every GPS-related topic imaginable. I cannot recommend it highly enough.

- You may also want to check out the British site **www.gpspassion.com**.

- Two newsgroups worth exploring: **groups.google.com/groups?group=alt.satellite.gps** and **groups.google.com/groups?group=sci.geo.satellite-nav**.

- A newsgroup for Garmin GPS products can be found at **groups.google.com/ groups?group=alt.satellite.gps.garmin**. Magellan products are discussed at **groups.google.com/groups?group=alt.satellite.gps.magellan**.

Find even more Internet discussion boards on a wide range of GPS models on Yahoo. Go to **groups.yahoo.com** and search for "Garmin" or "Magellan" and "GPS" to find active groups.

The better groups are moderated, keeping spam out of the mix. If your model is new or is not listed, search for it online, perhaps using the terms "discussion," "forum," or "message."

GPS/Software Compatibility
Before you purchase any software, check the software manufacturer's Web site to ensure compatibility with your GPS.

Firmware

All GPS units come with firmware—software that's embedded in the hardware. Firmware can be updated in most GPS units. To keep your firmware up to date, visit your GPS manufacturer's Web site often and download the most recent non-beta version.

Egypt, Utah

There are so many uses for GPS. People use these systems for everything from marking the location of a parked car at the mega-mall to locating graves in old cemeteries for family genealogical research. One guy even got in trouble for stalking his ex-girlfriend with a GPS-enabled cell phone taped to her car; she caught him when he tried to change the battery.

One important habit to adopt is using your GPS to mark your starting location or trailhead on each trip. Many people find it easier to navigate to a waypoint than along a track log.

Before we had a GPS, my wife and I descended the technical slot canyon Egypt 3, near Escalante, Utah. It turns out that one sure would have come in handy. The trailhead was about three-quarters of a mile from the end of the road. We parked, grabbed our ropes and other gear, and picked our way into the canyon. The descent was all we imagined, full of downclimbing, natural anchor setups, short rappels, pothole escapes, brief swims, tight narrows, and faded midget rattlesnakes! Upon exiting the canyon, we climbed the ridge for the drudgery of making our way back to our truck.

The slickrock terrain of southern Utah can be relatively featureless, undulating, and downright difficult to navigate. Though you can often see the head of a canyon from on top, it's best to stay away from the rim so as to avoid the numerous side canyons that can block your path, making your hike out circuitous and time-consuming — not to mention making it difficult to discern where you entered the canyon and parked your vehicle. We trended northeast on our exit, paralleling the canyon, thinking we would encounter the road somewhere past our trailhead. And we did — one-half mile past the trailhead. But the road ended less than 1,500 feet from where we hit it. I shudder to think how lost we'd have been, and what kind of danger we'd have faced, had we missed that road entirely. Needless to say, we always carry our GPS now when canyoneering, and we always mark the trailhead.

Updates to this book will be posted at www.MakeYourOwnMaps.com. Bookmark and visit often to see what's new in the world of digital mapping.

Accuracy, WAAS, and DGPS

Don't blindly trust the accuracy reading on your GPS. Accuracy readings are only estimates, which different manufacturers calculate in different ways. If you want to mark a very accurate waypoint, pay attention to the position of satellites. Ideally, you want four that are well positioned. Again, in ideal conditions (which seldom occur in the real world) you would want three satellites 120 degrees apart, relatively low in the sky (with no obstructions between them and your GPS) and another directly overhead.

Some GPS receivers use the terms "2-D" and "3-D" to indicate the quality of satellite coverage. It takes at least three satellites to give your coordinates—a 2-D position. It takes four satellites to also estimate your elevation, which adds the third dimension to your position.

Also be aware that GPS satellites are always moving. This means that on an out-and-back trip, though you may not be able to get a good fix at a trail junction on the way in, on the way back conditions may be much better.

WAAS and DGPS are two technologies used to enhance the accuracy of GPS. WAAS stands for Wide Area Augmentation Service. In general, I suggest disabling this option on your GPS, since it speeds up battery drain and is unlikely to give you improved accuracy in an area without a wide view of the sky. Under ideal conditions, though, WAAS can (in theory) provide accuracy of around three meters. For a good primer on WAAS, go to **www.gpsinformation.net/waasgps.htm.**

DGPS stands for Differential GPS. DGPS stations transmit correction signals in coastal U.S. and Canadian waters and on some navigable rivers. As such, DGPS is more commonly used in marine environments. DGPS requires that you attach a special receiver to your GPS unit. The results may be slightly less accurate than if you use WAAS. More information on DGPS can be found at **www.navcen.uscg.gov/dgps** and at **gpsinformation.net/main/dgps.htm.**

Antennae

A GPS antenna is typically one of two types—patch or quad helix. A patch antenna is flat and is manufactured like a circuit board; you can often see these in GPS units with translucent cases. A quad helix antenna is circular and is wrapped with wire. A few receivers on the market have quad helix antennae that can be rotated.

The important thing to remember about antennae is that orientation affects their performance. Patch antennae work best when held parallel to the ground in a horizontal plane. Quad helix antennae work best when oriented vertically.

Some GPS experts say that a quad helix is the best option under tree cover, but not all agree. Others say that size matters, that larger GPS receivers work better under cover because of slight differences in gain and sensitivity.

Perhaps more important is the question of how your own unit will be oriented. If it will be mounted on the handlebar of a mountain bike, a patch antenna might be preferable. If the unit is destined to travel in the outside mesh pocket of a daypack, you might choose a unit with a quad helix antenna. As long as we're discussing the theoretical performance of antennae, I should mention that patch antennae seem to be better at reading satellites closer to the horizon. This implies that patch antennae work better in automobiles, which feature good views to the sides but not overhead. Having said all this, I suggest paying closer attention to other features; I've seen no significant performance difference between antennae types.

Cables

Most GPS units come with a computer connection cable. If yours did not, you'll need to purchase one to perform even the most basic computerized mapping.

Until recently, most GPS units have relied on serial cables. New models, however, are appearing with Universal Serial Bus (USB) cables and memory cards.

GPS manufacturers have been slow to migrate from serial cables, while computer manufacturers have been quicker to embrace USB. You may find that your GPS unit comes with a serial cable, while your new laptop has only USB ports. You can easily resolve this problem by purchasing a USB-to-serial adapter. Beware, though, of cheap adapters, which often fail to work. I'm a big believer in saving money where possible by purchasing generic components, but you'll be better off buying a name brand adapter such as those from Keyspan (**www.keyspan.com**), which have an excellent reputation.

Two popular sources of cables for GPS users:
- **www.pfranc.com**
- **www.pc-mobile.net**

Let's say you've purchased a newer GPS with USB connectivity. Think you've solved the problem? Think again! As slow as GPS manufacturers have been to embrace USB technology, mapping software vendors have been even slower. As of this writing, several major mapping applications listed in this book still aren't compatible with USB-based GPS models. If you're stuck with incompatible software, one solution is to use a utility like G7toWin or GPS Babel, discussed in Chapter 26.

Memory Cards

Some newer GPS units use SD (secure digital) cards or MMC (multimedia cards) for storing data. Unless your computer has a built-in card reader of the appropriate type, you'll need to buy one. Some companies even say you need their own brand of card reader to successfully transfer map data between their software and GPS units, though other data such as waypoints should work with any memory card. The card is typically placed under the batteries to protect them from moisture, which means you have to remove the batteries whenever you want to transfer data.

Mounts

Mounts are available that attach many GPS units to bikes and motorized vehicles. Mounts are critical in cars, where a loose GPS placed on the dash can become a flying projectile, with fatal results. It's especially dangerous to place your GPS in an airbag deployment zone.

Most GPS manufacturers sell mounts. Ram Mounts (**www.ram-mount.com**) are a popular alternative.

Communications Protocols

Think of communications protocols as the language that your GPS uses to talk to computers. Most GPS units offer several communications protocols, including a proprietary format that bears the company name, and one or more NMEA protocols (standards developed by the National Marine Electronics Association). Always use the proprietary format whenever possible; proprietary formats typically transfer more types of data, such as elevation and time information, which can make a big difference in terms of data analysis once you return from the field. It is almost always possible to use proprietary formats. One exception is communication between your GPS and a handheld computer (such as a Palm or Pocket PC), which often requires NMEA. See Chapter 22 for more information on using your GPS with handheld devices.

Mapping software typically chooses the proper baud rates and parity, once you enter the type of GPS and/or the communications protocol you are using. NMEA baud rates should always be set to 4800.

Generally speaking, NMEA is used only for real-time tracking. Most GPS units cannot transfer waypoints, routes, and tracks using NMEA protocols.

Finding the proper COM port can be a little more challenging. Keep the following in mind if you have problems:

- The serial port on your computer is usually COM 1, unless you have changed it yourself.

- USB ports are typically COM 5 and higher.

- You can experiment until you find the proper port.

- Some mapping programs won't communicate with your GPS if other mapping programs are running.

- Hot Sync and other PDA synchronization programs can cause problems. If nothing else works, shut them down.

Using Your GPS for Real-Time Tracking

The NMEA standard data output format allows just about any GPS manufactured in the last five years to track your location in real time.

Try using proprietary communication protocols before switching to NMEA, unless you want to display detailed satellite information, which often requires you to use the NMEA protocol.

If you have problems getting your mapping software to recognize your GPS, try starting the program before you connect your GPS to the computer. You might also try disabling any PDA synchronization software.

Fun With GPS

There are all sorts of ways to have fun with your GPS. In fact, you're probably going to get a kick out of nearly everything you do with it. A couple of specific activities bear mention:

- **Geocaching.** This is a great sport that lets you use your GPS to locate hidden "treasures." The site **www.geocaching.com** allows you to search for caches all over the world, download waypoints, and transfer them to your GPS using programs such as EasyGPS (Chapter 6) and ExpertGPS (Chapter 13). A good online geocaching forum can be found at **forums.groundspeak.com/GC**.

- **Degree Confluence Project.** This project aims to have people visit every location across the globe where a full degree of latitude and longitude meet, and post photos of these locations online. See **www.confluence.org** for more information.

More Tips

- Don't forget to set up your GPS configuration files properly in the GPS unit itself and in the mapping software you are using. You'll find configuration procedures in each software chapter.

- Know your GPS unit's limits for numbers of routes, tracks, waypoints, and waypoint characters. You can usually find this information in your user's manual.

- Speaking of the manual, your GPS unit is a complex device. No matter how painful it may be, try to read through your manual at least once.

- You may want to consider using battery saver mode, especially if you're moving on foot. In this mode, your GPS will take a reading every five seconds or so and try to predict your location for the next reading based on your speed and direction of travel. If it fails to do so accurately, it will automatically read your location at more frequent intervals until it can accurately forecast your position.

- Though I've seen reports that color screens mean shorter battery life, this has not been my experience.

> Updates to this book will be posted at www.MakeYourOwnMaps.com.
> Bookmark and visit often to see what's new in the world of digital mapping.

Chapter 3 Hardware and Software Matters

Hardware

Just what type of computer do you need, given the graphics-intensive nature of computerized mapping applications? Most software manufacturers list specific requirements but, in general, the more current your hardware and operating system is, the better. I recommend at least 512 MB of RAM. (Note that this book focuses exclusively on PCs, although I've added a few words on Mac resources at the end of this chapter.)

A powerful graphics card will help if you want to do much 3-D work. For more information on this subject, see Chapter 21. A reasonably large monitor is also helpful if you'll be working with maps for any length of time.

Some programs allow you to use a mouse scroll wheel to zoom, which is a very helpful feature. You may find that you can draw smoother tracks with an optical or wireless mouse.

Printers and Paper

Most printers aren't limited to 8-1/2 x 11" letter size paper. Many can handle legal size (8-1/2 x 14") paper, giving you more than 25 percent additional map real estate. And if you're shopping for a printer, consider one that can print on 11 x 17" ledger paper, doubling the area covered by standard letter paper.

While it's nice to have a color laser printer, most of us aren't that fortunate. We're stuck with inkjets if we want color. Be aware that the ink on these maps will run if it gets wet, kind of like a treasure map with disappearing ink—not a good thing when you're trying to find your way back to the trailhead in a rainstorm! If moisture is a concern, many copy shops can make non-running color laser copies for around $1. Black-and-white laser photocopies won't run when wet either, but you lose important information represented by color, such as water courses and vegetation cover. Black-and-white maps can be much easier to read at night than color maps, however. If you don't need color, black-and-white laser printers are a reasonably priced alternative.

Alternative papers let you use an inkjet printer to produce maps that hold up better in moist conditions. One option is National Geographic's Adventure Paper, which is marketed as waterproof. Available in 8-1/2 x 11", 8-1/2 x 14", and 11 x 17" sizes, it lists at $19.95 per pack (10, 15, or 25 sheets depending on paper size). At this price, you may want to use both sides. For more information, see **maps.nationalgeographic .com/topo/adventure.cfm.** Another weatherproof paper is available from **www.riteintherain.com.**

Software

Some concepts apply to nearly every software package in this book, so let's look at these common issues. Since we just discussed printers, we'll start with pointers on printing.

Printing Tips

• Displaying and printing a UTM grid every 500 to 1,000 meters makes it easy to find your location on the map while you're in the field. Your GPS can be set to read out coordinates in UTM format. Unless you've been using latitude and longitude your entire life, I'm sure you'll find UTM easier to read. For more information on UTM, see Chapter 4.

• Most printers' setup options allow for previewing the print job. This can save you the hassle and waste of printing illegible maps. Some printer software lets you preview maps at multiple scales. Select 100% and take a careful look to see if the map appears as you expected.

The Copy Shop Option

Many of the programs in this book allow you to export map images as .jpg files or in other graphics formats. Some allow you to export a large area. Put this on a disk, take it to a computer-savvy copy shop such as Kinko's, and you can get a large-format map close in size to USGS quads.

Help Files

The "helpfulness" of help files varies widely. Some software help files are minimal or unclear, while others are clear and extensive.

Help files come in several formats. If your software follows the standard Windows help format, the index and search tabs are powerful tools. Looking for mention of digital elevation models (DEMs) in OziExplorer's help files? Type "DEM" into the index or use the search function.

If the only help file is in .pdf format, use Acrobat's **Find** or **Search** feature to locate the information you seek.

Occasionally, you may come across software that offers online-only help. I recommend two strategies in this case:

1. Most browsers have some kind of search feature. In Internet Explorer 6.0, select **Edit**, then **Find (on This Page)**. In Firefox 1.0, select **Edit**, then **Find in This Page**.

2. Another option is to add the Google Toolbar (available at **toolbar.google.com**) to your Web browser. To use the toolbar, enter a search term, then use the tool labeled **Find next occurrence of 'search term' in current document**.

Discussion Groups and Netiquette

Throughout this book, I refer to various online discussion groups as help sources. Keeping up with discussion boards that focus on your software and brand of GPS will greatly increase your knowledge and keep you current on developments in this rapidly changing field.

Observing the informal rules, or netiquette, that has developed for using these resources will enhance your experience. Before posting, always search the board for answers to your questions. You can learn an amazing amount this way. Many groups prefer that your first post include an introduction, telling people about your experience with the software or hardware discussed. Remember to thank people for their help, and follow up as appropriate to let them know how their suggestions worked. When you get to the point where you can help people, please contribute and offer a helping hand. Never use all-caps text (it's considered rude), and don't flame (attack) people. Keep threads on topic and don't start a new topic if you're responding on an established subject. Finally, label any queries with a descriptive header.

An excellent resource on netiquette is available at **www.albion.com/netiquette/corerules.html**, where you will find a lot of cyberspace wisdom, including such gems as "lurk before you leap."

Yahoo! and Google Groups

Many of the Yahoo! discussion groups mentioned in this book require you to have a free Yahoo! e-mail address. If you don't have a Yahoo! account, use the **Sign Up** link for any of its discussion groups at the top of the Yahoo! home page. When you sign up for a group, be sure to check the **No Email** delivery option, unless you want to be deluged. Some of the groups are very active. I find it much more convenient to view messages on each group's Web site.

Be sure to check out the **Files** and **Links** sections of Yahoo! discussion groups. These often contain a wealth of additional information.

Though Google newsgroups cover less ground than Yahoo! groups, they offer a much better search function.

File Management

Give some thought to how your files are structured and to how you assign names to files. The software chapters in this book detail how programs store data and offer specific hints to help you stay organized.

Saving Your Data

None of the programs discussed in this book have a background save feature. Losing massive amounts of work is incredibly frustrating, so while it's easy to get caught up drawing tracks and having hours of fun, remember to save your work as you go.

Likewise, few programs offer an undo button that recovers data. Be certain you want to delete an item before getting rid of it. There are usually ways to work around this. Some programs, such as OziExplorer and Terrain Navigator, allow you to clear items or layers from a map without deleting the data. With others, such as TOPO!, you may wish to use the **Save As** option as a safety mechanism. You can always use **Save As** again to reassign the original file name to the new work, after you are sure you haven't accidentally lost critical data.

One reason this is important is that some mapping programs are designed to use all of your computer's free memory. If you find that a program is sluggish or, worse yet, tends to crash, try using it without other programs running. And save your data frequently!

Other Software Tips

• The first thing you should do after installing any mapping software is check the company's Web site for updates. Whatever program you use, check back now and again for upgrades, which are generally free. Some programs are updated more frequently than others. This is a rapidly changing field and new and useful features are developed and released regularly.

• If you want to keep a good record of trails you've taken, download tracks from your GPS to your mapping software after every trek. You will see numerous inaccuracies in the track, due to lost satellites and other causes. Most software allows you to clean up these tracks. It may be easiest to simply "draw" another track over the one you download, correcting the inaccuracies as you go. Some of the programs discussed here let you change individual track points, while others allow you to split a track and delete the inaccurate section. Logging roads or ranch tracks often show up from above; if you trek one of these, try locating it on a aerial photo, then comparing the photo with your track to correct any inaccuracies.

- It may be worthwhile, after spending some time with a program, to go back to the configuration files or reread a chapter in this book. Quite frequently, you'll discover new features and options the second time around.

- Different sources of information may show different features. When planning a trip, you may find it helpful to view aerial photos, along with 1:24,000 and 1:100,000 scale maps. Many of the programs discussed in this book allow you to toggle between various views. If a road or trail is missing on one view, draw a track and move it to your final map.

- Take a look at Chapter 26, which covers utilities. Sometimes, utilities offer the only way to transfer data from one program to another. Transferring large track files with your GPS may truncate tracks; utilities give you another option.

- While many programs offer elevation profiles, all of them leave a lot to be desired. Whether the profiles follow a track you have drawn or a pre-existing road, a certain amount of error is introduced, resulting in a jagged profile. None of the programs reviewed here provide any sort of smoothing function to remove this error. Unfortunately, this leaves us with no simple way to estimate elevation gain. This is not a problem if you are following a route that is a steady climb, with no interludes of descent along the way. But if you find yourself planning a trek with plenty of ups and downs, estimating total gain is difficult. One way to do this manually is to note the major low and high points along a route and calculate the differences. You can do this by viewing an elevation profile and picking the low and high points, or you can establish temporary waypoints at these key locations. Either way, bring out the pad, pencil, and calculator, which still have a place near your computer. Perhaps by the next edition of this book, an enterprising software designer will find a good way to deal with this problem.

- If you really get into mapping and find yourself with multiple programs, keep in mind that some require registration codes at reinstall (as in the event of a hard disk failure, heaven forbid. You do back up, don't you?). Keep all those cards or e-mail printouts with registration numbers in one place.

- Most software companies pay close attention to customer feedback. If you have problems or suggestions, by all means e-mail the support staff.

- Finally, before you buy, check online. Many GPS software packages are available online at significant discounts.

About Macs

Though this book focuses almost exclusively on PC-based applications, I want to list a few mapping programs and related sources of information for Mac users.

One of the CD-based software packages discussed in this book, National Geographic TOPO!, is available in a Macintosh version. See **maps.nationalgeographic.com/topo/state.cfm** for more information.

The following programs, which allow you to import digital maps such as DRGs, are similar to the programs in Section Four of this book:

• GPSy: **www.gpsy.com**
• MacGPS Pro: **www.macgpspro.com**

Route 66, at **www.66.com**, offers automotive navigation products for the U.S. and Europe.

GPS Connect is a freeware program that allows you to transfer waypoints to and from a Garmin GPS. It is available at **www.chimoosoft.com/gpsconnect.html**.

Two additional sources of information on Mac-based GPS mapping:

• **gpsinformation.net/macgps.htm**
• A very active Yahoo group, MacMap, at **groups.yahoo.com/group/macmap**, discusses Macintosh-based GPS applications.

Updates to this book will be posted at www.MakeYourOwnMaps.com. Bookmark and visit often to see what's new in the world of digital mapping.

Chapter 4 Maps 101

Mapmaking is the science (and art) known formally as cartography. In this chapter, we'll explore the basics of maps and mapmaking, defining key terms. Nothing scary: think of it as akin to a freshman-level introductory course.

Latitude and Longitude

Lines of latitude run parallel to the equator, and are used to measure distance north and south of the equator. The equator is 0 degrees, while the north pole is 90 degrees north latitude.

Lines of longitude, also called meridians, measure distance east and west. The prime meridian, at 0 degrees longitude, is often called the Greenwich meridian because it runs through Greenwich, England. Opposite this imaginary line is the longitude on the other side of the earth. This is the location of portions of the international date line—which while quite straight in many segments, jogs here and there so it isn't one day on one side of an island and another day on the other side. Lines of longitude are expressed as being east or west of the prime meridian. For example, Los Angeles is located at roughly 118 degrees west longitude.

Timing is Everything
What was previously known as Greenwich Mean Time (GMT) is now called Coordinated Universal Time, or UTC for short. You may encounter these terms in your GPS setup menu. Fortunately, most manufacturers make it easy by telling you the time zone and UTC offset (e.g., "U.S. Pacific" and "-8 hours").

Lines of latitude and longitude each add up to 360 degrees (360º) as you circle the planet. Smaller increments are expressed in minutes, noted with an apostrophe (') and seconds, noted with a quotation mark ("). And though we're not talking time here, a degree is made up of 60 minutes, and a minute is made up of 60 seconds.

Using these smaller increments, you can be very precise, saying for example that the Golden Gate Bridge is located at 37º 49' 10" north and 122º 29' 2" west. (You'll sometimes see this format abbreviated as Dº M' S". These paired measurements of latitude and longitude are referred to as "coordinates.")

To further complicate matters, coordinates can also be expressed as decimals. For example, we could say that the Golden Gate Bridge is located at 37º 49.167'N and 122º 29.033'W. This notation is referred to as decimal minutes, which can be abbreviated as Dº M.M'. To carry this convention even further, we can use decimal degrees and give the location as 37.81944ºN and 122.48389ºW. This format can be abbreviated as D.Dº. Table 1 shows four common ways to abbreviate coordinate formats.

Table 1. Four common ways to abbreviate coordinate formats.

Position	37.81944º	37º 49.167'	37º 49' 10"
1	Degrees	Deg, Min	Deg, Min, Sec
2	Degrees.Degrees	Degrees, Minutes.Minutes	Degrees, Minutes, Seconds
3	D.Dº	Dº M.M'	Dº M' S"
4	hddd.dddddº	hdddº mm.mmm'	hdddº mm' ss.s'

Negative Numbers

Sometimes coordinates are given without cardinal directions (N, S, E, and W), relying on positive and negative numbers instead. Using this format, anything south of the equator or west of the prime meridian is negative. For example, our Golden Gate Bridge coordinates can be expressed as 37.81944º, -122.48389º. Keep this in mind, for any U.S. location will be west longitude and, if expressed in this manner, must therefore bear a negative number for longitude.

Now for the good news. You should never have to manually convert from one format to the other; your GPS and most software programs will do it for you. If you've been using Dº M' S" and your hiking buddy gives you a coordinate in D.Dº, simply go into the preferences or configuration section of the GPS or software, and change to D.Dº. Once you enter the coordinates, you can change back to Dº M' S". If for any reason you do want to convert coordinates manually, several Web sites offer converters. One is found at **www.directionsmag.com/latlong.asp**.

UTM

UTM stands for Universal Transverse Mercator, which provides an alternative way to read your position. Some people favor lat/lon format, while others prefer UTM.

UTM coordinates are metric—a scary word for many Americans, but one that really makes sense on a map, even if you have no concept of how long a kilometer is. The reason I say this is simple: UTM is based on the decimal system that most of us understand pretty well. We know that three is 3/10 of the way between zero and ten, right? But quick, what is 3/10 of a degree? Well, it's 18 minutes. Start adding in seconds and you'll quickly see that reading coordinates and trying to find your location on your map, in latitude and longitude, can be challenging at best.

Deciphering UTM

The UTM system divides the world into 60 zones, running north to south, with each zone covering six degrees of longitude (See Figure 4A). Zone numbers in the contiguous U.S. range from 10 on the West Coast to 19 in New England. Each zone is divided into 20 bands of latitude, starting with C in the south and moving to X in the north. Often these bands are not shown in UTM coordinate displays.

UTM coordinates are given as eastings (E), which represents a measurement of position on an east-west axis within the zone, and northings (N), which represent the position along a north-south axis. Sometimes UTM coordinates are given on a single line and sometimes on two lines. Using our Golden Gate Bridge example, here are two common ways UTM position can be stated:

Zone 10 4185911 N 545903 E

Zone 10 4185911 N
        0545903 E

Find more information on UTM at **erg.usgs.gov/isb/pubs/factsheets/fs07701.html**.

Almost all the software with print capabilities detailed in this book allows you to produce a map with a UTM grid superimposed on it. Print a map in this format, set your GPS to display UTM, and try it out yourself. You'll see how easy it is to ascertain your location in the field using UTM.

Having said that, UTM does have its drawbacks. Remember that the UTM grid for each zone is independent of other zones, which can cause problems if your trip crosses the boundary between two zones. I've heard one person call UTM "navigating for dummies." Still, I find it very useful for locating your position on paper maps.

Scales and Quads

Most of the programs discussed in this book are based on scanned images of 1:24,000, 1:100,000, and 1:250,000 scale maps. One inch on a 1:24,000 scale map (abbreviated 1:24K) represents 24,000 inches on the ground, or—to put it in terms you can visualize—one inch on the map works out to 2,000 feet on the ground.

These images are typically scanned from United States Geological Survey (USGS) maps. You may also see 1:24K USGS maps referred to as 7.5 minute quadrangles or quads. These maps display an area 7.5 minutes of longitude wide and 7.5 minutes of

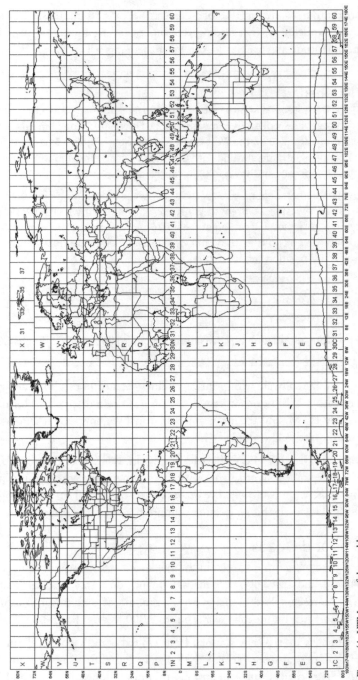

Figure 4A. UTM map of the world.
Map courtesy of Alan Morton (www.dmap.co.uk).

latitude high. Because lines of longitude converge at the poles, these quads are not true rectangles. A 7.5-minute quad covers 71 square miles in the southern United States and only 49 square miles in the north.

Just to add a little confusion, there are actually some 1:25K quads out there, mainly for Alaska and a few other parts of the U.S. There are also some 1:63K scale maps for Alaska.

> **TIP:** Want to find the name of a particular quad? Many of the mapping programs discussed in this book can display quad names, but if your program or programs don't, an excellent online resource is **www.topozone.com**. Search for a location and, once you load the map image, the quad name will be shown above the map.

Datum, Data, Datums

A datum is a mathematical formula used to compute the results of surveys, where coordinates are based on an ellipsoid model of the earth. Examples include WGS84 and NAD27. In some programs, you may see a range of NAD27 options. When using NAD27, most readers of this book. will want to choose NAD27 CONUS, which stands for North American Datum 1927 Continental United States.

Interestingly enough, for those of you who remember your Latin, *datum* is typically regarded as the singular version of the word *data*, but in the mapping world the plural is *datums*.

It is very important to use the correct datum, and to be sure that your GPS and map are set for the same datum. Otherwise, you could find yourself off by anywhere from 15 to 400 feet.

When you return home from an outdoor adventure and download waypoints and tracks, you may find that they don't fall on the map where you expected. If they are all off in the same direction and by the same distance, that's a dead giveaway that something has the incorrect datum—either your map, your GPS, or your download settings.

> **TIP: WHEN TO CHANGE YOUR DATUM** Displaying the Map Datum in your GPS is one of two instances when you may want to change the datum. The other is when you import and calibrate a map in one of the programs discussed in Section Four. Here the map should always be set to the datum it was drawn in. Basically, you always want the GPS display of coordinates and the grid on the map to be in the same datum. It's easy to change the map datum in your GPS; look for this option in your setup or interface menus.

> **TIP: WHEN NOT TO CHANGE YOUR DATUM** WGS84 is considered the standard for data transfer. Garmin and Magellan GPS units always use WGS84 to download and upload data, as do many Lowrance and Eagle units. Many software packages do not allow you to change the datum used for uploading and downloading data (such as waypoints), which almost always defaults to WGS84. If a software package does allow you to alter this option, think carefully before changing it.

Most mapping software for the U.S. defaults to WGS84. However, UTM coordinate systems are best used with the NAD27 datum. According to DeLorme, 95 percent of the USGS quads containing UTM grid lines use the NAD27 datum. Also, note that NAD83 and WGS84 are essentially identical. Finally, be aware that aerial photos may be in a different datum than maps of the same area.

> **Map Collar**
> Each standard USGS map has a white border around the edge called the map collar. The collar contains important information such as the scale, datum, contour intervals, and the date the map was created.

Magnetic Declination

True (or geographic) north is not the same as magnetic north. The location of the magnetic north pole changes over time, so maps are based on the geographic north pole. A diagram on the map collar shows the difference (declination) between magnetic north (abbreviated MN on USGS maps) and true north, indicated by a star (as in Polaris, the North Star). This diagram also shows the declination between true north and the UTM grid north (GN).

Magnetic declination is constantly changing, so the declination shown on the map may not be accurate. For an online declination calculator, see **www.ngdc.noaa.gov/seg/geomag/jsp/Declination.jsp**.

More About Maps

• Contour intervals vary depending upon the map. For example, on USGS 7.5' quads, some will have 20-foot contour intervals, others 40-foot, and some will be in meters.

• A map legend shows how symbols are used on maps. Legends are often included on map collars, though USGS 7.5' quads typically lack detail. USGS relies instead on a guide to map symbols, available at **erg.usgs.gov/isb/pubs/booklets/symbols**.

Chapter 5 Free Software: USAPhotoMaps

USAPhotoMaps is a shareware program created by Doug Cox. If you have a GPS receiver but aren't sure which software to purchase, it's an excellent place to start. USAPhotoMaps is also a great way to explore the world of computerized mapping, even if you have yet to purchase a GPS.

USAPhotoMaps is based on Microsoft's TerraServer Web site (**www.terraserver-usa.com**), from which it downloads topographical maps and aerial photos. Maps and photos you download using USAPhotoMaps reside on your computer. When you use TerraServer alone, however, you must download a map each time you view it. USAPhotoMaps also offers a friendlier interface, offline zooming (much faster than what can be done online), and GPS tools that allow you to work with waypoints, routes, and tracks. We'll take a look at a couple of other TerraServer-based programs in Section Three, but I wanted to introduce USAPhotoMaps early in the book since it is free and easily accessible.

This is a great program—even if you own several mapping programs, you may still find USAPhotoMaps comes in handy. Few programs allow you to switch back and forth between aerial photos and contour maps at exactly the same location; this feature alone makes USAPhotoMaps a great tool in your mapping arsenal.

Basic Information

COST
• The software is free, but if you like it please consider making a donation to developer Doug Cox. A "nag box" reminds you of this option each time you close the program. It goes away permanently once you make a donation.

SYSTEM REQUIREMENTS
• Windows operating system

GPS COMPATIBILITY
• Garmin and Magellan

TESTED VERSION
• 2.33

CONTACT INFORMATION
• jdmcox@jdmcox.com
• www.jdmcox.com

- **www.gpsinformation.net/waas/maps/usaphoto.html**
- **www.digitalgrove.net/USAPhotoMaps_Instructions.htm**
- **www.kimdara.com/usaphotomaps/index.html**

Advantages

- It's free (shareware).

- Aerial photos and maps are stored on your hard disk, eliminating the need to wait for downloads of frequently viewed areas.

- It offers coverage of almost the entire U.S.

- When you place a waypoint, you are automatically taken to the name field—no extra steps are required.

- Users can switch between aerial photos and topographic maps of the same location.

Disadvantages

- Printing capabilities are very limited.

- Downloads are slow without a broadband connection.

- There are no 3-D capabilities.

- Route-making tools are limited.

Installation

Installation is straightforward. Go to **www.jdmcox.com** and download the latest version of USAPhotoMaps. This will download the USAPhotoMaps.exe file. Run it and start the program, which will initially take you to a location in Washington, D.C. Be sure to check this out—it's one of the first U.S. urban locations represented by color aerial photos. See the Getting Started section of this chapter for details on how to view these stunning images.

Tutorial/Manual

To access the help file, choose **Help,** then **Using.** Though it is limited in scope, USAPhotoMaps is a simple program and most users will have little trouble figuring it out. You can find a separate GPS help file by choosing **GPS** and selecting **Help.** The three Web sites listed above in Internet Resources can provide additional assistance.

Configuration

There isn't a great deal to worry about in terms of configuration. In the **File** menu, choose **Preferences** to adjust the following:

• **Colors** (Figure 5A).

• **Waypoint & Position Dots** (Figure 5B). This allows you to set the size of these features at different zoom levels.

• **Route and Track Line Width** (Figure 5C).

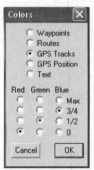

Figure 5A Figure 5B Figure 5C

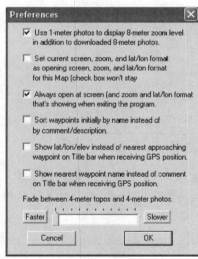

Figure 5D

• **Preferences** (Figure 5D). Here you will find options controlling the opening screen, waypoint lists, and moving map behavior. At the bottom is a slider that, when moved to the right, slows the fade when you switch between topo and aerial photos on the 4 meter/pixel screens. Before leaving this area, select **Always open at screen (and zoom and lat/lon format) that's showing when exiting the program.** You can change this setting later, but you'll need it to perform a little trick you'll find in the More Tips section of this chapter.

To set the coordinate format, choose **View**, then **Lat/Lon**.

The last configuration item you'll need to take care of is setting up your GPS. From the **GPS** menu, choose **Comm Port, Baud,** or **Protocol** to establish your GPS settings. Choose **GPS** and then **Help** for the GPS Help file, which contains information on the proper settings.

Getting Started

1. The first time you start USAPhotoMaps, you'll see the **New Map** window shown in Figure 5E. Click **OK** and then click **OK** again. Now press the **F** key to fill the screen.

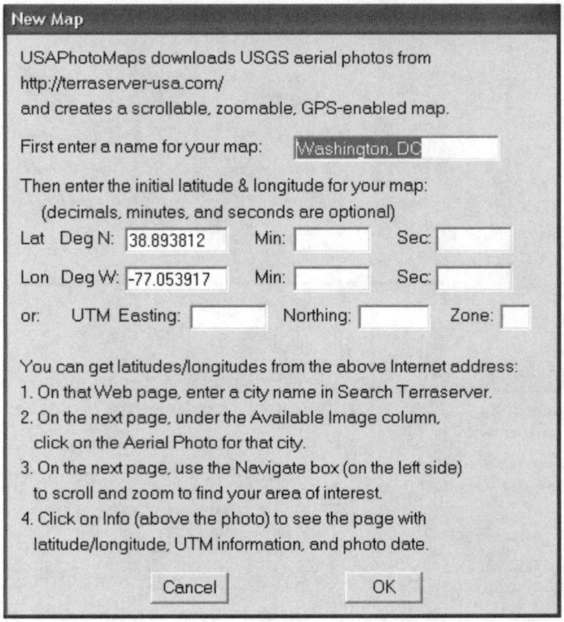

Figure 5E

2. Use the **T** and **P** keys to switch between Topographic map and aerial **Photo** screens. Once you switch to the aerial photo screen, you'll need to press the **F** key to begin downloading images again.

> **TIP:** If nothing appears on the screen, you may need to alter your firewall settings to allow downloads for USAPhotoMaps.

Finding Other Locations

If you want to view a different location right away, choose **File**, then **New Map File**. Enter the latitude and longitude of the location for which you want to download maps and photos. If you don't know the coordinates, use one listed in Table 1, which shows coordinates for the highest point in each of the 50 states. Alternatively, go to Microsoft's TerraServer site (**www.terraserver-usa.com**) and enter a place name or address. Select your view—aerial photo or topo map—and, when the image appears, choose **Info** at the top of the screen. Scroll back down to the map to see the coordinates, which are given in several formats. Now return to USAPhotoMaps, enter the coordinates, and click **OK**. Don't worry about the format for latitude and longitude; you can enter them as degrees, minutes, and seconds, as the format calls for, or as decimal degrees in the degree boxes.

Once you've entered the coordinates, a **Waypoint** box will appear on the screen. If you don't want to establish a waypoint at the coordinates you entered, click **Cancel**. Otherwise, type a **Description** and **(GPS) Name**, and click **OK**. The **(GPS) Name** is the waypoint name that will be sent to your GPS.

NOTE: If you type too many characters for the **(GPS) Name**, it will be shortened to the maximum number your GPS will hold.

USGS is now making available color aerial photos of a number of urban areas. These images, which are available in resolutions down to 0.25 meters per pixel, are available by pressing the U key and then pressing F. Pretty cool, huh? Note that this is new technology for USGS and there are reports that some location information (especially in Texas) may be inaccurate.

If you've already moved on to a different location, we can get back to the Washington map pretty easily. When you downloaded USAPhotoMaps, a map file was created for this area. From the **File** menu, choose **Open Map File**, select **Washington, DC**, and click **OK**.

Here are a few other tips for navigating USAPhotoMaps:

• Use your keyboard's arrow keys to pan the map. To download an adjoining area, simply scroll and then press F. This way you won't need to reenter latitude and longitude coordinates.

• Use the plus sign (+) key to zoom in, and the minus sign (-) to zoom out. Or use the PAGE DOWN key to zoom in and PAGE UP key to zoom out.

• Alternatively, choose **Zoom** and then select one of the zoom levels from the drop-down menu.

Table 1. Coordinates for the highest point in each state in the U.S.

ST	Rank	Peak Name	Elevation (feet)	Latitude (Degrees, Minutes, Seconds)	Longitude (Degrees, Minutes, Seconds)
AK	1	Mount McKinley	20320	63, 04, 12	151, 00, 17
AL	35	Cheaha Mtn	2413	33, 29, 08	85, 48, 31
AR	34	Magazine Mountain	2753	35, 10, 01	93, 38, 41
AZ	12	Humphreys Peak	12637	35, 20, 47	111, 40, 41
CA	2	Mount Whitney	14505	36, 34, 43	118, 17, 31
CO	3	Mount Elbert	14440	39, 07, 04	106, 26, 43
CT	36	South Mount Frissell	2380	42, 02, 59	73, 28, 58
DE	49	Ebright Azimuth	448	39, 50, 15	75, 31, 10
FL	50	Britton Hill	345	30, 59, 13	86, 16, 54
GA	25	Brasstown Bald	4783	34, 52, 28	83, 48, 40
HI	6	Mauna Kea	13803	19, 49, 14	155, 28, 05
IA	42	Hawkeye Point	1670	43, 27, 37	95, 42, 32
ID	11	Borah Peak	12668	44, 08, 15	113, 46, 52
IL	45	Charles Mound	1235	42, 30, 15	90, 14, 23
IN	44	Hoosier High Point	1257	40, 00, 01	84, 51, 03
KS	28	Mount Sunflower	4039	39, 01, 19	102, 02, 12
KY	27	Black Mountain	4145	36, 54, 51	82, 53, 38
LA	48	Driskill Mountain	535	32, 25, 29	92, 53, 47
MA	31	Mount Greylock	3487	42, 38, 13	73, 09, 57
MD	32	Backbone Mountain	3360	39, 14, 15	79, 29, 07
ME	22	Mount Katahdin	5266	45, 54, 16	68, 55, 17
MI	38	Mount Arvon	1979	46, 45, 21	88, 09, 19
MI	38	Mount Curwood	1978	46, 42, 11	88, 14, 23
MN	37	Eagle Mountain	2301	47, 53, 51	90, 33, 37
MO	41	Taum Sauk Mountain	1772	37, 34, 16	90, 43, 45
MS	47	Woodall Mountain	807	34, 47, 16	88, 14, 30
MT	10	Granite Peak	12807	45, 09, 48	109, 48, 27
NC	16	Mount Mitchell	6684	35, 45, 53	82, 15, 54
ND	30	White Butte	3506	46, 23, 13	103, 18, 08
NE	20	Panorama Point	5424	41, 00, 27	104, 01, 51
NH	18	Mount Washington	6288	44, 16, 14	71, 18, 12
NJ	40	High Point	1803	41, 19, 15	74, 39, 41
NM	8	Wheeler Peak	13167	36, 33, 25	105, 25, 01
NV	9	Boundary Peak	13143	37, 50, 46	118, 21, 04
NY	21	Mount Marcy	5343	44, 06, 46	73, 55, 25
OH	43	Campbell Hill	1549	40, 22, 13	83, 43, 13
OK	23	Black Mesa	4975	36, 55, 55	102, 59, 52
OR	13	Mount Hood	11248	45, 22, 24	121, 41, 45
PA	33	Mount Davis	3205	39, 47, 09	79, 10, 36
RI	46	Jerimoth Hill	808	41, 51, 00	71, 46, 45
SC	29	Sassafras Mountain	3551	35, 03, 55	82, 46, 37
SD	15	Harney Peak	7242	43, 51, 57	103, 31, 52
TN	17	Clingmans Dome	6643	35, 33, 46	83, 29, 54
TX	14	Guadalupe Peak	8751	31, 53, 29	104, 51, 39
UT	7	Kings Peak	13518	40, 45, 57	110, 22, 40
VA	19	Mount Rogers	5711	36, 39, 36	81, 32, 42
VT	26	Mount Mansfield	4393	44, 32, 38	72, 48, 51
WA	4	Mount Rainier	14410	46, 51, 12	121, 45, 36
WI	39	Timms Hill	1952	45, 27, 03	90, 11, 44
WV	24	Spruce Knob	4863	38, 42, 00	79, 31, 58
WY	5	Gannett Peak	13804	43, 11, 03	109, 39, 15

File Structure

You can create map files for a given area, allowing you to store locations by name. To do so, choose **File**, then **New Map File** to open the dialog box shown in Figure 5E. Notice that it asks you to enter the longitude and latitude for the location. Alternatively, you can navigate to the area by panning the map or locating a waypoint and then naming it, avoiding the need to enter coordinates manually. USAPhotoMaps uses the UTM Zone number as the default map file name. See Chapter 4 for information on UTM zones.

Choose **File**, then **Open Map File** to open an existing file.

Files are saved in the following formats:

• Routes are saved as .txt files.

• Waypoints are saved as .xml files.

• Tracks are saved as .csv files.

The default directory is C:\Program Files\USAPhotoMaps. Further information on USAPhotoMaps' file structure can be found by selecting **Help,** then **Using**.

Waypoints and Waypoint Management

To create a waypoint, select a point anywhere on the map. This opens a **Waypoint** dialog box in which you can enter a **Description** and **(GPS) Name**. Remember to limit the GPS name to the number of characters accepted by your GPS.

To view a list of waypoints, choose **Waypoints**, then **Open/New File**. A list of current map files will be shown. USAPhotoMaps assigns the UTM Zone as the default name for map file names. Select a map file and click **Open** to open the dialog box shown in Figure 5F. From here you have several options:

• Select **Name** or **Comment/Description** to sort waypoints by those fields and choose which field to optionally display on the map as a waypoint label.

• Select **Show Names/Comments on map** to show waypoint labels on the map screen. If you don't want waypoint labels shown on the map, you can still right-click any waypoint on a map to see its name.

• Click **Edit** to edit waypoint names.

• **Delete** a waypoint.

• Send an individual waypoint **To GPS**.

USAPhotoMaps offers limited waypoint management tools. If it's your primary mapping program, you may want to pair it with the stand-alone waypoint manager EasyGPS (see Chapter 6).

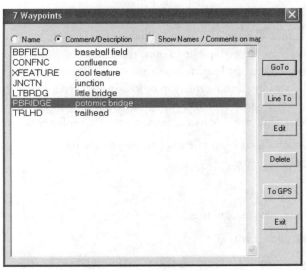

Figure 5F

Routes

1. To draw a route, from the **Route** menu, select **Create**, and then click anywhere on the map.

2. Continue moving the pointer along your route, clicking at each turn. If you make an error, press CTRL+Z to remove the last leg.

3. Double-click or press ESC to end the route and name it.

Also note the following:

• If you get to the edge of the map and wish to continue your route, press an arrow key to pan the map.

• You can transfer only a finite number of points per route to your GPS—typically up to 50. When creating a route, the number of route points is displayed in the upper left corner of the map each time you click.

• The cumulative route length is displayed in feet along the route, up to a length of 1000', and in decimal miles above 1000'.

Routes are saved as .txt files. Display a saved route by selecting **Route**, then **Display**.

> **NOTE:** It's easy to create freehand routes using USAPhotoMaps, but the program provides no way to create a route from a list of waypoints. This can, however, be done in EasyGPS—the process is described in detail in Chapter 6.

Select **GPS**, and then point to **Route**, for options to **Send** and **Receive**, for transferring route data with your GPS. Other options:

- **Convert to Tracks.** This converts the route to a track file. You will be prompted to choose a route (.txt) file. A new file will be created, using the same name with a .csv (track) file extension.

- **Append to Tracks.** This appends a route onto a track. You will be prompted to choose a route (.txt) file, and then to choose a track (.csv) file to append the route to. The track file you choose will be overwritten by the new track, incorporating the selected route.

> **TIP:** The **Convert to Track** option can come in handy for moving data between programs.

Tracks

Select **GPS** and point to **Tracks** for options to **Display** tracks and to **Send and Receive** them when transferring data between your computer and GPS. While USAPhotoMaps has no tool for drawing tracks, you can create a route and then select **GPS**, point to **Route**, and select **Convert to Track.**

When a track is displayed in USAPhotoMaps, two boxes appear in the upper left corner of the screen:

- **Go to Beginning of Tracks.** Click this to center the screen on the beginning of a track.

- **Edit Tracks.** Select this to display individual track points and to edit the track. When you click **Edit Tracks**, a third box, **Help**, appears. Click this to open a dialog box offering help with editing tracks.

GPS Interface

Select **GPS**, then either **Routes, Tracks,** or **Waypoints** for options to **Send and Receive** data. You can also select **Waypoints**, and then **Open/New File** to open a waypoint file, select an individual waypoint for transfer, and then click **To GPS.**

Printing

Lack of printing options is one of this program's main drawbacks. The only way to print maps in USAPhotoMaps is to capture the full screen in landscape mode for use in a graphics program, using one of two methods:

- Choose **File**, then **Copy to 'Screen01.jpg'**, which is saved to the USAPhotoMaps directory. Subsequent saves are named in numeric order.

- Press the PRINT SCREEN key, which will save the image to the Windows Clipboard as a .bmp file.

Moving Map

USAPhotoMaps provides real-time GPS support for your laptop. The moving map features are fairly simple:

- To start tracking, choose **GPS**, then **Show Location**.

- If you scroll the map or click the mouse, position updating will stop. To resume tracking, choose **Show Location** again.

- The name of the closest waypoint and the distance to it will be shown in the title bar, assuming you set this option in **Preferences**.

- A file, Position.txt, will hold four hours of tracking data before being overwritten. To view this on your screen, choose **GPS**, then **Display Position.txt**.

Working With Other Programs

Importing Data

From the **File** menu, you can import the following:

- Microsoft Streets & Trips .psp files

- Garmin ForeRunner Logbook .xml files

- Tracks in .gpx format

You can also import waypoints in .gpx format. Copy or move the desired .gpx file to your USAPhotoMaps directory. Now choose **Waypoints,** then **Open/New file**. In the **Open** dialog, select **Files of Type** and then ***.gpx**.

Exporting Data

You can export route (.txt), track (.csv), and waypoint (.xml) files by copying them from your USAPhotoMaps directory. The file extension on .xml waypoint files can be changed to .gpx and the files read in that format.

You can also export a map or photo as a one-meter-per-pixel image, using the BigJpeg utility available at **www.jdmcox.com**. You'll find instructions at **www.digitalgrove.net/USAPhotoMaps_Instructions.htm**.

More Tips

- Before I got a broadband connection, I used to let USAPhotoMaps run late at night, downloading image files for hours. Allowing the software to download when there is little need for an open phone line can be a good strategy if you rely on a dialup connection for Internet access.

- For roads that show up on aerial photos but not on topographic maps, create a route on the aerial photo, and then switch to the topo screen to see where it falls on the map. If you are using other mapping software, you may want to export this route to it. By first converting the route to a track, you will be able to export a simple track line rather than a route made up of waypoints. To do this, on the **GPS** menu, point to **Route** and select **Convert to Track**.

- Choose **View**, then **Grid On** to superimpose a UTM grid.

- To add text to a map, hold down the SHIFT key while drawing a line with your mouse. (Do not depress the mouse button.) An **Enter text** dialog box will open. Additional options are available from the drop-down **Text** menu. Note that text can be entered and viewed only at the one- and two-meter zoom levels.

- USAPhotoMaps Help files contain instructions on how to save (and read from) map and photo images on CDs, which saves hard disk space.

- Some aerial photos are missing from the TerraServer database. With the exception of some military bases, this is just missing data, and not likely to be a secret government research center!

- Want to see the date of an aerial photo? Find the same location on TerraServer (**www.terraserver-usa.com**) and the date will be shown. Aerial photos of most locations are shot every five years or so.

- For extensive additional information, select **Help**, then **Using**.

- USAPhotoMaps is frequently improved; check for updates often at **www.jdmcox.com**.

Adding Contour Lines to Aerial Photos

You can superimpose contour lines on an aerial photo:

1. First, download the Convert SDTS Data utility from **www.jdmcox.com** and place it in your USAPhotoMaps directory.

2. Press the X key while viewing an aerial photo. A **Cursor Location** box pops up. Note the bottom row of numbers. These are latitude and longitude coordinates, separated by a space.

3. Navigate to **http://64.83.8.153/SDTS_DL_b.htm**, scroll down, and type those numbers as latitude and longitude. Be sure to include the minus sign if one is displayed in the **Cursor Location** box.

4. Choose **Get Data**.

5. Click the link to download the 30 x 30 meter data to the USAPhotoMaps directory.

6. Navigate to that directory with **My Computer** or **Windows Explorer** and double-click **ConvertSDTSdata.exe.** You'll get a message saying that any .GZ files have been converted to .TAR files. Choose **OK**. You'll get another message saying "Done!" Choose **OK** again.

7. Now shut down USAPhotoMaps and restart it. Because you configured the program that way, you'll come back to the same area on the aerial photo.

8. Now press the C key, or select **View**, then **Contours On**. Contour lines, color-coded for elevation, will overlay the aerial photo, at levels up to eight meters per pixel.

For more detailed instructions on how to do this, go to **www.gpsinformation.net/ waas/maps/usaphoto.html**.

NOTE: When you downloaded the elevation data, you obtained it for a specific USGS quadrangle. If the contour lines do not cover the whole desired area, you'll need to scroll over with the arrow keys and repeat the process for an adjacent area.

Chapter 6
Waypoint and Route Management: EasyGPS

Let's take a brief side trip and explore EasyGPS™, a waypoint and route management program. Readers using even some of the more advanced software covered in this book may appreciate how this program provides a simple method for managing waypoints and creating routes.

Basic Information

COST
• Free

SYSTEM REQUIREMENTS
• Windows operating system

GPS COMPATIBILITY
• Garmin, Magellan, Lowrance, MLR, Eagle, Brunton, and Silva GPS units.

TESTED VERSION
• 1.3.7

CONTACT INFORMATION
TopoGrafix™
24 Kirkland Drive
Stow, MA 01775

• info2004@easygps.com
• www.topografix.com

AVAILABLE OPTIONS
• ExpertGPS is a TopoGrafix mapping program that uses TerraServer topo maps and aerial photos, just like USAPhotoMaps does. ExpertGPS, which has extensive capabilities, is covered in Chapter 13. As of this printing, it costs $59.95.

INTERNET RESOURCES
• There are no discussion groups devoted exclusively to EasyGPS, though you may find assistance from the Yahoo Map Authors group at **groups.yahoo.com/group/map_authors**.

Advantages

• The interface is very easy to use.

• Compiling routes from your existing waypoints in this software is a breeze.

• You can maintain a master list of all waypoints, without the 500-waypoint limit found in many GPS receivers.

Disadvantages

• EasyGPS is not mapping software; it is designed only for waypoint and route management. Nevertheless, it does what it was designed to do very well.

• EasyGPS does not allow you to enter coordinates in UTM or in degrees/minutes/seconds format.

• EasyGPS uses WGS84 as its sole datum. This is not a huge drawback, though, since WGS84 is the standard for data transfer. See Chapter 4 for more about datums.

Tutorial/Manual

A simple but useful tutorial is available at **www.easygps.com/tutorials.asp**. A help file is also provided with the program.

Installation

Download the EasyGPS Installer from **www.easygps.com**. Close any open programs and run the installer.

Configuration

When you first start EasyGPS, a **Preferences** window will appear (see Figure 6A). Alternatively, from the **File** menu, choose **Preferences**. Here you can enter your GPS receiver model and unit preferences.

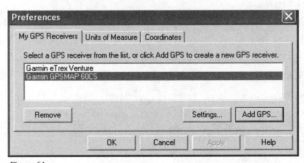

Figure 6A

On the My **GPS Receivers** tab, choose **Add GPS**. From the **Manufacturers** list, choose your brand and then, from the **Models** list, select the correct model and click **OK**. A **GPS Settings** dialog box will open. The **Port** and baud **Speed** will usually have defaulted to the correct settings. If you run into problems, check your GPS owner's manual for the correct baud **Speed**. (See the Communications Protocols section of Chapter 2 for more information on COM ports.) Click **OK** to finish setting up your GPS receiver. For additional configuration information, select **Help**, then **Contents and Index**, and then **Configuring your GPS Receiver**.

Now choose the **Units of Measure** tab and select either **Standard, Nautical,** or **Metric**. Click **OK**.

Finally, select the **Coordinates** tab and choose either **Decimal Degrees** or **Degrees, Minutes.Minutes**.

Getting Started

The Help file has a great section labeled "Getting Started with EasyGPS," which will take you through all the basic steps necessary to familiarize yourself with the software.

File Structure

Data can be saved in two formats:

- .loc (TopoGrafix Data File)

- .gpx (GPS Exchange File)

  Click **New** to open a blank file. Click **Open** to open an existing file.

The tabs along the bottom of the screen represent the currently open files.

Waypoints and Waypoint Management

While EasyGPS's waypoint management may not be any cleaner than that of some other programs, it does provide you with the ability to store a master list of all waypoints you have accumulated. Unfortunately, many GPS receivers carry a limit of 500 waypoints. EasyGPS is a great way to store and organize any number of waypoints.

 To create a new waypoint, click **Add** or select **Waypoint**, then **New Waypoint**. This opens the **Edit Waypoint** dialog box shown in Figure 6B. Enter the **Latitude** and **Longitude** (and **Elevation**, if known), along with a **Waypoint** name, and click **OK**.

I find it easier to use mapping software to create waypoints, rather than manually entering coordinates. But sometimes manual entry can't be avoided. Most other programs in this book allow you to input coordinates in UTM—unlike EasyGPS, which allows input of only lat/lon coordinates.

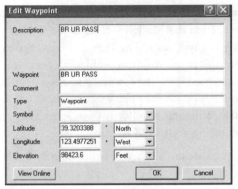

Figure 6B

TIP: From the **Edit Waypoint** dialog box, choose **View Online** to open an Internet browser window that offers a range of choices for viewing the waypoint location on maps and aerial photos. It also provides access to services from which you can purchase maps. By clicking either the aerial photo or the topo link to Microsoft TerraServer, you can see what year the image was created. You can also do this from the **Waypoint** menu, by choosing **View Waypoint Online**.

Routes

To create a route:

1. On the **Route** menu, select **New Route** to open the **Edit Route** dialog box.

2. **Name** the route, click **OK**, then click **Finished**.

3. On the Combo List screen, the lower of the three panes on your screen is the **Route List**. Go there and double-click the new route to set it as the active route. A red arrow will appear beside the route name.

4. You can now add waypoints to the route in one of three ways:

   • Drag a waypoint from the upper pane (the **Waypoint List**) to the center pane on your screen, which is the **Active Route List**.

   • Right-click a waypoint and select **Add Waypoint To Route**.

   • Select a waypoint and click **Waypoint**, then choose **Add Waypoint To Route**.

To edit a route, first double-click the route in the Route List to make it active. Then, in the **Active Route List:**

• Change the order of waypoints in the route by dragging the waypoint to a new location in the active route list.

• Delete a waypoint by right-clicking the route leg and clicking **Delete Leg.** Note the other options shown in Figure 6C.

Figure 6C

GPS Interface

You can send data to your GPS in one of two ways, either of which will transfer all the waypoints or routes in the currently open file:

1. Choose **Send** to open the **Send to GPS** dialog shown in Figure 6D. You can select whether to send only **waypoints, routes,** or both. The numbers of **waypoints** and **routes** shown in the dialog box represent the numbers in the currently loaded .gpx or .loc file, and the number that your GPS can accommodate.

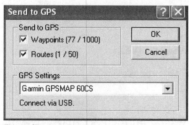

Figure 6D

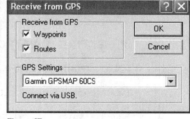

Figure 6E

2. Choose **GPS,** then **Send Waypoints to GPS** or **Send Routes to GPS.**

To transfer an individual waypoint or route, right-click it and select **Send Waypoint to GPS** or **Send Route to GPS.**

To transfer data from your GPS to EasyGPS, click **Receive,** which opens the **Receive from GPS** dialog box shown in Figure 6E. You can select to receive only **waypoints,** only **routes,** or both.

Alternatively, you can select **GPS**, then **Receive Waypoints from GPS** or **Receive Routes from GPS.**

Working With Other Programs

EasyGPS can import and export waypoints in .gpx and .loc formats.

More Tips

• To move data between files, select individual or multiple waypoints or routes, then select **Edit** and **Cut, Copy,** or **Paste.**

• Select **Waypoints,** then **Find Waypoints** to open the dialog shown in Figure 6F. This allows you to search for waypoints by **Description, Type, Elevation,** and **Distance to Point.** For the latter, you'll need to set a waypoint as active to find other waypoints within a certain distance.

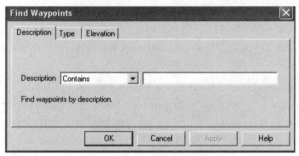

Figure 6F

TIP: SETTING A WAYPOINT AS ACTIVE

• Set a waypoint as active in one of three ways:

• Double-click a waypoint.

• Select a waypoint and choose **Waypoint,** then **Set Active Waypoint.**

• Right-click a waypoint and choose **Select Active Point.**

• To determine the firmware version of your GPS, connect it and turn it on. Select **GPS,** then **GPS Version Info.**

• You can download .loc files directly from **www.geocaching.com.** For more information, select **Help,** then **Contents and Index.** Choose **Geocaching,** then **Configuring your Web browser.**

Section Two Maps on CDs

W alk into your local outfitter and you'll likely find some of the software covered in this section, often side by side with the GPS units you've been drooling over.

The five software packages discussed here are generally easy to use, and typically cost around $100 each. For that, you usually get all the topo maps for an entire state or for regions such as the northeast and mid-Atlantic states.

The map images are high-resolution scans of significantly better quality than the TerraServer-based maps seen in USAPhotoMaps and the programs covered in Section Three. Some of the packages discussed offer 3-D views and access to aerial photography, and all have the ability to track your location in real time if you connect a laptop to your GPS. (Just remember, the laptop is for the passenger, not the driver!)

If you're not looking for a freebie, or if you don't have the time or technical inclination to deal with more complex programs, these packages can be a great solution. They also make a lot of sense if you don't have a broadband Internet connection for faster map downloading. All these programs have some strong advantages, so let's take a closer look at each one.

Chapter 7 National Geographic TOPO!

My first mapping software purchase was the National Geographic® TOPO!™ package for my state. I was a little reluctant to lay out $100, but I was excited by what I could do with it. I wasn't disappointed.

It's difficult to express exactly how cool it was the first time I plugged waypoints into a map, uploaded them to my GPS, followed the route on my mountain bike, then came back home and downloaded my track. It was exciting to see how close USGS was to getting roads and trails properly located on the map!

Basic Information

COST

- $99.95 per state (or group of states in a region)

- $24.95 packages available for groups of national parks or for specific regions

SYSTEM REQUIREMENTS

- Windows 95, 98, ME, 2000, XP, NT 4.0 and higher

- Macintosh OS 9.0 and higher or OS 10.2 and higher

GPS COMPATIBILITY

- Many Garmin, Magellan, and Eagle/Lowrance models.

- More detailed information is available at
  maps.nationalgeographic.com/topo/state.cfm.

TESTED VERSION

- Version 3.4.3

- This chapter is based on the state series. The regional series is slightly different.

CONTACT INFORMATION

National Geographic Maps
P.O. Box 4357
Evergreen, CO 80437-4357
800.962.1643 x130 (technical support)
topo@ngs.org (technical support)
maps.nationalgeographic.com/topo/

- Two packages that allow you to import TOPO! info into ArcView and ArcGIS, aimed at a professional market, are priced at $499 each. See Chapter 23 for more information on GIS software.

- For $19.95, the TOPO! Streets & 3-D Views Expansion Pack adds 3-D views, split-screen capability, updated roads, USB support, and access to updated maps.

- A $25 add-on module, Pocket TOPO!, allows you to transfer maps to a Pocket PC or Palm device and supports real-time tracking on your PDA.

INTERNET RESOURCES

- Although the Yahoo Topomap discussion group (**groups.yahoo.com/group/topomap**) is not extremely active, National Geographic TOPO! staff occasionally answer questions there.

Advantages

- Maps can be transferred from CDs to your hard disk.

- When you place a waypoint, you are automatically taken to the name field—no extra steps are required.

- Routes can be constructed from existing waypoints, retaining waypoint names.

- The Notes feature allows you to place notes and links to digital photos and Web sites.

- You can split tracks.

- A nice extra is TOPO!'s mapXchange Web site, at **maps.nationalgeographic.com/ topo/search.cfm**, where you can easily download a wide range of trails posted by other users, or post your own for others to enjoy.

- You can purchase a $19.95 expansion pack for 3-D viewing.

Disadvantages

- There is no free demo.

- You can't directly export tracks.

- You can't view aerial photos.

Tutorial/Manual

Choose **Info**, then **Help**, using TOPO! to open a fifty-page .pdf file that answers most questions. You may wish to print the guide for reference. Note, however, that as of this writing it appears to be slightly out of date.

A **Status Bar** provides context-sensitive help at the lower left corner of the screen as you move the pointer over tools and map features.

Installation

TOPO! Installation is straightforward. Shut down all other programs, load Disk 1 (the installer disk), and run it. Once you've finished the installation, you may want to visit **maps.nationalgeographic.com/topo/upgrades.cfm** and check for free upgrades.

Configuration

Point to **Preferences** to display the menu shown in Figure 7A. Most of the options are pretty straightforward. Note that **GPS Settings** can also be changed from the **Handhelds** menu. Choose the **GPS Receiver** and **Model** from the list. TOPO! will automatically configure the **Baud Rate** and **Receiver Limits**. If you have any problems finding the proper **COM Port**, see Communications Protocols in Chapter 2.

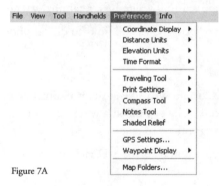

Figure 7A

Getting Started

Once you've installed the software, remove the installer CD and insert any other CD in the set. A **Welcome to TOPO!** window appears. Select one of the following options to open a map:

• **Start with a new map**

• **Browse for an existing map**

• **Return to map from previous session**

To open a map from within the software, click **Open Map**, or choose **File** and then **Open**.

TOPO! has five map levels, each representing a different scanned map at a different scale:

- **Map Level 1** shows a large section of the country, covering roughly 500 by 1000 miles. You can pan to view the entire U.S. at this scale, even though you may have purchased the maps for only one state or region.

- **Map Level 2** shows a smaller area, but still at a fairly large scale, covering roughly 200 by 100 miles. You can view this and smaller-scale maps only for the state(s) or region(s) you purchased.

- **Map Level 3** shows a 1:500,000-scale USGS map.

- **Map Level 4** shows a 1:100,000-scale USGS map.

- **Map Level 5** shows a 7.5' USGS map, usually at a 1:24,000 scale.

The scales often differ in the regional series.

To zoom in on the map, do any of the following:

- Click **Zoom**, then click anywhere on the map to recenter it and take you to the next most detailed of the five map levels.

- Right-click anywhere on the map to display the menu shown in Figure 7B. Select any of the **Levels** to zoom in or out, or select **Magnify Map** to reduce or magnify the current map image. The **Magnify** feature can be very helpful when you're trying to see a wider area on a detailed map or when you're working with routes and waypoints that are near each other.

Level 1 of 5, NG Reference Map
Level 2 of 5, NG Reference Map
Level 3 of 5, 500K Map Series
Level 4 of 5, 100K Map Series
✓ Level 5 of 5, 7.5' Map Series
Magnify Map ▶
About This Map…

Figure 7B

You can navigate using any of the following methods:

- Click anywhere on one of the large-scale regional maps to the right of the main map screen to recenter the map at that location.

- Move any tool to the edge of the screen and it will become an arrow. Click to move the map in the direction of the arrow.

- Click the **Centering** tool, then click anywhere on the map to recenter at that point.

- As shown above, you can click **Zoom,** then click anywhere on the map, to recenter the map and zoom to the next most detailed of the five map levels.

- Once you get to Level 5, the **Zoom** tool will stop working. Instead, click the **Centering** tool, then click anywhere to recenter the map at the level you are currently viewing.

- Click the **Traveling** tool and move the pointer over the map to display an arrow. Click to move the map in the direction of the arrow.

File Structure

TOPO! saves all data in a proprietary .tpo format. To save a .tpo file, choose **File**, then **Save As** (or **Save** if you're working with a new file). The saved file will contain all waypoints, routes, tracks, bookmarks, and labels that you created on the current map.

Unless you will have a very limited number of waypoints, plan to organize your waypoints and other data using separate .tpo files. These files are basically separate maps. For example, you may want a separate file or map for your home county, your favorite river basin, or that upcoming trip to the Yellowstone backcountry.

You can join two files by opening one, selecting **File,** then **Merge .tpo**, and choosing the second file.

You can use additional file management options to select certain types of data, such as waypoints or routes, to delete. Choose **File**, then **Delete Contents** to open the dialog box shown in Figure 7C. This is a permanent deletion, so consider choosing **Save As** first.

TOPO! previously used .tpg files, but newer versions have eliminated this file type. The default location for .tpo and .tpg files is C:\TOPO!.

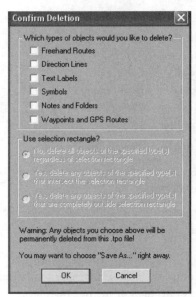

Figure 7C

Waypoints and Waypoint Management

To place waypoints, choose the **Waypoint** tool, then click anywhere on the map. This opens the **TOPO! Waypoint Editor** shown in Figure 7D. Give the waypoint a **Name** and click **OK**.

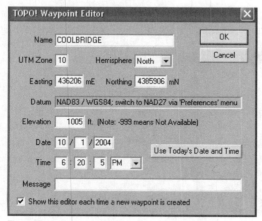

Figure 7D

TIP: Click the **Hotspot Magnifier** to create a magnified view of the pointer area on the lower right side of the screen. This can be a great aid for accurately placing waypoints. You can also find this option in the **View** menu.

You can also choose **View**, then **Coordinate Locator** to enter waypoints manually. If you find yourself having to do this, remember that it is easy to change units of latitude and longitude from the **Preferences** menu by choosing **Coordinate Display**.

Waypoint management is a little limited in this application, but it should readily meet most users' needs. As discussed earlier, waypoints and other data are saved to .tpo files.

Choose **View**, then **GPS Waypoint List** to open a pane in the lower portion of your screen that lists all current waypoints. You can right-click a waypoint and choose **Cut, Copy, Paste,** or **Delete**. These tools can be used to move waypoints to another .tpo file.

Finally, from the **Preferences** menu, choose **Waypoint Display** to bring up several waypoint label display options. When drawing a route in an area crowded with waypoints, clicking **Hide Waypoint Labels** may help you place the route more accurately.

Routes

TOPO!'s **Route** tool allows you to draw a freehand route on the map. It actually functions more like other programs' track tool than a route tool, allowing you to draw in a trail that may not be shown on USGS maps.

Click to begin drawing the route. When you finish, click again to bring up the dialog box in Figure 7E. Name the Route and click **OK**. Let's look at some of the other options here:

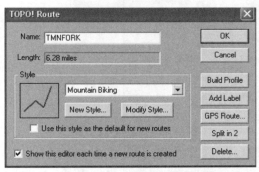

Figure 7E

- Choose **Build Profile** to display an elevation profile of the route as shown in Figure 7F. Any waypoints along the route are displayed as small diamonds. Use your mouse to move the crosshairs along the route and notice that the coordinates and elevation of any given point are displayed below the profile. Click at any point along the profile and a gold dot will appear there, as well as on the map at that location.

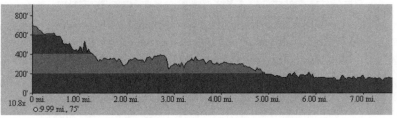

Figure 7F

> **TIP:** Use the profile to find major low and high points on a route. Creating waypoints for each of these key elevation locations may be helpful. Although it requires some manual calculation, adding the elevation change between these points will give you an accurate picture of the elevation gain for any given trip.

• Choose **Add Label** and a label showing the length of the route will appear on the screen. Right-click to open the **TOPO! Text** dialog box shown in Figure 7G. Notice the **Style** section; we'll talk about it a little later on.

Figure 7G

• Choose **GPS Route**, which opens the **TOPO! GPS Route Wizard** (see Figure 7H), to prepare a drawn route for transfer to your GPS. There are three sections to this dialog box:

1. **Number of waypoints.** The maximum number of **Waypoints** allowed was established when you configured your **GPS Settings** in the **Preferences** menu.

2. **Distribution of waypoints.** I prefer the default option, **Match the shape of the freehand route as closely as possible**, but you may prefer one of the other two.

3. **Optional waypoint name prefix.** Entering an **Optional Prefix** can help if you need to delete waypoints later. I often use this feature to export a track, and find that a prefix comes in handy. (More on this later.)

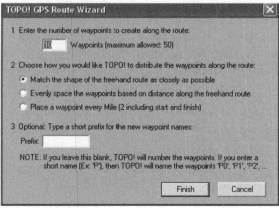

Figure 7H

Click **OK** to create the **GPS Route**, which will show up in the **Waypoint List** as the active route.

• To split routes, first close the **TOPO! Route** dialog box. Now place the **Route** tool over the route to be split, at the location where you want to create the break. Right-click to open the TOPO! Route dialog box (Figure 7E, page 54) again, and select **Split in 2**. This option allows you to split a route and delete just a portion of it.

• Choose **Delete** to delete a route.

• Choosing **New Style** or **Modify Style** allows you to select the color and line style for a given type of route. Each option opens the **Route Style Editor** shown in Figure 7I. Notice that you can change the levels the routes are **Displayed On**.

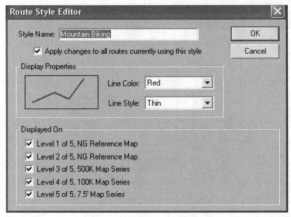

Figure 7I

Think carefully about how you organize styles. There is no way to remove route styles once you create them, and it's easy to overdo it. My styles include routes I have hiked and biked, trails and roads that show on Level 4 but not Level 5 maps, boundary lines, trails and roads that show up on aerial photos but not on maps, and so on.

• Finally, notice the two check boxes in the **TOPO! Route** dialog box. One is **Use this style as the default for new routes**. The other is **Show this editor each time a new route is created**.

Creating Routes to Transfer to Your GPS

TOPO! offers several ways to create routes that can be uploaded to your GPS:

• We've already seen one way to create a route for your GPS—a freehand route drawn using the **Route** tool can be converted to what TOPO! calls a **GPS Route** in the **TOPO! Route** dialog box.

• To create a route and its waypoints as you go, do the following:

1. Click the **Waypoint** tool.

2. From the **Handhelds** menu, choose **New GPS Route**. Notice that a new folder, titled **Empty**, has been created in the Waypoint List. It is red, which indicates that it is active.

3. Click to create a waypoint at the start of your route, name it, and click **OK**.

4. Repeat Step 3 as many times as necessary. If you want to be able to transfer the route to your GPS, don't exceed the number of waypoints per route that your GPS can accommodate.

• To create a route from existing waypoints:

1. Hold down the CTRL key and select the waypoints that you wish to use in the route from the **Waypoint List**.

2. Right-click any of the selected waypoints and select **Copy**.

3. From the **Handhelds** menu, select **New GPS Route**. A new active (red) folder, titled **Empty**, will be created in the **Waypoint List**. Right-click the folder and select **Paste**.

4. Unfortunately, the order of the waypoints is related to the order in which they appeared in the **Waypoint List**. The waypoints now appear underneath the active folder, which now has a name that incorporates the first and last waypoints. You can right-click waypoints and use **Cut** and **Paste** to change their order. Just remember the following two rules:

   – After using **Cut**, select a waypoint, right-click it, and select **Paste**. The waypoint will be inserted immediately before the one that was highlighted.

   – To move a waypoint to the start of a route, paste it onto the route folder.

Using the Route Tool as a Track Tool

TOPO!'s Route Tool actually functions much like other programs' track tools. This makes it excellent for highlighting trails or adding them to maps. Here are some tips on creating tracks or routes:

• If you want to extend a previously created route, hold the **Route** tool near the end you wish to extend. Once a plus sign (+) appears on the screen by the **Route** tool, click to start drawing, extending the route.

• To erase a portion of a route you just drew, hold down the right mouse button and move backward along the line. Release the mouse button to end the erase function.

• To create straight-line segments, hold down the SHIFT key and click the **Route** tool at the beginning of the desired route. The pointer will turn into a diamond with an anchor below it. Move the pointer to the desired end of the straight-line segment and release the SHIFT key; a line will be drawn connecting the beginning and end points. Hold down the SHIFT key again, move to the next location, and release the SHIFT key. Repeat as necessary.

• To view the length of a route, move the **Route** tool over a route; it will turn into a hand. A pop-up label will show the length in whatever **Distance Units** you set in **Preferences**.

TIP: Use the Route tool to trace roads shown on Level 4 (1:100,000-scale) maps that don't show up on Level 5 (1:24,000-scale) maps. You'll instantly have a more complete map than the standard USGS quads!

Tracks

To import tracks from your GPS, from the **Handhelds** menu, choose **Import (from GPS or .txt) Wizard**, opening the dialog box shown in Figure 7J. Select the first option, indicating that your GPS is connected, and click **Next**, opening the dialog box shown in Figure 7K. Select one of the following two options:

• Tracks (make a waypoint for each track point)

• Tracks (make a freehand route for each continuous track)

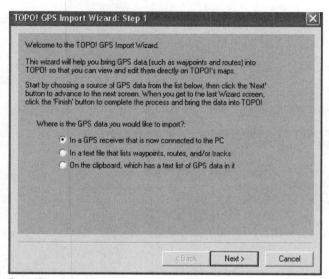

Figure 7J

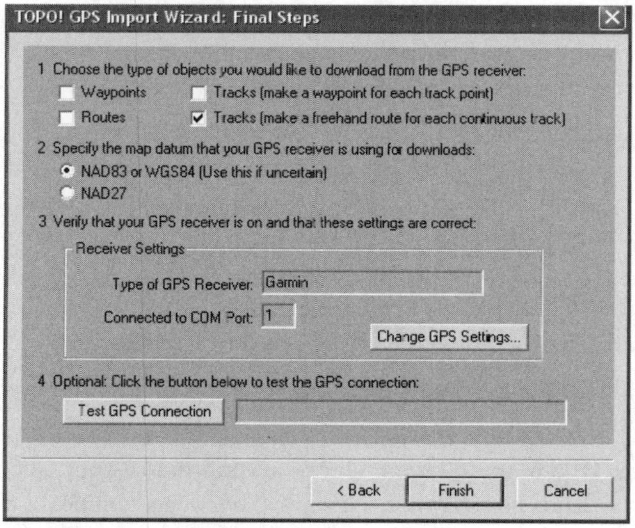

TOPO! GPS Import Wizard: Step 1 ✕

Welcome to the TOPO! GPS Import Wizard.

This wizard will help you bring GPS data (such as waypoints and routes) into TOPO! so that you can view and edit them directly on TOPO!'s maps.

Start by choosing a source of GPS data from the list below, then click the 'Next' button to advance to the next screen. When you get to the last Wizard screen, click the 'Finish' button to complete the process and bring the data into TOPO!

Where is the GPS data you would like to import?:

⦿ In a GPS receiver that is now connected to the PC
◯ In a text file that lists waypoints, routes, and/or tracks
◯ On the clipboard, which has a text list of GPS data in it

< Back   Next >   Cancel

TOPO! GPS Import Wizard: Final Steps ✕

1 Choose the type of objects you would like to download from the GPS receiver:
☐ Waypoints   ☐ Tracks (make a waypoint for each track point)
☐ Routes   ☑ Tracks (make a freehand route for each continuous track)

2 Specify the map datum that your GPS receiver is using for downloads:
⦿ NAD83 or WGS84 (Use this if uncertain)
◯ NAD27

3 Verify that your GPS receiver is on and that these settings are correct:
┌─ Receiver Settings ──────────────────────────────┐
│ Type of GPS Receiver: │Garmin│   │
│ Connected to COM Port: │1│   │
│   Change GPS Settings...   │
└──┘

4 Optional: Click the button below to test the GPS connection:
Test GPS Connection │   │

< Back   Finish   Cancel

Figure 7K

If you choose the latter, you'll be given three additional options, shown in Figure 7L:

• Make a single continuous route connecting all the track points

• Start a new route if a track point is (insert number) miles or further from previous track point

• Start a new route at each point the GPS receiver had to search the sky for satellites

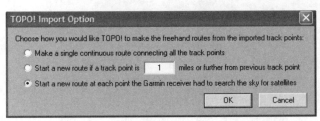

Figure 7L

Your choice may be dictated by whether or not your GPS was able to maintain satellite reception the entire time. If you were in the open, and it did, the first option may be fine. If not, you may find a long and suspiciously straight line connecting two portions of your route.

Finally, select the datum, which should almost always be set to WGS84. (See Chapter 4 for more information on this subject.) Now click **Finish**.

Once the tracks are downloaded, TOPO! treats them like routes. You can right-click for the options discussed in the Routes section of this chapter. You can also use the **GPS Route** feature to convert a track to a route, as discussed earlier. This is the only way to export tracks from TOPO! to your GPS.

GPS Interface

To initiate data transfer from the **Handhelds** menu, select either:

• **Import (from GPS or .txt) Wizard.** Details of this process are covered in the Tracks section of this chapter.

• **Export (to GPS or .txt) Wizard**. Once you confirm that your GPS is connected, you will see the dialog box shown in Figure 7M, offering a number of choices.

 Alternatively, you can choose **GPS and Handheld Options,** which opens the dialog box shown in Figure 7N.

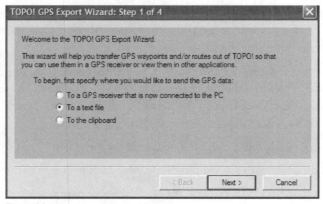

Figure 7M

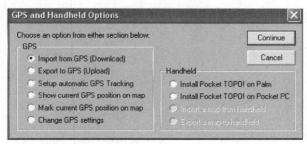

Figure 7N

Printing

> **TIP:** If you want a grid to appear on your printed map, first determine your grid settings. Choose **Grid Settings** to open the dialog box shown in Figure 7O.

Figure 7O

Like most of the software discussed in this section, TOPO! has an easy-to-use print interface. Click **Print or Export**, and a red rectangle with an X through it will appear on the screen.

The red rectangle shows the area that will be printed by default. You can now drag the center of the X to move the entire area to be printed, or drag the edges to expand or contract the area. Notice that on the right side of your screen there is an image, shown in Figure 7P, with the following features:

• The blue rectangle represents the area shown on the screen.

• The red rectangle with an X through it corresponds to the one on the map screen.

• The white background represents the blank sheet of paper.

• The dotted line represents the printable area.

Make sure that you keep the red rectangle within the dotted lines.

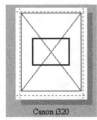

Figure 7P

In the frame below this (Figure 7Q), choose **Page Setup**, then **Portrait** (for a vertical map) or **Landscape** (for a horizontal map). Select your **Paper Size**. Note that you can reduce margin size in the **Margin** box, changing the dotted lines representing the printable area and giving you a larger map. Before leaving **Page Setup**, choose **Printer**, then **Properties**. Select **Preview before printing** if it's available, then click **OK**.

Figure 7Q

We're almost ready to print. But first let's take care of a few other useful things. The pane shown in Figure 7Q provides several printing options:

• Selecting **Select 1 Full Page** will ensure that the map fits the page to the fullest extent possible, given your margin settings.

• Under **Magnification**, choosing **Suggested** will print the map at 50 percent magnification, which strikes a good balance between readability and area covered. Choose **Custom** to bring up several other options, including retaining the original scale of the map (e.g., 1:24,000).

• You may wish to select **Scale Bar** and **North Arrow**.

• Selecting **Grid Label**s does not include the grid on the map—it only provides labels. To show the grid, from the **View** menu choose **Grid**, and select the options you wish to display.

• Other options include a **Header** (file name and/or other information), **Elevation Profile**, and **Notes**.

After making the desired choices, click **Print Map**.

Moving Map

TOPO! allows you to track your position in real time on a laptop. To start, do one of the following:

• Choose **Handhelds**, then **Show Current GPS Position**.

• Click **GPS and Handheld Options**, opening the dialog box shown in Figure 7N, and choose **Show current GPS position on map**.

To create a track of your position readings, choose **Setup Automatic Tracking** from one of the above locations to open the screen shown in Figure 7R. Select from the available options and choose **Start Tracking**.

Pocket TOPO!, a $25 add-on module, allows you to transfer maps to a Pocket PC or Palm device and supports real-time location tracking on your PDA. For information on this and other PDA-based moving map options, see Chapter 22.

3-D

For $19.95, the TOPO! Streets & 3-D Views Expansion Pack adds 3-D views, split-screen capability, updated roads, USB support, and access to updated maps.

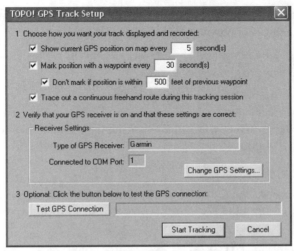

Figure 7R

Working With Other Programs

Use the following procedure to import data from a .txt file:

1. From the **Handhelds** menu, choose **Import (from GPS or .txt) Wizard** to open the dialog box shown in Figure 7J.

2. Select **In a text file that lists waypoints, routes, and/or tracks**. Click **Next**.

3. Choose a .txt file to import. This will open the dialog box shown in Figure 7S. Here you can select the format of the text file (comma-separated values, tab-delimited, and so on) and select the first data line in the import file. Click **Next**.

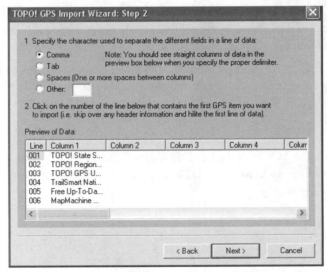

Figure 7S

4. In the dialog box shown in Figure 7T, select the type of objects to be imported and the datum. Click **Next**.

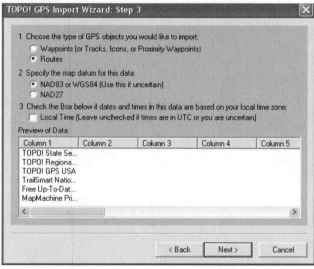

Figure 7T

5. In the next dialog box, shown in Figure 7U, select the data type by selecting the various column headers and making the appropriate choices. Click **Finish**.

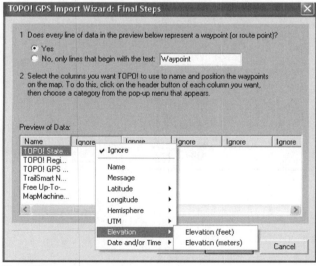

Figure 7U

Use the following procedure to export data to a .txt file:

1. From the **Handhelds** menu, choose **Export (to GPS or .txt) Wizard**, opening the dialog box shown in Figure 7V.

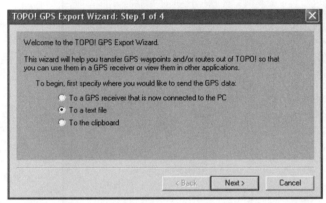

Figure 7V

2. Choose **To a text file** and click **Next**.

3. In the dialog box shown in Figure 7W, select the data you wish to export and click **Next**.

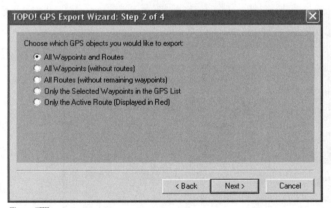

Figure 7W

4. Select the datum in the dialog box shown in Figure 7X, and click **Next**.

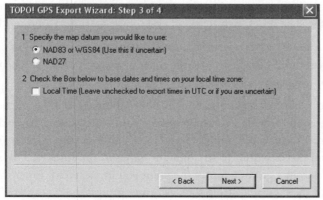

Figure 7X

5. Select the export **Format** from the choices shown in Figure 7Y.

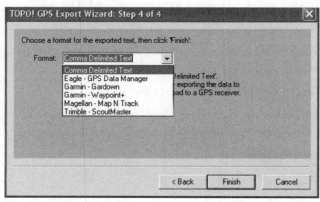

Figure 7Y

6. Name the file and select a location to save it to.

You can also export map images by choosing **File**, then **Export Map to Disk**. You can choose from various formats including .bmp, .eps, .gif, .jpg, .pcx, and .tif. (Note that this option is not available in the regional series.) Since TOPO! allows you to export areas larger than the screen, you can put these files on a disk and, with a quick trip to a computer-savvy copy shop, create a large-format map for field use.

More Tips

- Want to know the name of the quad you're looking at? If you're using a newer version of the state series, right-click a Level 5 map and select **About This Map**.

- To start a route or create a waypoint near another feature of the same type, simply hold down the CTRL key, move the route or waypoint tool to wherever you desire, and then release the CTRL key.

- To begin a name or feature search, click the **Compass** tool. An anchor will appear at the pointer. To provide a central point for your search, place the anchor by clicking anywhere on the map. From the **View** menu, choose **Find (Gazetteer)**, and select **Only find places within** (insert number) **miles of the Anchor**. This search will locate features within a given radius of the point you just selected. Enter the number of miles and then a search string such as "Hot Springs."

- Choose **Info**, then **Legend** to open the dialog box shown in Figure 7Z. This is a great way to learn important USGS map symbols.

- Choose **Shaded Relief**, to toggle this feature on and off.

- Use the **Note** tool to place links to notes, photos, and Web links.

- Use the **Symbol** tool to place symbols on the map. Place a symbol and choose **New Style** or **Modify Style** for a range of choices.

- Use the **Text** tool to place text labels on the map.

- Finally, don't forget to check out the trails other TOPO! users have posted to TOPO!'s mapXchange, at **maps.nationalgeographic.com/topo/search.cfm**.

Figure 7Z

TIP: LOAD MAPS TO YOUR HARD DISK

For convenient access to maps you frequently view, just load them onto your hard disk. This can also keep you from having to change CDs as you near the edge of coverage for an individual disk.

For the state series:

1. Insert any of the CDs (except the installer disk) into your computer's CD-ROM drive.

2. View the contents of the CD using **My Computer**.

3. Right-click on the folder called XX_DOX and select **Copy** (for example, CA_DO7 for California Disc 7).

4. Using **My Computer**, locate your hard disk, then the TOPO! folder.

5. Now locate the folder named TPO_DATA, right-click on it, and select **Paste**.

To do this for a regional series:

1. Open the folder called xxx_DATA (for example, CYN_DAT for TOPO! Grand Canyon).

2. You will see a number of folders. Choose **Edit**, then **Select All**. Now right-click and select **Copy**.

3. Using My Computer, find your hard disk, then the TOPO! folder. Now locate the folder named TPO_DATA, right-click, and select **Paste**.

Updates to this book will be posted at www.MakeYourOwnMaps.com. Bookmark and visit often to see what's new in the world of digital mapping.

Chapter 8 Maptech Terrain Navigator

Maptech™ Terrain Navigator™ is similar to most of the software packages in this section. It has some very nice features—my favorite is the way it displays the grid on printed maps. I always carry a printed map on my outdoor adventures, and it is usually a Terrain Navigator map. Most of the software packages in this book will superimpose a grid on the map. What Terrain Navigator does, in addition, is to place rulers along the perimeter. If you combine this with a UTM coordinate display, you end up with a map that makes it very easy to establish your location in the field.

Other highlights include 3-D viewing and the ability to view two maps side by side. The latter is useful if, for example, you wish to compare a 1:24,000-scale map to one at 1:100,000.

Basic Information

COST
• $99.95 per state or region

• Demonstration version available at **www.maptech.com** (click on **Downloads**)

SYSTEM REQUIREMENTS
• Microsoft Windows 95, 98, ME, NT, 2000, or XP

• Pentium-class CPU

• 32 MB of RAM

• 256-color display (16-/24-/32-bit color for 3-D)

• OpenGL Video Accelerator recommended for optimal 3-D performance

• CD-ROM drive

GPS COMPATIBILITY
• Terrain Navigator works with almost all Garmin, Lowrance, and Magellan models, although, as of this writing, support was not available for Garmin USB units. Other brands and models of GPS units may not be capable of storing, downloading, or uploading tracks and other information from Terrain Navigator. Maptech has excellent GPS compatibility information online at **ftp://ftp.maptech.com/downloads/ TN_GPSChart.pdf**. If you have any GPS compatibility problems with Terrain Navigator, you may be able to find the answer there.

TESTED VERSION
• 6.03

CONTACT INFORMATION
Maptech, Inc.
10 Industrial Way
Amesbury, MA 01913
978.792.1000
www.maptech.com/land/terrainnavigator/

OTHER AVAILABLE OPTIONS
• Terrain Navigator Pro, the subject of the next chapter, costs $299.95 per state or region, and includes significant additional features. Each package includes a one-year subscription that allows you to download aerial photos for the corresponding state or region to your hard drive. After the subscription period expires you must pay $99.95 per year to download additional or updated photos for that region. The program also allows you to export maps and photos to Photoshop and CAD/GIS programs.

• Maptech offers two PDA packages: Outdoor Navigator and Pocket Navigator. For more information on these, see Chapter 22.

• Maptech also offers a National Park Digital Guide and software for the Appalachian, Continental Divide, and Pacific Crest trails.

• Particularly noteworthy is Terrain Navigator 50/50, a digital guide to the highest point in each of the 50 United States. The $9.95 price makes it a great introductory package, especially for peak baggers.

INTERNET RESOURCES
• The Yahoo Map Authors group, at **groups.yahoo.com/group/map_authors**, lists Terrain Navigator as a product discussed on its message board.

• Maptech hosts a forum for Terrain Navigator support at **www.maptech.com/ support/forums/index.cfm**.

Advantages

• A demo version is available.

• You can view maps in three dimensions.

• A well-conceived way of showing the grid on printed maps makes it easy to read your location (especially when using a UTM grid) without cluttering the map.

• You can construct routes from existing waypoints, retaining waypoint names.

- Dual map windows let you view maps side by side—so you can, for example, compare maps of different scales or view a map and its corresponding 3-D image.

- You can capture a rotating 3-D animated image as an .avi file.

- It's easy to e-mail Terrain Navigator maps to friends.

Disadvantages

- GPS waypoint names you create in the program or export with the program are limited to six characters.

- Once you've placed a waypoint, it takes three extra steps to get to the name field.

- You cannot change the color or symbol associated with a group of waypoints after they are created, other than by changing them one at a time. The sole exception to this is route waypoints.

- You cannot view aerial photos.

- You cannot split tracks.

- You cannot start a track or directly start a route on an exiting waypoint.

> **NOTE:** The following disadvantages with version 6.03 are scheduled to be fixed in a free update, version 6.04, which was slated for release in March 2005:
>
> - You cannot load maps onto your hard disk.
>
> - You cannot eliminate the white background on marker labels, which masks a portion of the map.
>
> - The new version will allow you to place notes on the map.

Tutorial/Manual

Terrain Navigator has a comprehensive **Help** file, with few deficiencies. While there is no Print heading under **Contents**, you can get information on printing by choosing the **Index** tab and selecting **Printing Maps**. The **Help** button found in many dialog boxes provides context-sensitive help.

Terrain Navigator also comes with a helpful "Getting Started" manual. Yellow labels called **Tooltips** appear as you point to toolbar buttons or controls. And a **Help Line** is shown on the gray bar at the bottom of the map screen as you point to various menu items or controls.

Installation

1. First, shut down all other Windows applications.

2. Load and run the Installer CD. Follow the directions as they appear on your screen.

3. Following Step 2 you will be prompted to load a CD for the state set you purchased. Insert any of the CDs and choose **Install New CD**. You will then be asked if you want to add that state "to your library of map CDs." Click **Yes**.

4. You will next be asked to register and enter the product ID code found on your registration card. Do not throw this card away! If you ever have to reinstall your software, you'll need it again.

5. After you register the product, you will be prompted to load the CD titled "Geographic Data Enhancement." According to Maptech's documentation, this will provide "more accurate profiles, greater 3-D detail, and closer spot elevation approximations." The digital elevation data is based on 1:24K digital elevation models (DEMs), not the less-detailed 1:100K DEMs. This information will be placed on your hard drive. Map images, which take up much more disk space, are located on each of the disks in the Terrain Navigator set. For more information on DEMs, see Chapter 21.

Configuration

To configure Terrain Navigator, choose **File**, then point to **Preferences**. Now select **GPS Setup**, then select the appropriate GPS model. Before leaving **GPS Setup**, be sure to read the **Driver Notes** area, which provides important information about how your particular GPS model works with Terrain Navigator. Should you encounter difficulties, choose **Help**, then **Contents**, select the **Index** tab, and enter **GPS**. Select **GPS Troubleshooting** for helpful information on GPS connections.

From the **Preferences** dialog box you can configure other program options by selecting an item from the **Category** list.

> **TIP:** You can also open the **Preferences** dialog box by clicking the **Preferences** tool. For context-sensitive help, select **Help** on any category's **Preferences** dialog box.

Choose **General** to open the dialog box shown in Figure 8A. Here you can set your preferences for display of **Coordinates, Datum, Bearings,** and **Height**. For more information on datums, see Chapter 4. Setting **Height** to **Local** will utilize the same units for elevation that the map uses; if the map shows contour intervals in meters, selecting

Local will cause elevation to show in meters. Otherwise you can set **Height** to always show in **Feet** or **Meters**. The **Controls** area allows you to select toolbars and other control and help features. **Control Size** sets the size of the Toolbar, Compass Control Bar, and **Help Line**. Selecting **Small** will devote more screen area to maps and less to controls. **Live Scroll** allows the screen to update as soon as a scroll bar is moved; otherwise the screen will not update until the mouse button is released. This option works well with fast computers. Clicking **Edge Arrow** will convert any tool to a black arrow as you move near the edge of the screen. Once the edge arrow appears, you can use the mouse to scroll, or double-click to jump further on the map. Checking **Allow "Delete All"** will allow you to delete all layers of a given type, such as routes, in one operation. I recommend not checking this box—but if you do, a safety mechanism in the program will help prevent accidental deletions. If you select this option and later try to delete a layer, you will be asked to use SHIFT + DELETE.

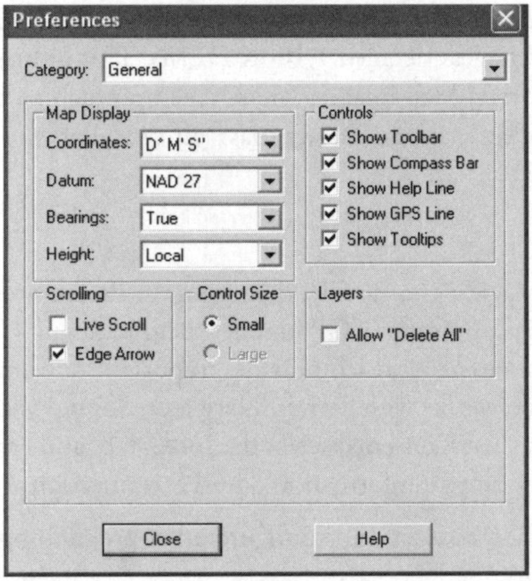

Figure 8A

The **Markers** category controls the display of markers, which effectively function as waypoints in Terrain Navigator. Options include changing the **Default Name** and resetting **Numbering**. You can also **Change Symbol** and change the symbol **Color**. Note that while you can change the marker **Color**, you cannot eliminate the white background for the label.

> **WARNING:** In the **Markers**, **Routes**, and **Tracks Preferences** dialog boxes, be cautious about resetting **Numbering**, which can result in duplicate marker names.

The **Routes** category allows you to set up a default **Route Prefix** and route **Waypoint Prefix,** or to **Reset Numbering** of waypoints. You can also select the waypoint symbol **Color**, and various symbol styles are available by clicking **Symbol**. Finally, you can select the **Line Color** for routes.

The **Tracks** category allows you to choose a **Default Name**. Options are **Text, Date,** and **Time**. If you choose **Text**, you can type a default **Prefix**. You can also select the **Line Color** for tracks and **Reset Numbering** of tracks.

Finally, for a discussion of the **3-D** and **GPS Tracking** categories, see the 3-D and Moving Map sections of this chapter.

Getting Started

Insert any of the map CDs (labeled "USGS Topographic Series") into your CD-ROM drive. Choose **Map Selector,** or choose **File** and then choose **Open Map**, which brings up an **Open Map** screen that shows a regional map. In the **Map Type** box, select the preferred scale, either 1:24,000/1:25,000 or 1:100,000, which brings up an outline of the quads at this scale for the CD in your drive. Choose **Seamless** to be able to scroll seamlessly between quads. Otherwise, you will see an exact scanned image of the USGS map with all the information found on the map collar. (You can also get to the **Seamless** and **Single-Map** choices from the main screen **View** menu.) In the **Single-Map View** a new navigation tool (Figure 8B) appears in the lower left portion of the screen. This tool allows you to click on adjacent quadrangles. In the **Coverage** box, select **CD** for a regional map that is zoomed in to the current CD. Choose **CD Library** to change CDs.

Figure 8B

Terrain Navigator lets you have two map windows open at once, side by side. The map or window you are currently working on is the **Active** map. Choosing **Replace Active** will replace the last map you were working on with the newly selected one, while choosing **Open Another** will open a second map window. If you already have two map windows open, the **Open Another** button will be replaced by one with a **Replace Inactive** option.

> **TIP:** Choose **Find** in the **Open Map** window, or choose **Find** from the main map screen, to search and open maps by a variety of feature types.

Navigating the Map

Terrain Navigator offers several ways to move around the map:

- Click the **Drag** tool and use it to drag the map to a new location.

- Click the **Center** tool, then click anywhere on the map to center the map at that location.

- In the **General** section of **Preferences**, if you selected **Edge Arrow**, any tool will change to a black arrow as you near the edge of the screen. Once the edge arrow appears, you can click to scroll the map, or double-click to jump a greater distance across the map.

To zoom:

- Use the **Zoom In** and **Zoom Out** tools.

- Use the **Zoom Level** button. Zooming options are limited to 1:1, 2:1, 1:2, and 1:4.

- Right-click anywhere on the map and choose **Zoom In** or **Zoom Out**.

To the left of the screen, several features, shown in Figure 8C, provide additional options for navigation and managing map display:

- Select a point on the compass to shift the map one-half screen in the chosen direction.

- The **Map Overview** window below the compass shows the entire quadrangle you are viewing. Click **Show Large Overview** to enlarge the **Map Overview** window. You can also right-click anywhere on a map and select **Overview** to open the large **Overview** window. This will bring up an overview of the entire 1:24,000 or 1:100,000 quad you are on, with a blue rectangle indicating the position of the main map screen. To move the main map screen to the new position, drag the rectangle to a new location and either double-click it or click **OK**. You can navigate in the same manner on the small **Map Overview** window in the pane on the left side of the screen.

Figure 8C

 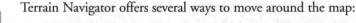

- Click **Two-Window Mode** to open a second map window—a useful feature for viewing maps side by side. In this mode, the title bar of the active map window will be highlighted. The active window is always the last one you were working with. Click **One-Window Mode** to close the second map window.

Waypoints and Waypoint Management

Terrain Navigator actually has two types of waypoints. One is used in routes, and will be discussed in the Routes section of this chapter. The other type is referred to as a Marker. **Markers** can be sent to your GPS and read as waypoints.

Click the **Marker** tool (or, alternatively, choose **Tools** and then **Marker**) and click anywhere on the map to place markers. Use the upper point of the triangle as a guide for placement. Once you've placed a marker, right-click the marker and then select **Edit**. This will allow you to edit the **Full Name** and **GPS Name**. Unfortunately, only six characters are allowed for the name sent to your GPS, even though your unit may be able to handle longer waypoint names. Imported waypoints can have longer GPS names, but longer names exported from Terrain Navigator back to your GPS will be truncated to six characters. If you have multiple names starting with the same six characters, only one will be saved to your GPS.

> **TIP:** G7toWin, a free utility discussed in Chapter 26, has a feature on the **Waypoints** menu to remove duplicate waypoints based on six characters. Users of Terrain Navigator may find this feature helpful.

From the **Edit Markers** dialog box shown in Figure 8D, select **Symbol** to open the **Symbol Editor** dialog box, which allows you to choose the marker symbol used on the map. You can also change the **Symbol Size** and **Color**. Changes you make here do not

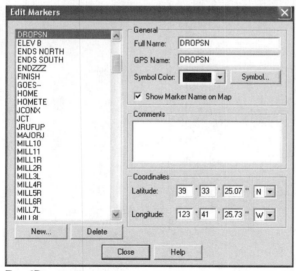

Figure 8D

affect the default settings you made in the **Preferences** dialog box. There is no way to remove the white background for marker labels in version 6.03, though this problem was scheduled to be fixed in version 6.04 (scheduled for release in March 2005).

To locate a marker at a specific longitude and latitude, first open the **Edit Markers** dialog box by either right-clicking an existing marker or choosing **Layers**, then **Markers**. Once in the **Edit Markers** dialog box, click **New** to open the **New Marker** dialog box shown in Figure 8E. Now type the marker's **Name** and **Coordinates**. Remember that you can change the coordinate format by clicking **Preferences**, then selecting the **General** category.

To delete a specific marker, right-click it, then choose **Delete**. Alternatively, open the **Edit Markers** dialog box (Figure 8D), select the marker(s) you want to delete, then choose **Delete**.

Notice that when you move the **Marker** tool over an existing marker, it will change from a triangle to a hand with a triangle. You can now drag the marker to a new location, or right-click for some of the options previously discussed.

Terrain Navigator limits zoom capability to 2:1, which can make it difficult to work with closely placed markers. You can mitigate this by hiding selected markers using Terrain Navigator's **Layer Visibility** feature. See Managing Layers later in this chapter for more information on this feature.

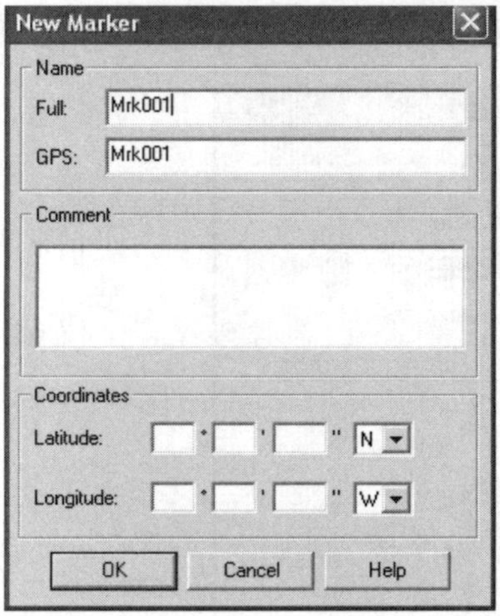

Figure 8E

Routes

You can create a route from existing waypoints and retain the waypoint names using the following procedure:

1. Choose **Layers**, then **Routes** to open the **Edit Routes** dialog box shown in Figure 8F.

2. Choose **New** to open the **Route Waypoints/Legs** dialog box.

3. Choose **New** to open the **New Waypoint** dialog box.

4. In the **Name** area, choose the **Full Name** drop-down menu and select the first waypoint in the route.

5. Repeat Steps 3 and 4 as necessary to complete the route.

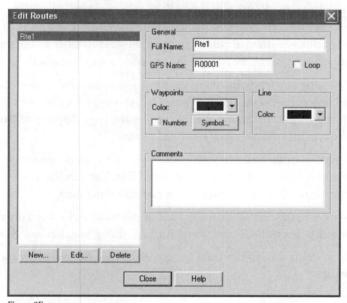

Figure 8F

> **TIP:** Once you've assigned waypoints to a route, you can change the color and symbol for all of them in a single operation using the **Edit Routes** dialog box.

Another way to create a route is to use the **Route** tool (which can also be accessed by choosing **Tools** and then **Route**). Once the **Route** tool is enabled, clicking anywhere on the map places a route waypoint. Subsequent waypoints are placed and named in consecutive order. Should you make an error, press the BACKSPACE or DELETE key to delete the last waypoint in the route.

Finish Route

Once you're finished, either select the **Route** tool again or choose **Finish Route**.

Right-click any waypoint along the route to bring up a menu that provides a number of options. Choose **Edit Route** to open the dialog box shown in Figure 8F. Give the route a **Full Name** and **GPS Name** of your choosing. Changes to **Waypoint Color** and **Symbol** here will alter all waypoints in the route. Choose **Number** to give waypoints consecutive numeric prefixes. You can also change the **Line Color** connecting route waypoints and select **Loop** to connect the first and last waypoints.

From the **Edit Routes** box, you can click **Edit**, which will allow you to give individual waypoints descriptive names, as well as change their symbols and colors.

To insert a waypoint mid-route, move the **Route** tool anywhere along the route. As it nears the route, the **Route** tool icon will change, and you can click to add a waypoint to the route. You can drag this and any other waypoint in the route to a new location. The waypoint you inserted will be assigned the next number in the route sequence. You can edit this number or assign the waypoint a name as described above.

Right-clicking any waypoint along the route gives you other options as well. **Toggle Route Loop** connects the final waypoint in the route with the first one, creating a loop. Click it again to remove the leg creating the loop. **Append to Route** allows you to add waypoints to a previously finished route.

 Note that you cannot place a waypoint on top of a marker unless you hide the marker. To do this, right-click the marker and click **Hide**. You can also choose **Toggle Layers** on the toolbar, which temporarily hides objects on the map.

To reverse a route, right-click a waypoint in the route and select **Edit Route Waypoints** to open the **Route/Waypoint Legs** dialog box. Choose **Reverse**.

Finally, to delete a waypoint from a route, right-click the waypoint and select **Delete Waypoint**.

Tracks

 To create tracks, choose the **Track** tool, or choose **Tools** and then **Track**. Then click anywhere on the map to start. The **Track** tool can be used in two ways:

1. Click at every bend in the track, essentially connecting a series of straight lines.

2. Hold down the mouse button and drag to create a freehand track on the screen.

When you're done, choose **Finish Track**. You can also finish by choosing the **Track** tool button again or right-clicking the track and selecting **Finish Track**.

  You can also create tracks by selecting one of the **Distance** tools, then right-clicking on the line created and selecting **Convert to Track**.

While you're drawing a track using any of these methods, you can erase the last section(s) drawn with the BACKSPACE or DELETE key. Once you choose **Finish Track**, however, you cannot further modify the track line.

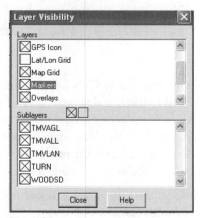

To assign a name to a track or change its color, right-click the track and select **Edit**. From the **Edit Tracks** dialog box, you can also convert a track to a route by selecting the **Route** button.

To create a loop, right-click a track and then choose **Toggle Loop** to connect the two ends of the track. Right-click a track and click **Information** to see the track length. This will even show the acreage of a toggled loop! To create an elevation profile, right-click a track and select **Profile**.

File Structure: Managing Layers

Choose **View**, then **Layer Visibility** to control which layers appear on the map. In the **Layer Visibility** box, select which layers you want to make visible. Choose **Markers**. The **Layer Visibility** box should resemble the one in Figure 8G. Now move down to the **Sublayers** area, where your markers will be listed. Next to the word **Sublayers** are two boxes. Choose the box on the left to select every item in the sublayer list and show them on the map. Choose the box on the right to clear every item in the sublayer list from the map.

Figure 8G

Unfortunately, there is no other way to manage data in Terrain Navigator. For that option, you'll have to fork over the extra $200 for Terrain Navigator Pro. Neither does Terrain Navigator offer any way to save a map project. This could be cumbersome if you have a great deal of data and want to show only part of it on a particular map.

Of course, you can code markers and other layer names with a prefix for a certain project or area. However, being limited to only six characters per name for items you send to your GPS limits your flexibility.

> **TIP:** If you find yourself placing temporary markers, or other temporary items, on maps for whatever reason, leave a blank space at the beginning of the name of any temporary item. These items will be the first to show up in the **Layer Visibility** list.

The default location for data in Terrain Navigator is C:\Program Files\Maptech\ Terrain Navigator. There are subfolders for markers, routes, and tracks. To transfer any of this data to another program, use the import and export functions described later in this chapter in Working With Other Programs.

> **TIP:** Terrain Navigator has no "save" button or command. Instead, it saves your work when you exit the program. If you're doing a lot of work, it's a good idea to close and reopen the program occasionally, especially if you have multiple programs running. Also, many mapping programs were designed to use all of your computer's free memory. If you find that the program is sluggish, or subject to lock ups or crashes, try using it without other programs running.

GPS Interface

To send markers to your **GPS** as waypoints, choose **GPS**, point to **Send to GPS**, and then choose **Send Markers**. In the **Send Markers** dialog box, you can select individual markers, or hold down the CTRL key while selecting several markers to send. You can also click a marker in the list, hold down the SHIFT key, and click another marker to select all markers in between. Once you have selected the markers to transfer to your GPS, choose **Send**. Tracks and routes are handled in the same manner.

There is a simpler way to send individual markers, waypoints, and tracks to your GPS: Right-click any of these features and choose **Send to GPS**.

To send waypoints from your GPS to Terrain Navigator as markers, choose **GPS**, point to **Receive from GPS**, then choose **Receive Waypoints**. Select the waypoints you wish to import and then click **OK**. Routes are imported in the same manner.

When importing tracks, after you choose **OK** you'll be presented with the opportunity to name each track. The **Track Name** dialog box will also allow you to create a **New** track, **Append** the track to an existing one, or **Overwrite** an existing track file.

Printing

There are two key printing options with Terrain Navigator. Choose **Quick Print** or choose **File**, then **Quick Print** to print only the area shown on the screen.

For greater flexibility, click the **Print** tool or choose **File**, then select **Print** to open the **Print** dialog box shown in Figure 8H. Let's take a closer look at some of the options and features in this dialog box:

- The area outlined in blue is the area that will be printed. You can drag the blue box to a new location.

- The size of the area can be enlarged or reduced by changing the **Scale**, although changing it from 100% will reduce readability.

- Select **Summary** to include a scale note (e.g., 1 inch = x feet) and a **Caption**, if you wish. The **Summary** option will reduce the size of the map area printed.

- To set the map quality, use the **Quality** and **Weight** options. The latter controls ink density.

- Select the **Layer** box to include markers, routes, tracks, distance lines, and a grid. Note that layers may show on the map overview but will not show on the printed map unless you check the **Layers** option. The **Small, Medium,** and **Large** options influence the size of marker names and symbols.

- Select the **Layer Information** box to print an additional sheet that shows layer data.

- To show gridlines on the map, you must select both **Rulers** and **with Gridlines**. If you select only **Rulers,** the grid coordinate system (e.g., UTM) scale will show on the perimeter of the map, but gridlines will not appear across the face of it. **Rulers** is an excellent feature, and I suggest you familiarize yourself with it. To select the grid coordinate system, from the **File** menu point to **Preferences** and select **General**.

- Select **North Arrow** to place a north arrow and another arrow showing magnetic north in the lower left corner of the map.

- You also have the option of placing **1" ticks,** or marks, along the edges of the map.

Updates to this book will be posted at www.MakeYourOwnMaps.com.
Bookmark and visit often to see what's new in the world of digital mapping.

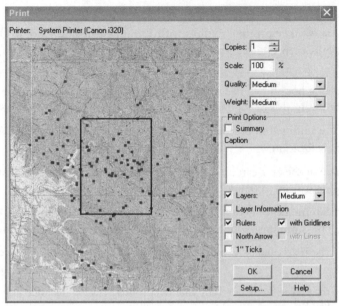

Figure 8H

Moving Map

Choose **Preferences** and select the **GPS Tracking** category to display the dialog box shown in Figure 8I. Here you can customize your **Position Icon** and **Screen** behavior, and establish how often **Tracking** of your location is updated.

From the GPS menu, point to **GPS Tracking** and choose **Start Tracking** to begin tracking your position. From the same menu, choose **Record Track** to display the dialog box shown in Figure 8J. Here you can **Name** the track file and choose from several options for collecting track **Points**:

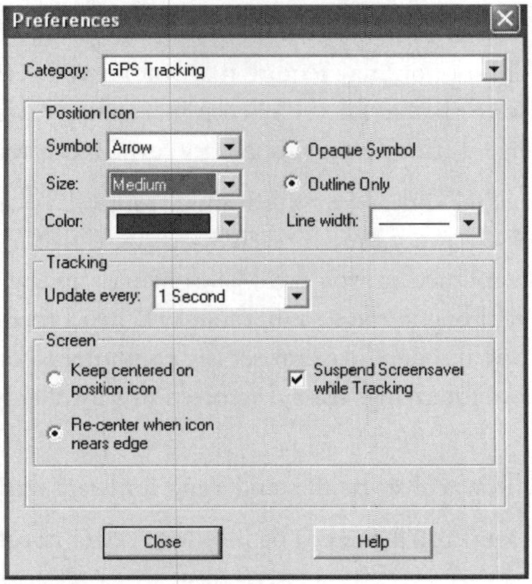

Figure 8I

Figure 8J

• **By time** (specify the time interval)

• **By distance** (specify the distance interval)

• **By direction change**

From the **GPS** menu, you can also select **Find GPS Location**—which is helpful if you don't know your position on the map, as it will center the screen at your location. You can also choose **Place Marker at GPS Position**.

Finally, on the **GPS** menu, point to **Utilities** for the following options:

- **Show Satellite Status.** This option may require that you set your GPS to NMEA data transfer. Be sure also to change the GPS Setup in Terrain Navigator Preferences. And don't forget to change it back to the proprietary format afterward.

- **Set System Clock to Satellite Time.** I love this feature. Your GPS's clock synchronizes with the GPS satellite clocks every time it receives signals. So your GPS receiver is probably the most accurate timepiece you own! Click here to update your computer's clock. There may be a slight bug in the system, though. When I tried it, my GPS was set to the correct time, but Terrain Navigator set my computer to one hour later, apparently because of daylight savings time. I resolved this by changing the computer hour manually.

- **Show GPS Unit Info.** This will give you the model and firmware version for your GPS.

- **Show Streaming GPS Data.** You'll need to be in NMEA data transfer mode for this as well.

Pocket Navigator, an added module priced at $99.95, lets you export Terrain Navigator maps to this Pocket PC-based application, which is capable of real-time tracking when connected to your GPS. For information on Pocket Navigator and other PDA-based moving map options, see Chapter 22.

3-D

Choose **Preferences** and select the **3-D** category to open the dialog box shown in Figure 8K. Here you can choose various options for Terrain Navigator's 3-D mode:

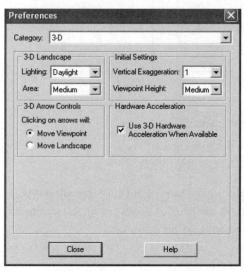

Figure 8K

- From the **Lighting** list, click **Daylight, Fog, White, Moonlight, Wire Frame,** or **Overhead.** Several of these effects are obvious, while others beg explanation. **White** and **Wireframe** both remove the topographic map image. **White** replaces it with a white and gray landscape, which Maptech compares to a moonscape, while **Wire Frame** replaces the image with a grid. **Overhead** brightens relatively flat areas and is designed to make map details more legible.

- Under **Area,** choosing **Large** will allow you to view a larger area in 3-D. If your computer's power is limited, you may prefer to set this to **Small.**

- Under **Initial Settings, Vertical Exaggeration** controls the height relative to horizontal distances. Values above 1 exaggerate the vertical. Set this to 1 to create the most realistic landscape. (Those mountains sure look a lot smaller on the computer screen!)

- **Viewpoint Height** changes the perspective from which you view the scene.

- **3-D Arrow Controls** affect how the arrow controls respond. The choices are **Move Viewpoint** in the direction of the arrow or **Move Landscape** in the direction of the arrow.

- Finally, choose **Use 3-D Hardware Acceleration When Available.** Choose **Help** and select the **Index** tab, then choose **Video Card Drivers** for information on hardware acceleration and improving Terrain Navigator's 3-D performance. For more tips on improving your computer's 3-D performance, and for information on other programs with 3-D options, see Chapter 21.

 To view maps in three dimensions, choose **Toggle 3-D View.** The area you were previously viewing in two dimensions will change to 3-D. To expand the area viewed, change the **Map Scale** to 1:100,000 or change the **Zoom Level** to 1:2 or 1:4, but watch out—this may slow your computer drastically. Remember that you can also control the **Area** viewed from the **3-D Preferences** menu.

 Use the **Drag** tool to rotate the screen and change the perspective.

 The 3-D tools on the left side of the screen, shown in Figure 8L, provide the following options:

- Zoom in and out by clicking the **Move Forward** and **Move Backward** arrows.

- Change the relative **Elevation** from which you view the 3-D image.

- **Rotate** the scene.

Figure 8L

- Change the relative height of landscape features by using the **Vertical Exaggeration** buttons.

- Use the **3-D Glasses View**, with the glasses that come with the program. (It's a little cheesy, but your kids will probably love it.)

- Use Terrain Navigator to create an animated .avi file of a rotating 3-D view. Open a 3-D view, adjust the viewing angle, and choose **Save Animation**.

> **NOTE:** The 3-D animation feature requires a codec (short for compressor-decompressor) that may or may not be available on your computer. Intel developed the particular codec required, called Indeo (which stands for Intel Video) but sold it to Ligos Corporation in 2001. This typically isn't a problem, but if you're running Windows XP with Service Pack 1 or 2 you may not have Indeo Video 5.2. If not, you'll need to lay out $15 for the codec, which you can find at **www.ligos.com/indeo.htm#xp.**

Working With Other Programs

From the **File** menu, choose **Import** or **Export**, then **Markers, Routes,** or **Tracks** to import or export these data sets.

Terrain Navigator allows you to import and export markers (waypoints) as marker export files (.mxf). You can also import .mtx files from the older TopoScout program, the predecessor to Terrain Navigator. You can convert waypoint data from other programs into this text file format. For more information, choose **Help** and **Contents,** then **Markers,** and then click **Marker Text File Format (.MXF).**

> **TIP:** FormatMXF, a marker import utility, is available as a free download from **www.maptech.com.** Click on the download button. This utility helps clean up .mxf and .txt files created for importing into Terrain Navigator. It also works with .csv files and files created with Excel. More information is available on the FormatMXF download page.

You can import or export routes in the route text file format (.rxf), or import older TopoScout .mtx route files. For more information on the .rxf format, choose **Help,** then **Contents,** and then select the **Index** tab. Now choose **Routes,** then **Route Text File Format (.RXF).**

Tracks can be imported and exported as track text file format (.txf). For information on importing tracks from other programs with text or Microsoft Excel files, choose **Help,** then **Contents,** and select the **Index** tab. Now choose **Tracks,** then **Track Text File Format (.TXF).**

> **NOTE:** All Terrain Navigator data import and export utilizes the WGS84 datum. For more information on datums, see Chapter 4.

You can export the map image shown on the screen to other programs, such as a graphics program, OziExplorer, or Fugawi (see Section Four). Choose **File,** then **Export,** and select **Active Map.** Terrain Navigator allows you to export image files in three formats—.tif, .bmp, and .jpg. You can also copy the image to Windows Clipboard and export an .avi video clip, as discussed in the 3-D section of this chapter. Note that you can export only the area shown on the screen, not an entire quad.

More Tips

- Click **Toggle Layers** to show or hide all layers, including markers, routes, tracks, and the map grid. You can also do this from the **View** menu by deselecting **Show Layers.**

- When using a tool, pressing the CTRL key will toggle to the **Drag** tool.

- Terrain Navigator makes it easy to send a map to a friend. Choose **File,** then **Send Map** to e-mail a .jpg image of the current screen. Since you'll be sending an image file, it will show any markers, routes, or tracks that are visible when you send the image. Select **File,** then **Send Link** to e-mail a link to a Maptech server, which will show the area you are viewing. While the map will not show makers, routes, or tracks, your friend will be able to zoom and scroll off the map to check out nearby areas.

- Want to view an area for which you don't have the CDs—perhaps just over the state line from your set? Click **Maptech MapServer** to view any of Maptech's maps.

- To create an elevation profile, right-click a track, a route, or a line created with a distance tool, and choose **Profile.** The small white dots on a profile represent waypoints along a route or locations you clicked on when creating a line with a distance tool.

- Select **Peak Names** to show waypoint names and the names of any major peaks crossed along the profile. Choose **Center Map** and click the profile to center the map at that point.

- Choose **View**, then **Bookmark this View** to save the same map view at the same scale. Give the map an appropriate name. To return to bookmarked locations, choose **Find**, then **Bookmark**. Select the bookmarked view you wish to open and Terrain Navigator will return to the location at the zoom level and scale you were using when you bookmarked it. Bookmarks are saved in the proprietary .btx format; you can import and export them from the **File** menu.

Using the Find Feature

- From the **Find** menu, you can search for places by name, zip code, coordinates, geographic feature, etc. You can also open the **Search all Place Names** dialog box by choosing **Find Place**. Many searches can be limited to the nearest 15 occurrences. If you choose **Replace Active** or **Open Another** to view a search result, a red **Find Circle** will appear. Move the pointer over the **Find Circle** and an X will appear. If you click at this point, the **Find Circle** will be removed from the map.

- From the **Find** menu, you can choose **Marker, Route,** or **Track** to quickly show the location of one of these on the map.

- Select the **Find** menu and, at the bottom of the menu, you will see the last five places you have searched for and viewed, including bookmarked locations. Clicking here is an easy way to return to a previous map.

- Ever wonder if you'll be able to see a particular location from the next peak you bag? Create a line from the peak to that location using the **Distance** tool, **Track** tool, or **Route** tool. Now right-click the line and select **Line of Sight.** This will tell you whether or not you'll have a clear sight line.

- Click the **Information** tool, then select any marker, track, or route for additional information on the selected item and the quadrangle being viewed, including the date the map was created.

- If you love Terrain Navigator so much that you end up buying a set of disks for another state, you can install them from the **File** menu by selecting **Install Map CD**.

- Finally, an excellent help section titled **USGS Map Symbols** provides detailed explanations of these important symbols. To view it, select **Help**, then **Symbols Glossary**.

Chapter 9 Maptech Terrain Navigator Pro

Maptech™ Terrain Navigator Pro™ is very similar to Terrain Navigator, the subject of the previous chapter. Among other things, it adds the ability to download black-and-white aerial photos, and comes with a one-year aerial photo subscription for the state or region you purchase. You can store downloaded photos on your hard drive. After the year's subscription expires, you must pay $99.95 per year to download additional or updated photos. A broadband Internet connection makes a big difference in your ability to utilize this feature. The program also allows you to export maps and aerial photos to Photoshop and CAD/GIS programs.

Terrain Navigator Pro has features that make it useful for professionals, such as realtors, who need to develop presentation products. MapTech appears to be targeting this product toward these and other professionals, such as wilderness guides and search-and-rescue teams.

To avoid mind-numbing repetition, I will occasionally refer to this product as TN Pro. If you purchase TN Pro, I urge you to read Chapter 8 on Terrain Navigator, which covers features common to both programs, before you read this chapter.

Basic Information

COST

- $299.95 for most states

- $299.95 regional packages available for New England (CT, MA, ME, NH, RI, and VT) and mid-Atlantic states (DC, DE, MD, and NJ)

- $99.95 annual subscription required after year one to download aerial photos

- Demonstration version available at **www.maptech.com** (Click on **Downloads**)

SYSTEM REQUIREMENTS

- Microsoft Windows 98, 2000, ME, NT, or XP operating system

- Pentium-class processor

- 32 MB of RAM

- CD-ROM drive

- 256-color display (16-/24-/32-bit color for 3-D)

- Open GL Video Accelerator recommended for 3-D

- Garmin, Lowrance, and Magellan models work best with Terrain Navigator Pro. Limited compatibility is offered with some Brunton, DeLorme, Furuno, Northstar, Standard Horizon, and Trimble units.

- Maptech has excellent GPS compatibility information online at **ftp://ftp.maptech. com/downloads/TN_GPSChart.pdf.** If you have any GPS compatibility problems with Terrain Navigator Pro, you may be able to find the answer there.

TESTED VERSION
- Version 6.03

CONTACT INFORMATION
Maptech, Inc.
10 Industrial Way
Amesbury, MA 01913
978.792.1000
www.maptech.com/land/terrainnavigatorpro/

AVAILABLE OPTIONS
- A network version is available with a five-user license for $995.00 per state or region.

- A free ArcGIS extension allows direct use of TN Pro maps in ESRI products such as ArcView, but only if you have ArcGIS installed on your computer. These are very expensive software packages typically used by professionals. For more information on GIS, including some lower-cost options, see Chapter 23.

INTERNET RESOURCES
- The most active online forum on TN Pro is hosted by Maptech at **www.maptech.com/support/forums/index.cfm.**

- The Yahoo Map Authors group, at **groups.yahoo.com/group/map_authors**, lists Terrain Navigator Pro as a product discussed on its message board.

Advantages

In addition to the advantages listed for Terrain Navigator, TN Pro's pluses are:

- Aerial photos are included.

- You can copy maps to your hard drive.

- As you move the pointer over a given area, street addresses are shown.

- You can attach digital photos to specific map locations.

- Pop-up GeoTips can provide additional information on map features.

Disadvantages

• After the first year, you'll have to pay a $99.95 annual subscription fee, per state or region, to obtain more or updated aerial photos.

• Aerial photos open at a different scale than do topo maps, making it impossible to toggle back and forth between the two. (This is mitigated somewhat by the two-window viewing option, which, when combined with zooming, can bring the images to the same scale.)

• GPS waypoint names created in the program or exported with the program are limited to six characters each.

• Once you place a waypoint, it takes three extra steps to get to the name field.

• You can't split tracks.

• You cannot start a track or directly start a route on an existing waypoint.

Tutorial/Manual

See this section in the preceding chapter.

Installation

Installation is almost exactly the same as for Terrain Navigator, except that after you load the CD titled "Geographic Data Enhancement," you can install any or all of the following:

• Internet access to aerial photomaps

• Enhanced digital elevation data

• Street and address database

• Updated NGS data sheets

Unless you are severely limited in terms of hard disk space, I suggest installing all of the above.

> **TIP:** TN Pro CDs, despite the price of the package, come in paper sleeves. Spring for some jewel boxes or a CD wallet to keep them from getting lost or damaged.

Configuration

GPS Setup, GPS Tracking, and **3-D Preferences** are handled in the same manner as they are in Terrain Navigator (discussed in Chapter 8).

For other configuration options, choose **File** and point to **Preferences,** then choose **General** to open the dialog box shown in Figure 9A. **Coordinates** and **Datum** are found here, as they are in Terrain Navigator, but this dialog box also lets you alter the size of the **Aerial Photos Cache** and the line width of the **Distance** tool. **TIFF Export Options** are discussed under Working With Other Programs, near the end of this chapter.

Figure 9A

The **Markers** category, shown in Figure 9B, provides a few additional options over those found in Terrain Navigator:

• The **Default Name** can be **Text, Date,** or **Time.** If you select **Text,** you can type the label default into the box at the right.

• You can choose to automatically insert certain information before or after the **Default Name** with the **AutoText** feature. The **AutoText** box on the right defaults to **None;** click the drop-down arrow to select from **Coordinates, Street Address, Elevation,** or **Grade.** In the box on the left, select **Append** to have this data show after the marker **Default Name,** or **Prepend** to have it displayed before the marker name. The **AutoText** data is automatically updated if you move the marker to a new location.

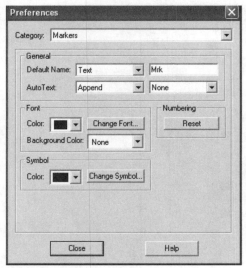

Figure 9B

- As with Terrain Navigator, you can select **Symbol Color.** But Terrain Navigator Pro also allows you to **Change Font** and select the **Font Color,** though this works only for newly placed markers. In other words, you cannot change the color and font of existing markers by making a change here; you must change them individually.

- You can change or eliminate the **Background Color** for marker labels.

> **WARNING:** In the Markers, Routes, and Tracks Preferences dialog boxes, be cautious about resetting **Numbering,** since doing so can result in multiple markers, routes, or tracks with the same number.

The **Routes** category, shown in Figure 9C, also provides options not found in Terrain Navigator:

- **Default Names** and **AutoText** work exactly as described under configuration of markers, except that you can choose **Default Names** for both routes and route markers.

- Additional **Line** options include **Style, Width,** and **Highlight.**

- **Font, Color,** and **Background** options are available for labeling route markers.

- You can also use a route to create a closed loop and choose the **Loop Interior Pattern** and **Color.**

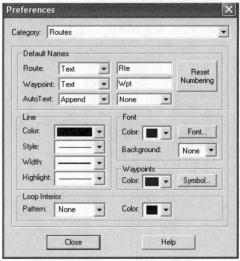

Figure 9C

Here are the additional options in **Tracks Preferences**, as shown in Figure 9D:

• Additional **Line** options include **Style, Width**, and **Highlight**.

• You can create a closed loop and choose the **Loop Interior Pattern** and **Color**.

TN Pro offers a number of features not included in the basic package, including GeoTips, Labels, Range Rings, and Range/Bearing Lines. Setting **Preferences** for these features is covered under Additional Features later in this chapter.

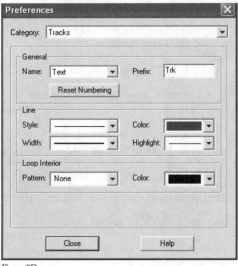

Figure 9D

Getting Started/Aerial Photos

Opening and navigating maps is done the same way as in Terrain Navigator, described in Chapter 8. The key difference is that with TN Pro, you have access to aerial photos.

As noted earlier, the first time you try to download aerial photos, you will be prompted to register. From any topographic map, click **Map Type**, then select **Aerial**. Unfortunately, all aerial photos are 1:12,000 scale, so you won't be looking at exactly the same area as you were on the topo map. The center of the image will be the same, however.

The best way to work around this is to open a second window and look at the topo map and aerial photo side by side. View a 1:24K scale topo map at the 1:1 **Zoom Level** in one window and a 1:12K aerial photo at the 1:4 **Zoom Level** in the adjacent window. No, those numbers don't add up—but for some reason that's what it takes to view them at the same scale. This is most likely because of scanning differences (dpi) and the fact that the resolution on aerial photos, one meter/pixel, is different from topographic map resolution.

Click **Preferences** to open the **Preferences** dialog box. In the **Aerial Photos** Category, you'll see that the **Aerial Photos Cache Size** defaults to 200 MB. You can increase this setting, which indicates the amount of disk space dedicated to caching aerial photos downloaded from the Internet. Once you exceed this amount, the software will start to overwrite older photos.

Fortunately, TN Pro allows you to store aerial photos or topo maps on your hard drive. If you have enough disk space, you can download all the aerial photos you want for your state or region. This way, if you don't need access to a new area, or to any available updated images, there is no immediate need to renew when your subscription for aerial photos expires. When you do renew, the cost will still be $99.95 per year, with no penalty for letting your subscription lapse.

Transferring maps to your hard drive will also keep you from having to load one or more CDs every time you use Terrain Navigator Pro. This is especially useful if you use one CD more than others, or if you find yourself constantly shifting back and forth between two CDs at the edges of their coverage range. Here's how to do it:

1. Choose **File**.

2. Choose **Share Maps Across CDs**.

3. In the **Map Type** box, you can select either **1:12,000**, **1:24,000/25,000**, or **1:100,000**. Choosing **1:12,000** will download and copy aerial photos to your hard drive. Choosing either of the other options will copy that scale of topo maps to your hard drive.

4. Choose the **Map Name**, or click the map, to select the quad you wish to download. Notice that if you select 1:12,000, instead of seeing one quad name, you'll see a set of four, each one followed by NE, NW, SE, and SW. This is because USGS divides topo quads into four sections for aerial photos, since the files are so big. These are called Digital Orthophoto Quarter Quadrangles (DOQQs). It may be tempting to choose **Select All** and download a large area to your hard disk, but a set of four DOQQs takes up about 26 MB of disk space. Check your download speed and available storage space before getting carried away.

5. I suggest that you not check **Include Related Non-Map Data**. According to Maptech, while this will include elevation data, more current information is included in the **Geographic Data Enhancement CD** that comes with TN Pro.

6. Now click **OK** and a **Copy Maps** or **Copying Map from the Internet** dialog box will appear. You can press ESC to cancel the operation.

TIP: The **Share Maps Across CDs** option is preferable to the one labeled **Copy Maps to Hard Drive**. Let's say you load all the 1:24,000-scale maps from one CD onto your hard drive. When you place a CD for an adjacent area in your CD-ROM drive and choose **Open Map**, you'll see the quads for that area. If you have copied maps to your hard drive using the **Share Maps Across CDs** option, you'll also be able to click on those quads from the **Open Map** dialog box. (If you used the **Copy Maps to Hard Drive** option, however, you'll have to choose **CD Library**, select the CD for your home area, and click **OK**. You still won't have to load the CD, but you will have extra steps.) Note that if you own TN Pro for multiple states this simplifies viewing areas that straddle state lines.

Finally, be aware that there are a few areas of the country for which there is no TN Pro aerial photo coverage. A coverage map is posted at **www.maptech.com/land/terrainnavigatorpro/docs/photo%20areas.pdf**.

File Structure

TN Pro, like its little brother Terrain Navigator, maintains a master list of all layer information, making it available at any time. This can be cumbersome when you must scroll through long lists of markers, routes, and so on.

With TN Pro, though, you can create **Projects**, storing only the layer information associated with each individual project. To create a Project, choose **Layers**, then **Change Projects**. From the **Projects** dialog box, choose **New** and name the project. New layers are added to the active Project until you change projects.

Unfortunately, there is no easy mechanism for sharing layers between multiple projects. See Working With Other Programs toward the end of Chapter 8 for information on how to export and import layer files. In addition to allowing you to share files with other programs, this lets you move layers between projects.

Changing projects is also an easy way to save your work. If you're manipulating a great deal of data, I suggest doing so every now and then.

Waypoints and Waypoint Management

The relationship between waypoints and markers is explained in the previous chapter. Some additional waypoint options have been added to Terrain Navigator Pro. To explore these, click the **Marker** tool, then click on the map to place a marker. Right-click and choose **Edit**, opening the dialog box shown in Figure 9E. In addition to the features found in Terrain Navigator, you now have the ability to alter the **AutoText, Font, Font Color,** and **Background Color** settings for individual markers. Changes made here affect only the marker you are currently editing, and do not change the default **Marker** settings you made in the **Preferences** dialog box.

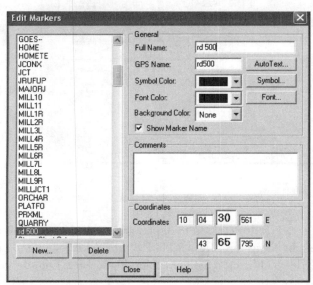

Figure 9E

Routes

TN Pro adds route options not found in Terrain Navigator. Right-click a route way-point and select **Edit Routes** to open the dialog box shown in Figure 9F. Once again, **AutoText, Font, Font Color,** and **Background Color** are added to the available choices. You can choose whether or not to show the **Waypoint Name** and alter various **Loop Interior** and **Line** characteristics. Remember that you can also make changes to indi-vidual waypoints in routes by choosing **Edit** in the **Edit Routes** dialog box, or by right-clicking a route on the map screen and choosing **Edit Route Waypoints**.

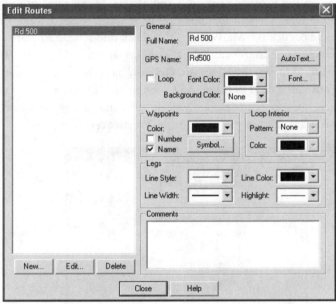

Figure 9F

Tracks

Right-click a track and select **Edit** to display additional track options not present in the basic Terrain Navigator software. TN Pro provides the ability to **Loop** tracks and alter **Line Style, Width,** and **Highlight** color; it also offers **Loop Interior** options.

The **Loop Interior** options may be useful for land managers and other professionals. Use the **Toggle Loop** feature to create an enclosed polygon and highlight the area with a **Pattern** and **Color**. Right-click the track and choose **Information** to ascertain the enclosed acreage.

Additional Features

Terrain Navigator Pro offers a number of features not included in the basic Terrain Navigator package, including Benchmarks, GeoTips, GeoPins, Labels, Range Rings, and Range/Bearing Lines.

Benchmarks

A benchmark is a marked point of known elevation. **Benchmarks** are shown in TN Pro as red triangles. They can be turned off by choosing **View**, then **Layer Visibility**. Click the **Benchmark** check box to clear it.

GeoTips

GeoTips are labels that appear temporarily as you point to various features on the map. Terrain Navigator Pro allows you to choose what information is displayed through **GeoTips**. While still in the **Preferences** dialog box, in the **Category** list choose **GeoTips** to open the dialog box shown in Figure 9G. In the **GeoTip for** list, select the GeoTip you wish to configure. Select an item from the box labeled **When cursor is held over,** and then choose what information the GeoTip should display by selecting an item in the **Display this information** box.

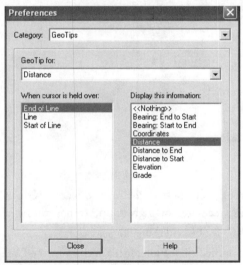

Figure 9G

Labels

Select the **Label** tool, then click anywhere on the map to place a label. To configure labeling options, click **Preferences** and, from the **Category** list, choose **Labels** to open the dialog box shown in Figure 9H. For **Default Name** you can choose between **Text,**

Date, and **Time.** If you select **Text,** you can type the label default into the box at the right. **Auto Text** options are available as previously described in the **Markers** section of the Configuration information. Labels can be dragged to resize them or to move them to a new location. You can also select the type of **Border** you prefer. If you choose a balloon style, the **AutoText** location information is based on the location that the "tail" points to. You can also **Change Font** and select the **Text Color** and **Background Color.**

When you place a label on the map, right-click the label to display a menu with options to **Edit, Hide, Delete,** or **Lock** its location, so that it cannot be accidentally dragged to a new location. By choosing **Edit,** you can alter many characteristics for an individual label without changing the default settings in the **Preferences** dialog box.

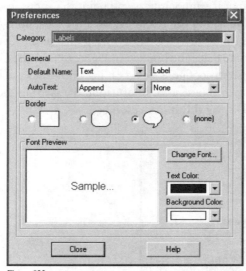

Figure 9H

Range Rings

Select the **Range Rings** tool, then click on the map to place a series of range rings. These are concentric circles, centered on a given point, that can be labeled with the distance (or time) from that point for each ring.

To configure range ring options, click **Preferences** and, from the **Category** list, choose **Range Rings,** opening the dialog box shown in Figure 9I. **Ring Interval** can be **Set By Distance** or **Set By Time,** and you can specify the interval. You may find the **Set by Time** option useful when doing real-time tracking of your location. You can also alter the **Ring Color, Line Style,** and **Line Width**, and specify the **No. of Rings. Show Name** allows you to display the range ring name as a label at the center point. **Show Ring Interval** displays the distance or time interval.

![Figure 9I - Preferences dialog box]

Preferences dialog showing:

Category: Range Rings

Ring Interval
- ● SET BY DISTANCE:
- Draw a ring every
- 0.200000 Miles
- from center.
- ○ SET BY TIME:
- Show distance traveled every
- 6.000000 Minutes
- if traveling at this speed:
- 2.000000 MPH

Display Options
- Ring Color:
- Line Style:
- Line Width:
- No. of Rings: 5
- ☐ Show Name
- ☐ Show Ring Interval

Close   Help

Figure 9I

As with many features in Terrain Navigator Pro, you can right-click a range ring to display a menu with various options. With range rings you can choose from **Edit, Information, Hide, Delete,** or **Lock.** The last selection prevents the range ring from being accidentally dragged to a new location. As with labels, by choosing **Edit** you can alter many characteristics for an individual range ring, without changing the default settings in the **Preferences** dialog box.

Range/Bearing Lines

Select the **Range/Bearing Line** tool, then click anywhere on the map to place a range/bearing line originating from that point. This feature allows you to determine and display the range, which is the distance to a given point measured in a straight line, and the bearing or compass heading to that point.

To configure options for this feature, click **Preferences** and, from the **Category** list, choose **Range/Bearing Lines,** opening the dialog box shown in Figure 9J. Under **Range,** choose **Set By Distance** and select the length you wish to establish as the default for range/bearing lines. Alternatively, choose **Set By Time** if you wish to use range/bearing lines as a predictor of distance traveled, perhaps in conjunction with real-time tracking of your location. Select the default **Bearing, Line Color, Line Style,** and **Line Width.** You can select **Show Name** to display the saved name of the range/bearing line (at the tail end of the arrow) and **Show Range and Bearing** to display this data at the tip of the arrow.

Once again, right-click any **Range/Bearing Line** and choose **Edit** to alter its characteristics.

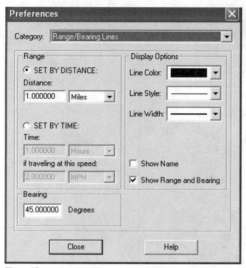

Figure 9J

GeoPins

GeoPins serve as links to documents, URLs, digital photos, etc. Select the **GeoPins** tool, then click anywhere on the map to place a GeoPin. When you do this the dialog box shown in Figure 9K will open.

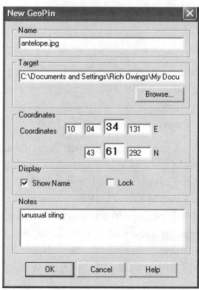

Figure 9K

GPS Interface

See this section in the preceding chapter.

Printing

See this section in the preceding chapter.

Moving Map

See this section in the preceding chapter.

3-D

Viewing maps and aerial photos in 3-D works exactly as in Terrain Navigator, so once again I refer you to the previous chapter.

I do want to call your attention to one thing, however: Since you have access to aerial photos with TN Pro, check out the **Lighting** options in **3-D Preferences**. Some of these options give you very cool effects.

Working With Other Programs

Import and export of marker, route, and track data is handled as discussed in Chapter 8, Terrain Navigator.

TN Pro also allows you to export georeferenced maps for use in GIS programs, and in programs such as OziExplorer and Fugawi. Should you find yourself migrating to one of these programs, you may want to try exporting maps from TN Pro instead of downloading them from USGS. (If you're ready to export maps, you might also want to look at Chapter 14, which discusses projections and georeferencing.)

To export maps, choose **File**, point to **Export**, and then choose **Active Map**. This will open an **Export** dialog box (Figure 9L) for the quad you are currently viewing.

Alternatively, choose **File**, point to **Export**, and choose **Multiple Maps** to export multiple quads. Terrain Navigator Pro automatically makes the choices it considers most appropriate, but let's take a closer look at some of the information you can control:

• You can choose **Scale** and **dpi** resolution from the **Export** dialog box. Terrain Navigator Pro maps have been scanned at 160 dpi, the default setting. Altering this will result in a less-clear image.

• When selecting **Projection** for export, make sure that the program in which you will ultimately use the map supports that projection.

• The **Zone** options will vary based upon the chosen **Projection**.

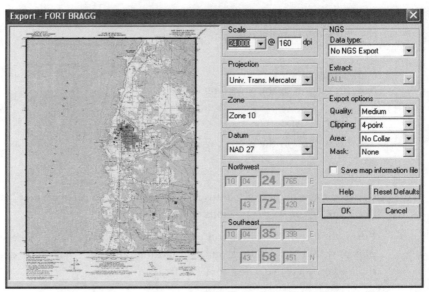

Figure 9L

- **Datum** choices are limited to **NAD27**, **NAD83**, and **WGS84**.

- **Northwest** and **Southeast** corner coordinates will not be asked for unless you choose a **User Defined Area**.

- **Data type** allows you to export National Geodetic Survey data (vertical control, horizontal control, etc.).

- You can also choose the **Quality** of the reprojection. The only thing you sacrifice by choosing **High** is speed of export.

- TN Pro's help section suggests considering **2-point Clipping** for UTM projections and **4-point** for images that will be stitched together.

- For **Area**, choose between **Entire Map** (with collar), **No Collar**, or **User Defined**.

- When a map is reprojected, the collar or other non-map data may appear along portions of the perimeter. You can **Mask** this material in several ways. **Color** replaces the material with magenta (which is never used on USGS maps, making it easier to remove in graphics programs without affecting the map image). See **Exporting Maps** in **Help** for the exact color specifications. **Adjacent Map** fills in these spaces with images from the adjoining quads. Choosing **None** may result in the appearance of some non-map information.

- **Save Map Information File** creates a file with the chosen projection, zone, and datum information.

Choose **Help**, then **Contents**, and then choose **Exporting Maps** for additional information on each of these options. If you have made any changes and decide instead to let TN Pro determine the export parameters, choose **Default**. Otherwise, choose **OK** to open an **Export Map As** dialog box. Here you can choose to export in any of the following file types:

- **TIF – Arc/Info (TFW)**. Also creates a .tfw georeference file.

- **TIF – MapInfo (TAB)**. Also creates a .tab georeference file.

- **TIF – GeoTIFF (Geographic)**. Incorporates georeference information in the image file.

- **TIF – GeoTIFF (Projected)**. Incorporates georeference information in the image file.

- **TIF – TIFF 6.0**. Does not export any georeference information.

- **TIF – DRG (FGD)**. Some programs may require a .fgd file to properly georeference a DRG.

- **TIF – TIF 4.0**. Does not export any georeference information.

- **BMP – Windows Bitmap Format**. Does not export any georeference information.

- **JPG – JPEG Format (JGW)**. This is an ESRI-supported format.

Once again, the **Help** section titled **Exporting Maps** has information on all of the available choices, many of which are also discussed in Chapter 14.

 Before exporting any .tif files, click **Preferences**, then select **General** and ensure that you have checked the proper **TIFF Export Options** at the bottom of the **Preferences** dialog box. Check the software in which you will be using the .tif images to see what export method is preferred. **Compressed** sends the .tif file as one image, using a Pack Bits file compression method, while **Tiled** breaks it into pieces.

More Tips

- See the Tips section in Chapter 8, Maptech Terrain Navigator, for tips common to both programs.

- Additional **Find** options, not covered in Terrain Navigator, are offered in TN Pro. To locate an address, choose **Find**, then **Street Address**. You can also use the **Find** feature to search for **GeoPins**, **Range Rings**, and **Range/Bearing Lines**.

- Consultants Rick Hood and Stu Bristol occasionally offer workshops on using Terrain Navigator Pro. For more information go to **www.maptech.com/training/index.cfm.** Attendees often receive significant discounts on software. Even steeper discounts may be given for search-and-rescue, first responders, fire department, and appropriate 501(c)(3) personnel.

Chapter 10 DeLorme 3-D TopoQuads

This package is somewhat similar to the others we have reviewed. But while the other programs in this section show both 1:24K and 1:100K scale maps, DeLorme® 3-D TopoQuads™ shows only 1:24K maps. For larger-scale displays it uses vector maps.

We'll get into more detail on vector maps in the next chapter. For now, realize that vector maps aren't scanned images. Rather, they are composed of lines and points. Because of this, vector maps look different than standard USGS quads.

Basic Information

COST
• $99.95 for most states and regions. Exceptions are California, Montana, Nevada, New Mexico, Oregon, and Wyoming, which are priced at $199.90, with packages that cover half of each state available for $99.95. The package for Texas comes in three sections, priced at $99.95 each (or $299.85 for the entire state).

SYSTEM REQUIREMENTS
• Microsoft Windows 98, 2000, ME, or XP; or Windows NT 4.0 (with Service Pack 4 or later)

• Intel Pentium II (or equivalent) 233 MHz or higher processor (300 MHz recommended)

• 64 MB of RAM (128 MB recommended)

• 300 MB of free hard disk space (for minimum installation; more recommended)

• 3-D graphics accelerator card recommended for 3-D map viewing

GPS COMPATIBILITY
• DeLorme lists the following GPS units as compatible: "Earthmate®; GpsTripmate®; or any fully-compatible NMEA receiver, including GARMIN®, Magellan™, Rockwell/Conexant, Lowrance/Eagle, and Trimble Scoutmaster™."

TESTED VERSION
• Version 2.0.0

CONTACT INFORMATION
DeLorme
Two DeLorme Drive
P.O. Box 298
Yarmouth, ME 04096
800.561.5105 (sales)
www.delorme.com

AVAILABLE OPTIONS
• DeLorme offers 10-meter-resolution satellite images for $99 per state or region.

INTERNET RESOURCES
• The Yahoo Map Authors group, at **groups.yahoo.com/group/map_authors**, lists DeLorme 3-D TopoQuads as a product discussed on its message board.

Advantages

• This software has 3-D capability.

• The **Drag** and **Zoom** features make it easy to navigate maps.

• Maps can be transferred to your hard disk, eliminating the need to load CDs.

• When you place a waypoint, you are automatically taken to the name field—no extra steps are required.

• You can search for street addresses.

• 3-D TopoQuads includes an **Undo** button that allows you to go back to previous map views as many as 256 times. It also includes an **Undo** button for **Draw** functions.

• Waypoint display is very flexible in terms of fonts, sizes, and colors.

Disadvantages

• There is no demo version, though DeLorme does offer a 30-day, money-back guarantee.

• Print options are limited.

• Waypoint management tools are limited. There is no way to view a list of waypoints.

• Aerial photos are not available, though satellite imagery is (at an extra charge).

• You cannot view USGS 1:100,000-scale maps, though a comparable scale vector map is provided.

• You cannot click on existing waypoints on a map to form a route and retain the original waypoint name when you send the route to your GPS. Nor can you create a route from a list of waypoints. Because of the latter issue, EasyGPS might be a good companion program to use with 3-D TopoQuads.

Tutorial/Manual

The help manual seems to be thorough, though you may have to dig a little to find what you're after. From the **Title Bar**, click **Help** to bring up an array of options. The **User Guide** is a 132-page .pdf file, with content very similar to that of the **Help Topics**.

3-D TopoQuads also includes context-sensitive help for the tabs. Select any tab, then click **Help on tab** to bring up information about it.

Installation

Installing this software involves several steps:

- First, you'll be asked for your name.

- Since 3-D TopoQuads requires DirectX, you'll be asked if you need to install it or not, or if you want to install only the 2-D version.

- You'll be given the option to register.

- You'll see a warning letting you know that shaded relief can slow the display on some computers and that you have the option of turning it off.

- The installation will then require you to restart your computer.

- Finally, a command window will appear. It may take a couple of minutes to go away.

Configuration

Most configuration options are found on the **Map Display** and **GPS** tabs.

The Map Display Tab

The **Map Display** tab has two buttons:

- **Features** (see Figure 10A). Most features are on by default, but you may want to select others. The **Grids** feature is one to note; if you want to include a grid on your printed map, you must select this option prior to printing. Another useful feature is **USGS Quadrangle Coverage.** If you need the names of the quads in a given area, this is a simple way to obtain them.

Figure 10A

• **Units.** Here you can set the format for coordinates (UTM, etc.). The **Datum** box offers only two choices, WGS84 and NAD27. Though these options are not as thorough as those in some other programs that allow importing of map images, they should suffice for the United States.

The GPS Tab

Choose **Device,** then select the proper **Device,** opening the pane shown in Figure 10B. Make sure that your selection matches the interface set on your GPS. The **Port** and **Settings** boxes will automatically default to the manufacturer's settings. When you're finished, choose **Done.**

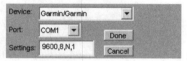

Figure 10B

Custom Map Features

You can customize the features displayed on your maps to an even greater degree. From the **Map Display** tab, select **Features,** then **Use Custom Map Features.** Now choose **Customize Features.**

You'll see four types of features to select from (**Image, Line, Point,** and **Polygon**). Clicking the plus sign (+) beside any feature will expand it to reveal the full list of categories within that feature, as shown in Figure 10C. Notice that each category can be expanded even further.

Let's make a custom map. Choose **None** underneath the features list. Now type Stream in the Search box. The lengthy list of types that appear, from which you can select individual items, should give you some idea of the power of this feature. Choose **All.** The tab manager should appear (see Figure 10D). Choose **Done,** and you should have a custom map that includes only streams.

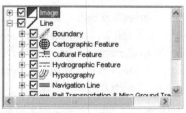

Figure 10C

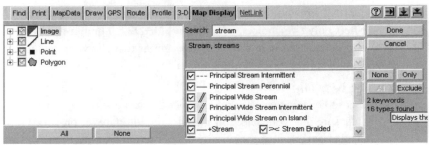

Figure 10D

Getting Started

Insert any of the state or regional CDs into your CD-ROM drive.

3-D TopoQuads provides several convenient ways to navigate or pan the map:

- In the lower right corner of the screen is a regional **Overview Map**. Click anywhere on the **Overview Map** to recenter the screen. A black box highlights the area shown on the main map pane.

- In the **Overview Map**, moving the pointer inside the black box brings up a **Drag Map** symbol. Once this symbol appears, you can drag the black box to a new location.

- In the main map pane, clicking anywhere on the map recenters it.

- Move the pointer to the edge of the map and the **Hand Panning** tool appears. You can now drag the map to reposition it.

- The **Control Panel**, the pane to the right of the screen, has a globe with a group of nine buttons, as shown in Figure 10E. Choose any of the outer buttons with yellow triangles to pan the map in that direction. I prefer clicking to recenter or using the **Hand Panning** tool.

Figure 10E

You can also zoom in multiple ways:

- The **Drag and Zoom Tool** certainly deserves top billing here. Available any time another tool is not selected, it's easy to use and lets you pan and zoom at the same time. To zoom in using this tool, point to the upper left corner of the area you wish to view, then drag the pointer toward the lower right. When you release the left mouse button, the map will zoom in on the rectangular area you just defined.

- To zoom out, you can proceed in reverse, dragging from lower right to upper left. As you do this, a stair-step pattern will appear. Each step will zoom out one full "data zoom" level, moving, for example, from 9-0 to 8-0.

This is a good place to look at 3-D TopoQuads' Zoom Level controls. At the top of the Control Panel is the Data Zoom box. Notice that it displays two numbers (e.g., 9-0). Moving from 9-0 to 10-0 zooms the map in one full zoom level, represented by the number on the left. The number on the right is a smaller increment, which DeLorme terms an octave. An octave in this case is defined as a group or series of eight. For example, a full zoom level consists of levels 9-0 through 9-7. You really don't need to worry about this; the key thing to know is that the Zoom Level box allows you to select smaller changes in zoom level, one octave at a time.

- The three buttons below the **Zoom Level** box on the **Control Panel** are labeled, left to right, **Zooms out three levels**, **Zooms out one level**, and **Zooms in one level**. These controls take you to the next full step. For example, if you are on level 8-3 and you click **Zooms in one level**, it will take you to level 9-0.

TIP: Below zoom level 13-0 you are viewing vector maps. At levels 13-0 and above, you are viewing standard USGS 7.5' quad maps.

File Structure

On the **MapData** tab, choose **File**, then **New** to create a new **Project**. A **Project** stores your current map view and associated data such as waypoints, routes, or tracks. The next time you open a saved Project, it will open to the same location and zoom level, and will contain all routes and draw files present the last time it was saved. Projects are saved in the DeLorme Docs\Projects folder with a .tq2 extension.

You can also open or save **Projects** from the **MapData** tab, by choosing **File**. You will see options labeled **New, Open, Save,** and **Save As**.

TIP: 3-D TopoQuads data is stored in a DeLorme Docs folder on your hard disk. The default location is C:\DeLorme Docs. For information on which subfolders contain which data, click **Help** and choose **Help Topics**. On the **Contents** tab, choose **Welcome**, then **3-D TopoQuads 2.0 File Directories**.

To manage other data, you will generally be working with two types of files—draw files and route files. These will be discussed in Managing Draw and Route Files; for now, let's move on to waypoints.

Waypoints and Waypoint Management

Let's create a new waypoint file. Choose the **Draw** tab, then select **File.** Choose **New** to create a new draw layer. The layer will appear in the box to the left with a name like **DrawLayer** or **DrawLayer1**. Select the name to rename it with a descriptive name for the group of waypoints you are about to create. Now click **Done**.

 To add a waypoint to the file, select the **Draw** tab, then click the **Symbol Tool**. Move the pointer and click anywhere on the map to place a waypoint. A text box will appear. Type a name or numbers for the waypoint and press ENTER. You are not limited to a set number of characters for waypoint names although, if you get carried away, the names may be truncated when you send it to your GPS.

Now let's try editing a waypoint. Right-click the waypoint and you will be given the option to **Delete Draw Object**. To edit the waypoint text, right-click the waypoint and select **Edit Draw Object**.

 More options are available if you use the **Select Tool** to edit. On the **Draw** tab in the **Tools** area, click **Select**. Click any waypoint and an edit box will appear. Notice that, on the **Draw** tab, you can select from a wide range of symbols. You can choose various fonts, styles, and sizes for waypoint names. What if you've placed several waypoints and want to change them all? Simply hold down the SHIFT key while clicking waypoints with the **Select Tool**.

 TIP: You can also create your own set of symbols using DeLorme's **XSym Tool**. You can find information on this in the **Help** files by searching for XSym. To open XSym, click Window's **Start** button, point to **All Programs**, then to **DeLorme**, then to **3-D TopoQuads**. Then select **DeLorme XSym**.

You may wish to create a waypoint from coordinates. To do so, from the **Draw** tab, select **Symbol**. Now enter the coordinates in the appropriate boxes on the right side of the **Draw** tab. Remember, you can change units on the **Map Display** tab if necessary. Once you have entered the coordinates, select **Apply**.

3-D TopoQuads is fairly weak when it comes to waypoint management. You cannot access a list of waypoints; you can only display them on a map. Nor can you create a route from pre-existing waypoints.

Managing Draw and Route Files

File...

Let's look at one more aspect of managing waypoint files. From the **Draw** tab, click **File**. You should see the waypoint or draw layer you have been working with. Click the check box to the left of the name to remove the check mark. All the waypoints in the file will disappear from the map.

To add an existing waypoint file to a map, choose the **MapData** tab, then **Data,** then **Add.** This will bring up a box labeled **Add Data to Maps**. Notice that all draw files carry .an1 as the file extension. Since all draw files, including waypoints and tracks, are included here, you may want to name files so that you know whether they are track or waypoint files. Another option is to create subfolders to hold various types of files. The default location for saving **Draw** files is the DeLorme Docs\Draw folder.

Route files are handled in the same way, except they carry a .rtd file extension. The default location for saving Route files is the DeLorme Docs\Navigation folder.

Saving and naming files in 3-D TopoQuads can be a little confusing. The key is understanding the software's use of layers, which are also known as draw files or routes.

Choose the **Draw** tab, then select **File**. You will see a box (Figure 10F) showing all the draw layers associated with the current **Map File**. Once again, if the box next to its name is checked, the layer is visible on the map. User-created draw layers (waypoints and tracks) can be edited only if the **Active** button is clicked. Several draw layers can be shown on the map at one time, but only one layer of that type can be active. And see the **Delete** button to the right of the layer window? Click that and whatever layer is selected at the time is gone forever.

While 3-D TopoQuads' file structure can be confusing, one simple but important piece of information will help you understand it: One draw layer can contain multiple waypoints or tracks, and one route layer can contain multiple routes.

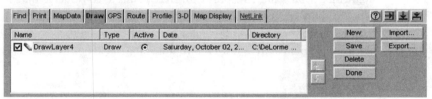

Figure 10F

Routes

To create a route, choose the **Route** tab, then select **New**. Highlight the name in the box and then type in a new route name. Click the green **Start** button and then click the map where you want the route to begin. Next, click the red **Finish** button, then click where you want the route to end. A text box, termed a Route Tag, will appear next to the **Finish** point. If you wish to hide these tags, clear the check mark from the **Show Route Tags** box.

You can use the yellow **Waypoint** tool to create waypoints along the route, though you cannot control how the waypoints will be named. They will show up in your route list as something like "(1) Wpt."

You can also create vias, to direct the route through certain locations. Vias will show on the map only when the white **Via** tool is in use.

All of these route-creation tools are available from any tab, not just the **Route** tab. Simply right-click and point to **Create Route**.

To delete a route, right-click it and then choose **Delete Route**. If you right-click a start point or finish point, you will be given the option of deleting them as well. Right-click a waypoint and you will see an option to **Convert to Via.** You will also see **Delete Stop**, which actually deletes the Waypoint. With vias displayed, you can right-click them to **Delete Via** or **Convert to Stop,** which converts the via to a waypoint.

You can also drag a start point, waypoint, via or finish point to a new location, but only if the corresponding button is depressed in the **Create/Edit** area. For example, click the **Start** button and you can drag the starting point of a route to a new location.

Finally, you can hide a route by right-clicking it and then selecting **Hide Route**. To have it reappear on the map, choose the **MapData** tab and select the box next to the route name.

Remember, you cannot use pre-existing waypoints to construct a route in 3-D TopoQuads. The disadvantage here is that your GPS will direct you to waypoints such as "(3) Wpt," rather than to waypoints with familiar names you have created. You can, however, use an ancillary program such as EasyGPS (featured in Chapter 6) to create such routes.

Tracks

You can download tracks from your GPS and, though it's a little awkward, you can also draw a track on the map, then export it back to your GPS. To do this, first choose the **Draw** tab, then select **File**. If you wish to create a new file, select **New**, which will create a file with a name like **DrawLayer** or **DrawLayer2**. Select the **Name** of the new file and rename it. If you want to use an existing file, make sure that the file layer is active. (Only one draw layer at a time can be active.)

Click **Done** and then click the **Line** button, in the upper right corner of the **Tools** area. If, instead of **Line**, you see the **Arc** or the **Spline** button, click it and hold until the **Line** button appears. Once you click **Line**, you can click anywhere on the map to start placing a track. You can either click at each point, creating a track from a series of straight lines, or you can hold down the mouse button and drag the mouse to draw freehand.

GPS Interface

You can exchange waypoints, routes, or tracks with your GPS from the **GPS**, **MapData**, or **Draw** tabs.

From the **GPS** tab, you can exchange information with your GPS by choosing **Exchange**. Notice that in the **Device Type** area you can choose from **GPS**, **Palm OS**, and **Pocket PC**. The last two options are designed to be used with DeLorme's Street Atlas USA software. Choose **Send to Device**, and under **Object Type** you'll see options for sending **Route Points**, **Route Directions**, and **Draw Files**. If you want to export a route to your GPS, select **Route Directions**. **Route Points** are DeLorme's route waypoints, discussed previously. Unfortunately, on the GPS with which I tested 3-D TopoQuads, a Garmin Etrex Venture, the software would export only the start point, finish point, and last waypoint in the route. It did export all waypoints when I selected **Route Directions**.

Use **Draw File** to export a track or waypoints. Now click **Next** and choose the route or draw file you wish to send to your GPS. There is a check box that, unfortunately, must be cleared each time unless you wish to **Prefix a Number to the Waypoint Name**. Finally, choose **Send to Device** and then click **Finish**.

To receive information from a GPS, select **Receive from Device**, then select **Route**, **Track**, or **Waypoints**. The **Save As** box will automatically default to the proper format. Now click **Next**, and choose from an existing **Draw File** or create a new one. If you choose to create a new draw file, type the name in the **New Draw File** box. Now select **Receive from Device** and then click **Finish**.

Printing

Before beginning your print job, decide if you want to display a grid, such as UTM, on the map. If so, select **Map Display**, then **Features**, then select **Grids**. Choose **Units** to select the type of grid to display.

To print a map, choose the **Print** tab, then select **Map**. Now center the map on the area you wish to print and select the **Zoom Level** at which you wish to print. USGS maps are shown only at level 13-0 and higher. Now click **Lock Print Settings**. This allows you to pan without changing the center of the printed map. Notice that the label at the top of the **Print** tab is now red. If you pan the map to the edge of the area to be printed, you'll see that it is outlined in red.

Choose **Print Setup,** then select either **Portrait** or **Landscape** to change the orientation of the printed image. While here, if your printer supports it, choose **Properties**, then **Preview before printing**, then click **OK**, and **OK** again.

The last step is to select the **Scale**. Note that you are not limited to the options presented; you can type in any scale you wish.

Be aware that you can reduce the scale to the point that the map becomes illegible. To a certain extent, this problem can be compensated for by changing waypoint fonts on the map. Unfortunately, this must be done from the **Draw** tab. You also have the option of changing track line widths from the **Draw** tab.

On the **Print** tab, when you click **Map**, you will also see a **Layout** area. Choose **2 X 2** to print the area on a series of four pages. The diagram in the **Layout** area shows the boundaries of each page. Selecting a quadrant in the **Layout** area will cancel the printing of that quadrant; click again to print it. The **3 X 3** option works in the same manner.

Moving Map

3-D TopoQuads has a nice moving map feature. To begin real-time tracking, connect your GPS to your laptop. (For information on cables, see Chapter 2.) Choose the **GPS** tab and select **Settings** to display the information shown in Figure 10G. Let's look at a few options:

• **Start GPS.** Select this to start real-time tracking. Once selected, this button toggles to **Stop GPS.**

• **Turn Pan On**. This option toggles to **Turn Pan Off**. If panning is enabled, the screen automatically follows your location. Your navigator may wish to disable panning to view upcoming sections of the map. If panning is enabled, you can pan manually, but the map will return to your position after five seconds.

• **Clear Trail**. This clears your track.

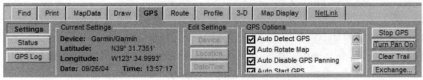

Figure 10G

In the **GPS Options** section:

• **Auto Detect GPS**. This helps the program automatically locate your GPS.

• **Auto Rotate Map**. When selected, this option orients the map in the direction of travel. If you are used to maps that are oriented north, it may be best to leave Auto Rotate Map unchecked. Many people find other orientations very confusing.

- **Auto Disable GPS Panning.** Regardless of your choice here, you can still control this feature with the **Turn Pan On/Turn Pan Off** button.

- **Auto Start GPS.** This option doesn't turn on your GPS from your computer; it just automatically starts real-time tracking each time you start 3-D TopoQuads.

If you are traveling at more than three miles per hour, an arrow will indicate your direction of travel. A green arrow indicates a strong signal, a yellow arrow indicates a weak (2-D) signal, and a red arrow indicates that you are not receiving enough satellite data to ascertain your location.

When you select **Start GPS**, the **Status** dialog box (Figure 10H) will display. You can also switch to this dialog box with the **Status** button. This screen displays your speed, heading, position, and elevation.

Select **Satellite Info** for information on the satellites your GPS unit is receiving and the precision of the datastream. A number of the options here will work only with DeLorme GPS units, while others will work only when using the NMEA communications protocol.

Figure 10H

To record your track:

1. Choose **GPS Log** to open the dialog box shown in Figure 10I.

2. Choose **Clear Trail** to clear all tracks from the screen.

3. Choose **New** to create and name a new file, or select an existing **Log**.

4. Choose **Record** to begin logging your track.

5. Click **Stop Recording** to end logging.

To play back the log file, choose **GPS Log** and select a file from the **Log** list. Select a **Playback Speed** and choose **Play**.

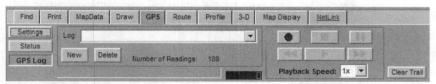

Figure 10I

Here are few other moving map tips for 3-D TopoQuads:

• HotSync, a software program designed to transfer data between a desktop PC and a handheld computer, can occasionally cause problems in GPS communication. If you experience problems with your laptop recognizing your GPS, exit HotSync.

• You can open a second window to show a 3-D view or a different scale.

• To follow a route you have created, from the **Route** tab, choose **Directions**. Double-click the route you wish to follow. Select **GPS Track** to highlight the current leg of the route.

• According to 3-D TopoQuads' help files, Magellan GPS units using this software will not display any data unless you are actually moving.

3-D

To display a map you are viewing in 3-D, choose the **3-D** tab, shown in Figure 10J, then select **View 3-D Map** to open a second window on the left side of the screen. Here are some tips for using the 3-D map:

• If you pan or zoom the map on the right, the 3-D map on the left will also reflect those changes.

• The zoom tools located above the 3-D map, control the 3-D map independently of the 2-D map on the right.

• On the **3-D** tab, use the **Pitch** control (in Figure 10J) to change the angle of perspective.

• Select **Horizon** to extend the 3-D area and add a blue-sky background.

• A **1x Vertical Exaggeration** makes horizontal distances and vertical elevation changes appear as they are in nature. To exaggerate the vertical, use 2x, 4x, or 8x.

• Choose **Rotation** and click anywhere on the adjacent compass rose to change the direction from which you view the 3-D image.

• Choose **Use Hardware Acceleration** (in Figure 10J) if your computer has a 3-D graphics acceleration card. This will improve the 3-D performance and resolution. For more information on 3-D hardware and on other options for 3-D viewing, see Chapter 21.

• To close the 3-D window, click **Show/Hide left map**.

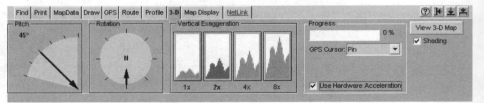

Figure 10J

Working With Other Programs

Solus Mark File (*.txt)
Topo USA 2.0 (*.ano)
Street Atlas USA 9.0 (*.sa9)
Street Atlas USA 8.0 (*.sa8)
Street Atlas USA 7.0 (*.sa7)
AAA Map'n'Go 7.0 (*.mn7)
AAA Map'n'Go 6.0 (*.mn6)
AAA Map'n'Go 5.0 (*.mn5)
GPS Log File (*.gpl)
Text File (*.txt)

Figure 10K

From the **Draw** tab, select **File**, then **Import** for the option to import the file types shown in Figure 10K.

Select **Export** to export draw files as .txt files.

Transfer files are .dmt files, which contain route, draw, and waypoint files. They are saved to the DeLorme Docs\Projects folder by default. To create a transfer file, open the map you wish to transfer; from the **MapData** tab, select **Transfer**, then **Create**. Name the file and choose **Create**. You can e-mail a .dmt transfer file by selecting **Transfer**, then **Email**.

More Tips

- To avoid having to load disks into your CD-ROM drive, you can load them onto your hard disk. For details on how to do so, click **Help** on the title bar, then select **Help Topics**. Choose **Welcome**, then **Frequently Asked Questions**. Finally, choose **How do I save my 3-D TopoQuads data to my hard disk drive?**

- If the map is slow to redraw, try disabling shaded relief. To do so, choose the **Map Display** tab, then select **Features**. **Shaded Relief** is the first item in the **Features** list.

Draw Tab Tips

- From the **Draw** tab, double-click any draw layer to center the map on it.

- The **Draw** tab provides options to add a **MapNote**, **Text Label**, **Polygon**, **Rectangle**, **Circle**, **Highlight**, and **Line**.

- You can use the **Select Tool** in conjunction with many of the **Draw** tab tools. For more information, choose **Help** on the title bar, then select **Help Topics**. Choose **Index** and enter the words "Select Tool."

- To create an elevation profile for a road, trail, track, or route, choose the **Profile** tab. Select any of these objects on the map. To select multiple objects, hold down the SHIFT key while selecting the objects to profile.

- Using the **Profile Info** button, on the right side of the **Profile** tab, to select the type of information to display. To display additional information, choose **More**.

- Choose the **Find** tab to locate addresses and zip codes.

Chapter 11
A Different Kind of Map: DeLorme Topo USA

All the map programs we've looked at so far are raster-based. Raster maps are scanned images, and all the previous programs are based on scanned USGS maps. They take up a lot of room on your hard disk or in whatever media they are stored. That is why it takes ten CDs to cover all of California. These maps are very familiar; they look exactly like standard USGS 1:24,000—and 1:100,000-scale paper maps. Each point on these maps is represented by a single pixel of a certain color. If you try zooming in on an image of, say, a 1:24,000-scale map, you quickly lose resolution.

DeLorme™ Topo USA™, on the other hand, is a vector-based program. It has more in common with the Geographic Information System software we'll look at in Chapter 23 than it does with the programs covered in the previous chapters. Vector maps take up a lot less storage space than do raster maps. DeLorme has packaged the entire United States in a six-CD set, at a resolution and scale that is in some ways comparable to 1:24,000 maps. How is this possible? Remember, raster images must assign a color to every pixel. Vector maps consist of data, not scanned images, so to construct a map of contour lines, the software must establish only the lines, not the background.

While this sounds great, there are some drawbacks. These maps simply don't have the look and feel of USGS maps. While contour lines, streams, and roads may be represented, other features, such as buildings and waterfalls, may be missing. If you purchase aerial data packets (ADP) for a given area, you will also receive the corresponding 7.5' USGS quads. See Available Options, on page 124, for more information on ADPs.

You can do a lot more with this program than you can with the ones we've looked at so far, but the learning curve is steeper. If you need or want those extra features, it may be worth it—and I'm going to help make that learning curve a little less steep. Topo USA does have a significant advantage for those of us who have a degree of wanderlust in our souls. If you find yourself engaging in outdoor activities in multiple states, $100 for the whole country is one heck of a deal.

This program's other strong advantage is that it offers autorouting. If you are looking for a program that does double duty in the backcountry and as an automotive navigational aid, the autorouting feature could sway you toward Topo USA.

> ### What is Autorouting?
> Autorouting allows you to enter a trip's starting and destination points; the program then automatically generates turn-by-turn direct ons. It is a common feature for GPS-based software that is designed for automotive use, but it's more unusual in topographic software.

Topo USA shares many features with 3-D Quads, covered in the preceding chapter. Features common to both programs are covered in that chapter, so you may wish to read it in its entirety.

Basic Information

COST
• $99.95 for the entire United States, or $49.95 for the Eastern or Western U.S.

SYSTEM REQUIREMENTS
• Microsoft Windows 98/2000/ME/XP

• Pentium III (or equivalent) 300 MHz or higher processor (600 MHZ recommended)

• 64 MB of RAM (256 MB recommended)

• For Windows XP: 128 MB RAM (256 MB recommended)

• 700 MB of available hard-disk space

• DVD-ROM drive for DVD version; CD-ROM drive for CD version; Microsoft Internet Explorer version 5.0 or later

GPS COMPATIBILITY
• DeLorme lists the following GPS units as compatible: "DeLorme Earthmate®, GpsTripmate®, or any fully-compatible NMEA receiver from GARMIN, Magellan, Lowrance/Eagle, Rockwell/Conexant, Brunton, or Trimble."

TESTED VERSION
• Topo USA 5.0

CONTACT INFORMATION
DeLorme
Two DeLorme Drive
P.O. Box 298
Yarmouth, ME 04096
800.561.5105 (sales)
www.delorme.com

- Aerial Data Packets (ADPs) containing USGS aerial photos, 10-meter-resolution satellite imagery, digital elevation models, and USGS 7.5' topo quads are available for download at extra cost. At publication time, DeLorme was including $50 worth of free ADPs with Topo USA. (See "Aerial Data Packets [ADPs]" under the More Tips section of this chapter. For information on other ways to obtain aerial photos, including free downloads directly from USGS, see Chapter 20.)

- 3-D TopoQuads, discussed in Chapter 10, adds USGS 7.5' topographical quad maps.

INTERNET RESOURCES

- DeLorme has its own online forum at **forum.delorme.com/index.php?c=12**.

- The Yahoo Map Authors group, at **groups.yahoo.com/group/map_authors**, lists DeLorme Topo USA as a product discussed on its message board.

Advantages

- The entire United States is included for the price you would pay for a single state in many other packages.

- This software includes 3-D capability.

- You can obtain aerial photos for the program (at an additional cost).

- The program's **Drag and Zoom** feature makes for a convenient way to navigate the map.

- Topo USA is the only program reviewed in this book that includes autorouting, a feature that automatically designs a route to get you from point A to point B. This could be a nice plus if you want a program that doubles as a navigational aid while driving.

- You can transfer maps to your hard disk, eliminating the need to load CDs.

- When you place a waypoint, you are automatically taken to the name field—no extra steps are required.

- You can search for street addresses.

- Waypoint display is very flexible in terms of fonts, sizes, and colors.

- You can attach aerial photos to maps.

- Topo USA includes an **Undo** button that allows you to go back to previous map views as many as 256 times. It also includes **Undo** and **Redo** buttons for **Draw** functions.

- The 3-D Map Center View could come in handy if you are trying to visualize the horizon from atop a peak or lookout tower.

- An online trail exchange makes it easy to trade waypoints, routes, and tracks with others.
- Though few people are likely to need or desire the feature, Topo USA can display coordinates in U.S. State Plane Coordinate Systems and in the Military Grid Reference System.

Disadvantages

- There is no free demo version, though DeLorme does offer a 30-day, money-back guarantee.
- Aerial photos obtained through the ADP program are expensive.
- You cannot click on existing waypoints on a map to form a route, and retain the original waypoint name when you send the route to your GPS. Nor can you create a route from a list of waypoints.
- The program has a steep learning curve.
- Waypoint management is limited. There is no way to view a list of waypoints in the program. If you use Topo USA, you may want to consider EasyGPS as a waypoint manager. For more information on EasyGPS, see Chapter 6.
- Topo USA maps do not have the familiar appearance of USGS maps.
- Many items found on USGS maps, such as structures and waterfalls, are missing from Topo USA.

Tutorial/Manual

The help manual seems thorough, though you may have to dig a little to find what you're after. Choose **Help** on the title bar at the top of your screen. This brings up an array of options:

- The contents of the **User Guide**, a 178-page .pdf file, are very similar to those of **Help Topics.**
- The **Frequently Asked Questions (FAQs)** are worth taking a look at, perhaps after you have explored the program for a while.
- The **Online Tutorials** are limited to specific topics. Unfortunately, there is no general tutorial to help you learn this deep and complex program.
- Also note the options to **Reset All Pop-up Tutorials and Shut Off All Pop-up Tutorials.**

The context-sensitive **Help on tab** feature is certainly the easiest way to get assistance with features on the tab pane. Select any tab, and then choose **Help on tab**, for context-sensitive help. On some tabs, you'll get different information depending on which buttons or tools you are using. For example, choose the **Map Display** tab, then select

Features, then choose **Help on tab**. This will bring up a screen showing map feature options. Now go back and choose **Display** and then choose **Help on tab**, which will take you to a help topic about changing the map display.

Installation

1. Shut down all Windows programs that are running.

2. Load the Install disk and follow directions.

3. You'll be presented with several options:

• You'll be asked if you want to register. You can skip this step, but you'll have to register later to obtain your $50 worth of free ADPs.

• There will be a notice that shaded relief may affect the speed of some computers.

• You'll have an opportunity to customize the tab display, though this can be done later from within the program.

4. You'll be prompted to restart your computer.

Configuration

> **TIP:** You can decide which tabs to show and change the tab order. Choose **Help** on the title bar at the top of your screen, then choose **Tab Manager**. You'll need to restart the program before the changes take effect.

Most configuration options are found on the **Map Display** and **GPS** tabs. Options for the latter are exactly as they were presented in Chapter 10.

The Map Display Tab

Choose **Map Display**, then select each of the following buttons to configure various options:

• **Features** (see Figure 11A). This tab is similar to the one found in 3-D TopoQuads, but with a few more options. Be sure to read Custom Map Features in the previous chapter, too. A few more choices are included here.

• **Display**. Because we are not viewing scanned images of maps, but rather vector data, more details show on maps as you zoom in more closely. There may be times when you want to maintain the features shown on a given map, yet magnify the image. To do so, in the **Magnification** box, choose the magnification level of your choice.

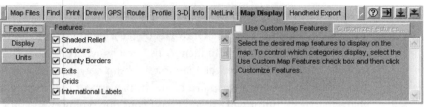

Figure 11A

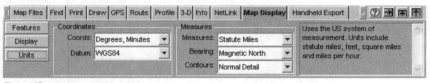

Figure 11B

• **Units** (See Figure 11B). Here you have more choices than you do in 3-D TopoQuads, especially in the **Coords** box. In addition to the standard choices, you'll also find a host of other acronyms. As you make your selections, keep an eye on the message box on the right side of the tab pane. MGRS stands for Military Grid Reference System, and USNG stands for U.S. National Grid. Note that if you select the latter, a dialog box will come up suggesting you switch to NAD83 datum. (For more information on datums, see Chapter 4.) Lastly, SPSC stands for State Plane Coordinate System. Each of the 50 states uses a different coordinate system. Choose this option and you will be asked to select the zone associated with your state. In many cases a state will have multiple zones to choose from.

I also want to call your attention to the **Contours** box. Here you can change the contour intervals on the map. Zoom in as far as you can, set this option for high detail, and you can actually display ten-foot contour intervals. This is a great example of the flexibility a vector-based program provides.

Getting Started

You can move around the map and zoom exactly as described in the previous chapter, with two exceptions:

• Topo USA allows you to use the mouse wheel to zoom. To do this, first ensure that the mouse is focused on the main map screen by either clicking anywhere on the map or pressing the F12 key. Rotate the mouse wheel forward to zoom in one octave (e.g., from 8-0 to 8-1). Rotate the mouse wheel backward to zoom out one octave. Hold the SHIFT key down while rotating the mouse wheel to go to the next full data zoom level.

• The other exception is in terminology. The Zoom Level box in 3-D TopoQuads is called a **Data Zoom** box in Topo USA.

Waypoints and Waypoint Management

To add a waypoint, choose the **Draw** tab, then click and hold the **Routable Road** button. This will display a group of hidden icons (see Figure 11C). Now choose the **Waypoint tool** and click anywhere on the map to establish a waypoint. A text box will appear, and in it you can type a waypoint name. It may appear that the box is limited to six characters or so, but it will expand if you continue typing. Remember, however, that a long name will be truncated when you send it to your GPS. Once you've typed in the waypoint name or number, press ENTER. One of the advantages of Topo USA's vector-based maps is that waypoint labels are often much clearer.

Another advantage is that Topo USA allows you to select from a range of waypoint symbols and text fonts, colors, sizes, and so on. These options are available in the **Draw** tab once you select the **Waypoint Tool**.

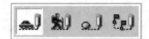

Figure 11C

TIP: You can import or create new waypoint symbols by choosing **Edit**. More information on these options can be found by choosing **Help** on the title bar, then selecting **Help Topics**, choosing the **Index** tab, typing **XSym** in the keyword box, and clicking **Display**.

To edit an existing waypoint, choose the **Draw** tab, then the **Select Tool**. Now click on a waypoint and a box will appear around it. You can now change the text font, color, size, and so on from the **Draw** tab. Click the waypoint a second time to display the text box for editing the waypoint name or number. Press ENTER when you are finished, or simply click outside the waypoint box.

Topo USA lets you correct any editing errors you make, using the **Undo** and **Redo** buttons. You can find these on the **Draw** tab.

To create a waypoint from coordinates, choose the **Draw** tab, then select the **Waypoint Tool**. Now type the coordinates in the appropriate boxes on the right side of the **Draw** tab. If you wish to change the format, to UTM for example, you can do this from the **Map Display** tab. Once you enter the coordinates, choose **Apply**.

Unfortunately, Topo USA is somewhat weak when it comes to waypoint management. You cannot access a list of waypoints; you can only display them on a map. Nor can you create a route from waypoints.

Routes

Topo USA takes a different approach to routes than do other programs we've reviewed. Topo USA automatically creates a route from point A to point B, the way trip-planning software designs a route for you to drive. Initially, this may appear to complicate backcountry routing, but it definitely has its advantages.

We'll look at how to make a route along a road or trail that already exists on the map, and how to construct a route where roads and trails are not shown.

1. Choose the **Route** tab. Let's say you're planning to mountain bike or four-wheel a logging road or mining track.

2. Now choose **New/Edit**, then **File**, then **New**.

3. Type a name for the **Route** in the **Name** box.

4. To the right of the **Route** tab is a box labeled **Select the type of route to calculate.** Select **Road-Quickest** or **Road-Shortest**.

5. Click the green **Start** button and select the point at which the route starts on the map.

6. Next, click the red **Finish** button and select the point at which you want the route to end. The software may highlight the correct route immediately, or it may automatically show a different way to get from **Start** to **Finish** than the one you had in mind.

7. You can correct this by choosing the white **Via** button. But first, take a look at the second box to the right of the **Via** button, and make sure it says **Add**. As long as it does, all route points you add will be in the order you place them, from start to finish. So choose the **Via** button and start clicking on the map to insert points, perhaps at key intersections along the route you wish to take. If you decide later to insert a point somewhere else along the route, click the arrow to the right of the **Add** button, and select **Insert** (see Figure 11D). Now you can click anywhere along the route to insert a via point.

Figure 11D

> **NOTE:** The Start and Stop points will be at the same location if you are constructing a loop.

WARNING: Be sure to use the correct type of via. If you **Add** a via when you meant to **Insert** one, the route will not change colors to alert you that you have doubled back on yourself. The best way to be sure you have not done this is to make sure that the vias appear in the route in the correct numerical order (0-1, 0-2, 0-3, etc.).

 The **Stop** feature works just like **Via**, except that it inserts a symbol of a different color (yellow instead of white). Where you insert the first stop, the numbering system will change: The stop will be labeled 1-0 and the next via 1-1.

Routes along trails can be constructed the same way as routes along roads. Simply select **Trail** instead of one of the **Road** options from the **Select the type of route to calculate** box. If you're adventurous enough to seek routes that don't show up on the map, choose **Direct.** (If you know of a road or trail not shown on the map, there is a way to create a routable road or routable trail. We'll get to it shortly.)

There are some advantages to the way Topo USA calculates routes. Other programs draw a straight line between waypoints, which can result in a confusing map. With Topo USA, the route follows the road or trail precisely. Want to hike the high Sierra from Mt. Whitney to Yosemite and along the way visit a lake your fishing buddies recommended? Plug in the **Start** and **Finish** stops, add a via at the lake, and the software will lay out the shortest route.

Ah, but there is always a price to pay. Try connecting the logging road with a trail along the same route. It won't work. You cannot join a road to a trail. You can handle this by creating a route along the road and then another route along the trail, but you'll have to switch the routes on your GPS partway through your trip. And your route won't be composed of familiar waypoint names, either. Instead of JOESLAKE, you may get "(0-3) Via." Topo USA basically treats starts, finishes, vias, and stops as waypoints. You can create waypoints with whatever name you like or import waypoints, placing starts, finishes, vias, or stops on top of them, but Topo USA will still name each route point something like "(0-3) Via."

No software package is perfect, though, and neither are its users. Which brings us to methods for correcting errors. If you erroneously place a via, right-click the via on the map, point to **Manage Route,** and select **Delete Via**. Notice that you are also given the options **Convert to Stop**, **Hide Route**, and **Delete Route**, among others. The latter two options are also available when you right-click anywhere on a route.

> **TIP:** You can edit only an active route. Inactive routes appear as broken orange segments (see Figure 11E), while active routes are solid (see Figure 11F). To activate a route, select it, point to **Manage Route,** then select **Activate Route.**

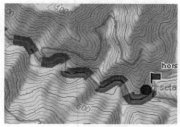

Figure 11E

Figure 11F

Creating Your Own Routable Roads and Trails

No software package has every road or trail, so let's assume that you know, and can accurately place, the location of a road that does not show up on the map. Using this knowledge, you can update the network of roads and trails on your maps and use them to create routes using Topo USA's autorouting capabilities.

1. Choose the **Draw** tab.

2. Look at the upper left button in the **Tools** area. Unless you've been using another of the tools here, it defaults to **Routable Road**. Choose **Routable Road** and, though you can start your road anywhere, we'll assume it ties into an existing road on the map.

3. Move the pointer to the spot on an existing road at which you wish to create an intersection, starting the new road, and a **diamond** will appear. Click the diamond and then draw in the new road with the mouse. You can click on every point at which you wish to change the angle of the road, or drag the mouse to draw freehand. Double-click to finish. If you end at an existing road, another diamond will appear when you move the pointer over it. Congratulations! You've just created a routable road.

Now go back and click and hold **Routable Road**. To the right you will see a **Routable Trail** button, allowing you to create routable trails in the same manner.

You can create routable roads and trails only at a data-zoom level of 11-0 or greater. In Topo USA, routable roads and trails are called **Draw Objects**, as are waypoints and tracks.

In the Draw tab, use the **Undo** or **Redo** buttons if you make a mistake while placing a point in a draw object.

Tracks

To manually place tracks on the map, choose the **Draw** tab, then the **Track** tool. Click at each turn in the track, or hold the mouse button down while drawing freehand. Choose **Done** when you're finished. You cannot construct a route using these tracks, though your GPS is capable of following a track without making it into a route. And, as we just saw, you can draw routable roads and trails on the map.

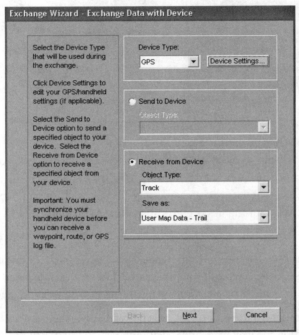

Figure 11G

When you transfer tracks from your GPS, you can specify whether you want them to download as routable roads, routable trails, tracks, or draw files. To begin sending tracks from your GPS to Topo USA, choose the **GPS tab**, then select **Exchange**, opening the **Exchange Wizard** shown in Figure 11G. In the **Device Type** box, select **GPS**, then **Receive from Device**. In the **Object Type** box, choose **Track**. In the **Save as** box, select your choice of formats. If the track is a road or trail you might use in a future route, select either **User Map Data–Road** or **User Map Data–Trail**.

You can modify the **Style** of line used to represent the track, as well as the line **Width** and **Color.** To use these options, select the **Draw** tab, then **Select**, and choose the track you wish to modify. You can find these options in the center of the **Draw** tab.

File Structure

Let's first take a look at how to create a map—what Topo USA refers to as a Topo Project.

 To create a new Topo Project, choose the **Map Files** tab, then select **Create a new Topo Project**. Alternatively, you can select **File**, then **New**. A Topo Project is basically a map file. The next time you open the project, it will open to the same location and zoom level, and will contain all the routes and draw files that were present the last time it was saved.

Topo Projects are saved in the Projects folder with a .tpx extension. The default location is C:\DeLorme Docs\Projects.

 To open an existing Topo Project, select **Open a Topo Project**, or select **File**, then **Open**.

While you're still on the **Map Files** tab, choose **File**, then point to **Current View**. Now choose **Contents**, and the name of the current Topo Project will be displayed on the **Map Files** tab. Underneath it will be the names of any route and draw files contained in the Topo Project file. You can control which ones are displayed on the map with the check boxes on the left side of the contents box.

Now choose **File** again, then point to **Current View**, and this time select **File Info**. The box in the center of the screen will display the directory location of the current Topo Project file, when it was last modified, and the number of route and draw files it contains.

Saving and naming files in Topo USA can be a little confusing. The key is understanding the software's use of layers, draw files, and route files. Let's take a look.

Choose the **Draw** tab, then select **File**. You will see a box (Figure 11H) showing all draw layers associated with the current map file. Once again, if the box next to the name is checked, the layer is visible on the map. User-created roads, tracks, trails, waypoints, and draw layers can be edited only if the **Active** button is clicked. Several layers of a given type (e.g., roads) can be shown on the map at a time, but only one layer of that type can be active. The next option you'll see is the **Lock** check box; if selected, it will prevent changes from being made to that layer. Lock will NOT prevent you from deleting the layer. (See the **Delete** button to the right of the layer window? Click that and whatever layer is selected at the time will be gone forever.)

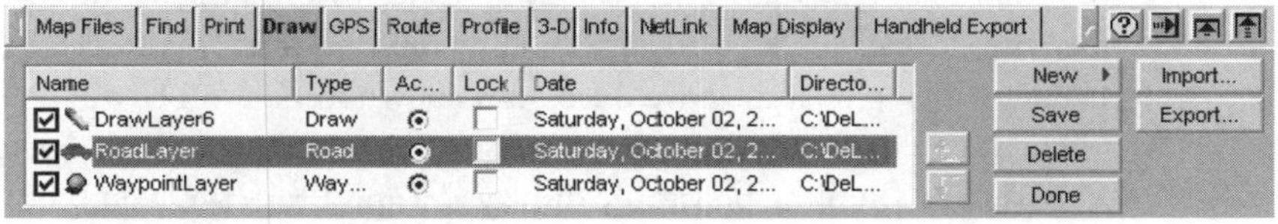

Figure 11H

While Topo USA's file structure can be confusing, one key idea will help you understand it: One layer can contain multiple trails, roads, tracks, and routes. That's it: a very simple but important statement.

To illustrate this, let's create a new layer:

1. Choose the **Draw** tab, then **File**, then **New**.

2. Let's make a trail on the map. Choose **Trail**. In the layer window to the left, you'll notice that the trail layer you just created is active, and has been automatically named "TrailLayer"—or if there is a pre-existing trail layer, it will be named something like "TrailLayer2" or "TrailLayer3."

3. Select that name and rename the layer, perhaps something like "Test." If you want to rename it later, you can do so by right-clicking the name.

4. Now choose **Done**, which will take you back to the main **Draw** tab.

5. Choose **Routable Trail**. If this button is not visible, click and hold the **Routable Road/Waypoint/Track** button, then click **Routable Trail**.

6. Type a name in the **Trail Name** box, and then draw a trail on the map. You can click at each bend or hold down the mouse button to draw freehand.

7. When finished, choose **Done** to save your work and the trail name.

8. Now type a different name in the **Trail Name** box, draw the trail, and choose **Done**.

9. Now choose **File**, and find "Test" (or whatever you named the layer you were just working on); uncheck the box next to it. Both trails you just drew will disappear from the map. Check the box and they will reappear.

The point of this exercise is to illustrate that you can place multiple features (trails in this case) into one layer file. Keep this in mind as you create your maps.

Now let's look at a couple of items found on the **Map Files** tab. Choose the **Add** button, then select **Draw Files**. Here you can add a draw layer (road, track, trail, or waypoint) to a **Topo Project**. You can hold down the CTRL key to add multiple layers to the map. Note that all draw files carry an .an1 file extension.

We're almost done here, honest! Before we finish, let's start a new **Topo Project**. From the **Map Files** tab, select **File**, then **New**. Since this will open a new project and close the current one, you'll be asked about any unsaved files. If you select **Yes** in the **Save Changes** dialog box, the **Save** dialog box shown in Figure 11I will open, allowing you to check any draw or route files you wish to save. The new **Topo Project** will open, and all draw files from the previously displayed **Topo Project** remain, but not route files. You can use this to your advantage when working on multiple projects in the same area.

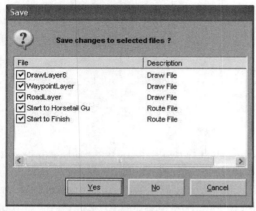

Figure 11I

Finally, I suggest giving careful thought to how you name draw layers. They should be descriptive enough so that you can easily find the information you are looking for. There are many ways to organize your data—by trip, by location, and so on. You might also want to get into the habit of locking layers so they can't be accidentally modified. To do this, choose the **Draw** tab, select **File**, and then select the **Lock** check box for individual layers.

Editing Tracks, Roads, and Trails

Sometimes, tracks don't show up in exactly the right place on the map. Perhaps the number of satellites your GPS was tracking affected accuracy. Perhaps there are errors on the base map. If you're anything like me, you will want your tracks to be placed as accurately as possible. In Topo USA, you can easily edit any track, road, or trail you place. To do so, the layer must be active. If it's a track you just downloaded, it will automatically be active. If you are working with an inactive layer, select the **Draw** tab, then **File**, and click the **Active** button for the layer you wish to edit.

Edit routable roads, trails, tracks, and draw objects by first choosing the **Select Tool** and choosing the object you wish to edit. Points appear as magenta squares (see Figure 11J), each of which you can drag to a different location. To delete the entire draw object, right-click the object, point to **Manage Draw**, then select **Delete Draw Object**. To add to an existing routable road or trail, click the appropriate draw button, such as **Routable Road**, place the pointer over the end you wish to extend so that a diamond appears, click there, and resume drawing.

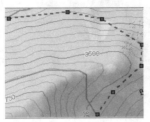

Figure 11J

Two lines of the same type, such as two trails or two roads, can be joined. To do this, from the **Draw** tab choose the **Select** tool, hold down the SHIFT key, and choose the two objects you wish to join. Alternatively, you can use **Select** to draw a box around the two objects you wish to join. Now press CTRL + N on the keyboard to join the lines. Alternatively, once you select the lines you wish to join, you can right-click anywhere on the screen, point to **Manage Draw**, then choose **Join Lines**.

You can also break a line into two sections, which can come in handy for calculating distance or viewing an elevation profile. To do this, choose the **Select** tool, then click on the line you wish to break. Click the magenta square where you wish to split the line. The square will turn red. Now right-click it, point to **Manage Draw**, and then select **Break Line**. Alternatively, once you select the square, you can press CTRL + B.

GPS Interface

From the **GPS** tab, you can exchange information with your GPS by choosing **Exchange**. Notice that in the **Device Type** area you can choose from **GPS**, **Palm OS**, or **Pocket PC**. The last two options are designed to be used with DeLorme's Street Atlas USA software.

Sending Data to Your GPS

Choose **Send to Device**, and under **Object Type** you'll see options for sending way-points, tracks, and routes, if those types of data are present in the current Topo Project file. If you want to export a route to your **GPS**, select **Route Directions**. Sending **Route Points** will send the **Start**, **Finish**, and any **Stop** route waypoints.

Select **Next** and, under **Source**, choose the name of the file to export. Depending on the type of data, you will be given some additional options such as naming or numbering the route or track file in your GPS. For all data types except tracks, you will see an option to **Prefix a Number to the Waypoint Name**. You must clear this check box each time unless you wish to add a numeric prefix to waypoint names. Finally, select **Send to Device**, and then **Finish**.

Receiving Data From Your GPS

For information on the various ways to receive track and other data, see the Tracks section of this chapter.

Note that you can create a new layer to send data to or you can transfer data to an existing layer.

Printing

To print a map, select the **Print** tab, then choose **Map**. Select **Screen** to print just the area shown on the screen. While this limits your options, you can select the **Map Display** tab, then choose **Display** for magnification options. While you are there, you may want to select **Features**, then **Grids**, to display a grid on the map. Choose **Units** to select the type of grid to display.

To avail yourself of even more print options, first center on the area you wish to print. Select the **Print** tab and choose **Page**. Now select **Lock Print Center**. This allows you to pan without changing the center of the printed map. Notice that the label at the top of the **Print** tab is now red. Now zoom to the desired level. Be aware that certain features, such as roads and trails, may not show on the map below level 11-0. Now choose **Print Preview** to see the outline of the area to be printed. (This is not the same as your printer's **Preview before printing** option.) Select the **Photo Zoom** scale option, which allows you to print the desired area. Note that you are not limited to the options presented; you can type in any scale you wish to use.

Keep in mind that you can reduce the scale to the point that the map becomes illegible. To a certain extent, you can compensate for this by changing waypoint fonts on the map. Unfortunately, you must do so from the **Draw** tab, where you can select groups of waypoints to change. And while roads, trails, and tracks you have placed on the map can be shown with a thicker line, pre-existing roads and trails cannot.

Whether you choose to print using the **Page** or **Screen** option, select the **Displays printer, orientation, and paper options** button, found in the lower right corner of the **Print** tab. You'll be taken to the printer setup dialog box. I strongly recommend that you click **Properties** if it's supported by your printer, then select **Preview before printing**. This will give you an opportunity to preview what the map will look like on the printed page.

Moving Map

Topo USA has an excellent moving map feature. To begin real-time tracking, connect your GPS to your laptop. For information on cables, see Chapter 2. Choose the **GPS** tab and select **Settings**, then **Options**. In the **Options** dialog box (Figure 11K) you'll see a number of ways to configure Topo USA's moving map options:

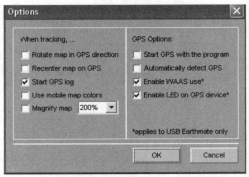

Figure 11K

- **Rotate map in GPS direction**. Check this option to orient the map in the direction of travel. If you're used to maps that are oriented north, it's best to leave this box unchecked. Many people find other orientations very confusing.

- **Recenter map on GPS**. When you pan the map, this returns your position to the center of the screen after five seconds. If your navigator (you're not trying to control the laptop while driving, are you?) wants to check out the next turn on the route, and needs to pan to do so, he or she should clear this box unless equipped with very fast fingers!

- **Start GPS log**. This creates a log file, which allows you to play back the trip on your computer at a later date.

- **Use mobile map colors**. This option darkens the screen. Many users will find that this makes it easier to view the screen at night.

- **Magnify map**. There are a range of settings in this option.

- **Start GPS with program**. This doesn't mean the computer will turn on your GPS; it will just automatically start real-time tracking each time you start Topo USA.

- **Automatically detect GPS**. This can make it easier for your laptop to connect to your GPS, especially if you are using a USB connection.

- The last two options, **Enable WAAS use** and **Enable LED on GPS device**, apply only to DeLorme's USB Earthmate GPS units.

The above is a one-time process unless there are items you wish to change. When you have finished establishing settings in the **Options** dialog box, click **OK**.

From the **GPS** tab, choose **Device** and select your GPS from the **Device** list. Whenever possible, it's best to use the proprietary communications protocol featuring the GPS manufacturer's name. You might have to experiment with the **Port** settings to find the right communications port. The other communication **Settings** should configure automatically based on the **Device** settings. For more information, see Communications Protocols in Chapter 2.

Click **Start GPS** and real-time tracking will begin! The screen will switch from **Settings** to **Status**, as in Figure 11L, showing your speed, heading, bearing, coordinates, and elevation. Units are displayed according to settings on the **Map Display** tab, as discussed previously in the Configuration section of this chapter. It's interesting to compare your speedometer with the **Speed** display, though I'm not sure a judge will let you off on the basis of your GPS log.

Figure 11L

Choose **Sat. Info** for information on satellites being received and the precision of the datastream. A number of the options here will work only with DeLorme GPS units, while others will work only when you're using the NMEA communications protocol.

Choose **Sun/Moon** to view sunrise, sunset, moonrise, moonset, phase of moon information, and whether the moon is waxing or waning.

 I mentioned earlier that you can create a GPS log file while tracking your position. To play back the log file, choose **GPS Log** and select a file from the **Log** list. Select a **Playback Speed** and choose **Play**.

Here are few other moving map tips for Topo USA:

• HotSync, a software program designed to transfer data between a desktop PC and a handheld computer, can occasionally cause problems in GPS communication. If you experience problems with your laptop recognizing your GPS or transferring data from it, exit HotSync.

• You can open a second window to show a 3-D view or a different scale.

• According to Topo USA's help files, Magellan GPS units will not display any data unless you are actually moving.

Moving Maps and Routes

We discussed route creation in the **Routes** section of this chapter, but I want to mention a couple of ways that routes integrate with the moving map. If you create a route and are tracking it in real time, you can select the **Route** tab to see turn-by-turn directions, including the distance to the next turn. Highlight a turn and select **Go To**, or simply double-click on the turn, and the map screen will move to that location. The directions give the time and distance to your next turn.

You can customize Topo USA so that it knows how fast you drive on various types of roads, and what types of roads you like to avoid. To begin this process, from the **Route** tab select **Advanced**, then **Route Prefs**. Under **Route Type**, select **Road**. Select a choice from the **Road Types** list, and enter your average **Speed** and an average **Urban Speed**. Under **Routing Preference,** for each **Road Type** choose **Preferred**, **Standard**, or **Avoid**. Select **Review** to see the entire list. When you're finished, click **Done**.

You should now see an **Edit Roads** button. Topo USA allows you to use this feature to edit road characteristics, making roads one-way or two-way, or prohibiting turns in a given direction. To begin, select **Edit Roads**, then the **Select Tool**, and select the road you wish to edit.

Finally, DeLorme's Street Atlas 2004 allows you to export Topo USA maps to a Palm or Windows CE-based handheld device. For more information on this and other PDA-based moving map options, see Chapter 22.

3-D

To display a map you are currently viewing in 3-D, select the **3-D** tab, then **View 3-D Map**. This will open a second window on the left side of the screen. If you pan or zoom the map on the right, the 3-D map on the left will also reflect those changes.

Use the **Zoom Tools**, above the 3-D map, to control the 3-D map independently of the 2-D map on the right.

Let's look at a few features on the 3-D tab:

• A **1x Vertical Exaggeration** makes horizontal distances and vertical elevation changes appear as they are in nature. To exaggerate the vertical, select **2x**, **4x**, or **8x**.

• Use the Pitch control (see Figure 11M) to change the angle of perspective.

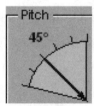

Figure 11M

• Select **Horizon** to extend the area viewed in 3-D to the horizon and add a blue-sky background. This is a very nice feature that makes the 3-D views seem much more realistic.

• The **Map Center View** section of the **3-D** tab provides a choice of **Orbit** or **Rotate**. Choose **Orbit**, then click anywhere on the adjacent compass rose to change the direction from which you view the 3-D image. Choose **Rotate** to change the perspective from the map center looking out. This feature could come in quite handy when you try to visualize what you might see from a lookout tower.

• Choose **Use Hardware Acceleration** if your computer has a 3-D graphics acceleration card. This will improve the 3-D performance and resolution. For more information on 3-D hardware and other options for 3-D viewing, see Chapter 21.

To close the 3-D window, choose **Show/Hide left map**.

Working With Other Programs

From the **Draw** tab, select **File**, then **Import** for the options to import the file types shown in Figure 11N.

Choose **Export** to export **Draw** files as .txt files.

Transfer files are .dmt files. These contain route, draw, and waypoint files. They are saved to the DeLorme Docs\Projects folder by default. To create a transfer file, from the **Map Files** tab open the map you wish to transfer. Select **File**, then **Transfer**, then **Create**. Name the file and click **Create**.

```
Solus Mark File (*.txt)
Topo USA 2.0 (*.ano)
Street Atlas USA 9.0 (*.sa9)
Street Atlas USA 8.0 (*.sa8)
Street Atlas USA 7.0 (*.sa7)
AAA Map'n'Go 7.0 (*.mn7)
AAA Map'n'Go 6.0 (*.mn6)
AAA Map'n'Go 5.0 (*.mn5)
GPS Log File (*.gpl)
Text File (*.txt)
```

Figure 11N

TIP: EXCHANGE DATA WITH OTHER TOPO USA USERS
Go to Topo USA 5.0 Trail Exchange (**forum.delorme.com/index.php?c=12**) to share your maps with others or download theirs. You can share trails (*.an1), routes (*.anr), GPS Log files (*.gpl), or DeLorme Transfer Files (*.dmt) with other Topo USA 5.0 users.

Topo USA data is stored in a DeLorme Docs folder on your hard disk. For information on which subfolders contain certain types of data, choose **Help** on the title bar, and then select **Help Topics**. On the **Contents** tab, double-click **Getting Started with Topo USA 5.0** and then select **Topo USA 5.0 File Directories**.

More Tips

- If you've also purchased 3-D TopoQuads, you can view these images side by side with Topo USA images by choosing **Show/Hide left map**, and then selecting **USGS Quads (3DTQ)** from the **Select map data** box at the top of the left window.

- You can avoid having to load map disks in your CD-ROM drive by loading the maps onto your hard disk. Load the map disk for the desired region in your CD-ROM drive, select **Start**, then **Run** and run the setup.exe file. That's all there is to it!

- If a map is slow to redraw, try disabling shaded relief. To do so, choose the **Map Display** tab, then select **Features. Shaded Relief** is the first item in the **Features** list.

- If you load a CD for a new region and it doesn't show up on the screen, select the **Find** tab and do a search for a town or feature near the area you want to display.

- To create an elevation profile for a road, trail, track, or route, select the **Profile** tab. Click an object on the map. To select multiple objects, hold down the SHIFT key. Using the **Profile** button on the right side of the **Profile** tab, **select the type of information to display**. To display additional information, choose **More**.

- Planning a trip to some great destination and wondering what the climate is like in a given month? Choose **Help**, on the title bar, then choose **Weather Almanac**.

- The Draw tab also provides options to add a **MapNote, Text Label, Image, Polygon, Rectangle, Circle, Line, Arc,** or **Spline**.

Section Three Downloading Maps: More Microsoft TerraServer-Based Programs

Programs based on Microsoft TerraServer, like USAPhotoMaps in Chapter 5, give users access to aerial photos and topographic maps for nearly the entire U.S., through images downloaded from www.terraserver-usa.com. Since images are downloaded, these programs work best with a broadband connection. It's not mandatory, though; before broadband came to my isolated area, I downloaded tons of images late at night when I didn't mind tying up the phone line. Once you download images, they are cached on your hard drive, so it's relatively easy to compile a good set for your favorite haunts.

These programs have some great advantages. You don't have to pay more for images from each state, as with programs in the preceding chapters. Also, TerraServer-based programs give you fast and easy access to aerial photos.

There are a few disadvantages, however. The images tend to be a little less sharp than the high-resolution scans found on CD-based maps. And printing options are limited in these programs, though with any luck that will change as the developers improve their products.

There are a few other things you should know about TerraServer images. The aerial photos may date back 10 years or more. Occasionally, you may come across areas TerraServer doesn't cover. In these cases a blank area will appear on the screen. With the possible exception of some military bases, it's not a government plot—just gaps in coverage. Finally, color imagery is coming to TerraServer! See Chapter 5 for examples in Washington, D.C.

Fuzzy Images
While you can zoom with TerraServer-based programs, there are some limitations. Images are available at the resolutions listed below. Zoom in beyond these points and things will get fuzzy, until you get to the next-listed level.

512 meters/pixel (topo only)
64 meters/pixel (aerial photos and 1:250,000-scale topo)
16 meters/pixel (aerial photos and 1:100,000-scale topo)
4 meters/pixel (aerial photos and 1:24/25,000-scale topo)
1 meter/pixel (aerial photos only)

Chapter 12 TopoFusion

TopoFusion™ is one of the newer entries in the field of mapping software that interfaces with Microsoft's TerraServer. A free demonstration version of the program is available for download at **www.topofusion.com**. The only limitations in the demo version are that a certain percentage of the map will be covered by the word "Demo," and you will be able to load only three files at any one time.

TopoFusion is designed to access and download TerraServer images quickly—it may be worth the cost for this reason alone. The designers chose to use the .gpx format for storing data, which retains the time record for every track point. This has allowed for the development of some great features such as the **Log Book** and **PhotoFusion**. The Log Book feature is a great way to store your data, analyze trips, and maintain a historical record of your outings, while PhotoFusion automatically links to the location digital photos were taken. Both features are covered in the More Tips section near the end of this chapter.

Basic Information

COST
- $40 for the registered version, which includes all future upgrades. A demo version is also available.

SYSTEM REQUIREMENTS
- Microsoft Windows 95/98/ME/2000/XP

- Intel Pentium processor or equivalent (or faster)

- 16 MB of RAM

- Microsoft DirectX 7.0 or higher

- 1 MB video card

- Internet connection (can also be used offline)

GPS COMPATIBILITY
- You can send waypoint and track data to, and receive it from, Magellan and Garmin units.

- Supports moving map/real-time tracking with any NMEA-compatible GPS unit and with Garmin's PVT protocol.

TESTED VERSION
• Version 2.1

CONTACT INFORMATION
www.topofusion.com

AVAILABLE OPTIONS
• None

INTERNET RESOURCES
• TopoFusion has an active support message board at **topofusion.com/cgi-bin/forum/ ikonboard.cgi**. You can also access the board via a link at **www.topofusion.com**.

Advantages

• There is a free demo version.

•The Log Book captures a history of your trips in a calendar format, and is one of several sophisticated tools you can use to save, analyze, and manipulate track data.

• You can switch between topo, aerial photo, and combination views of the same location.

• You can see 3-D views of topographic maps or aerial photos.

• Waypoint fonts and colors are flexible.

• The combination of Pan Map mode and mouse wheel zooming offers an excellent way to move about the map.

• The Simplify Track Tool can be used to reduce the number of track points.

• You need to perform only one extra step to get to the name field after placing a waypoint.

• You can split and merge tracks.

• The PhotoFusion feature lets you automatically link digital photos to the location at which they were shot.

Disadvantages

• TopoFusion does not support map printing, although **www.topofusion.com** lists the feature as in development.

• Route creation tools are limited.

Tutorial/Manual

TopoFusion's only manual is located online at **www.topofusion.com/manual.php**. Though the manual is at times incomplete, the main problem is its online location, which requires you to use your browser or add-ons to search help files. Here are a couple of ways to go about it:

1. Most browsers have some kind of search feature. In Internet Explorer 6.0, select **Edit**, then **Find (on This Page)**.

2. Another approach is to add the Google Toolbar to your Web browser. It is available at **toolbar.google.com**. Once you install the toolbar, you can enter a search term and then use a tool on the right side of the toolbar labeled **Find next occurrence of 'search term' in current document.**

Fortunately, the **Help** button on many dialog boxes provides context-sensitive help.

Installation

• First, be sure your computer has the current version of Microsoft's DirectX (version 7.0 or higher), available at **www.microsoft.com/windows/directx/default.aspx**.

• Download the demo file from **www.topofusion.com** and run it to install. If you like what you see, pony up $40 to purchase the full version. You will receive registration instructions by e-mail.

Configuration

Choose **Options**, then select **Preferences** to bring up the **Options** dialog box, with the following tabs:

• **General** (Figure 12A). A number of settings here can affect the speed of your work. The **Tile cache size** affects the speed at which you can scroll the map—the higher the number, the faster the scrolling. You can also change the default directories for storing maps, tracks, and DEM data. You must restart the program for changes to take effect. I suggest leaving the settings as is, since the directory in the panel to the far left of the active files lists defaults to the TopoFusion directory, regardless of changes that you make here. See the File Structure section of this chapter for tips on efficiently organizing your data. The **User Type** feature lets you select an icon for track playback. It's a little cheesy, and many users may choose **No Icon**. Click **Show Trackseg Breaks** to show where satellite coverage was lost while recording tracks.

• **Units.** The choices here are mostly self-explanatory. They include **Units of Distance**, **Coordinate Type**, and **Datum Selection**. Click **Show Scale on Map** to place a scale bar at the lower right of the map screen.

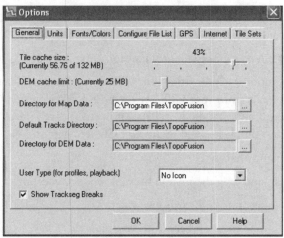

Figure 12A

- **Fonts/Color**. Here you can select track colors and waypoint fonts and colors. More information on some of these choices is provided in the Waypoints section of this chapter.

- **Configure File List**. This tab lets you select which columns appear in the **Active Files** list, shown below the map on your screen. You can also select their order and the width of each column.

- **GPS**. This is where you configure communication with your GPS unit.

- **Internet**. Here you can configure your Internet connection to **Use Proxy Server**. You can also customize the **Server Connection** to make the most effective use of your Internet connection speed, whether it is a slow dialup connection (use a low setting) or fast broadband connection (use a setting greater than 10).

- **Tile Sets**. TerraServer-based images are available at various scales (four meters per pixel, for example). These scales are shown in the drop-down menu at the upper right of the screen. TopoFusion refers to these as tilesets. If you select **Topo 4M,** you will notice that the images are based on USGS 1:24,000-scale maps. Select **Topo 8M** and the images will be based on 1:100,000-scale maps. To provide intermediate zooming, TopoFusion must shrink or expand the tilesets. Shrinking tilesets provides a higher-quality image but loads the image more slowly, while expanding tilesets is faster but produces a lower-quality image. Move the **Tileset Preference** slider accordingly, taking into account your hardware capabilities. The **Zooming Smoothness** slider controls the number of intermediate maps that will be drawn between standard tilesets. In effect, this controls how many clicks it will take to move from one tileset to the next, using the **Zoom Box**.

Getting Started

To begin using TopoFusion, do one of the following:

• Choose **Goto**, then select **Goto Coordinate** and enter a specific location.

• Import a waypoint or track list from your GPS or from a .gpx file. To learn more about importing data from your GPS, see the GPS Interface section later in this chapter. When you import data, it will appear in the **Active Files** list. Double-click the file name, or right-click it and then select **Center Map on File.**

To navigate the map, you can:

• Choose **Pan Map** and drag the map to move it to a new location.

• Scroll the map using your keyboard's arrow keys.

To switch between topo maps and aerial photos, press the T key. To cycle between aerial photos, topo maps, and combination images, press the A key. In urban areas where color aerial photography is available, press the C key to toggle between color and black-and-white aerial photographs.

To zoom the map:

• Use the drop-down menu at the upper right of the screen. Notice that here you have access to topo maps, aerial photos, urban color photos, and combination images.

• Use the scroll wheel on your mouse, if yours is equipped with one.

• Use the plus sign (+) and minus sign (-) keys.

• Use the **Zoom Box**. Once you have enabled this tool, click anywhere on the map to zoom in and recenter the map at that location. Right-click to zoom out. This feature is called a Zoom Box because you can also use it to drag a box on the map, which will zoom the map to that particular location.

To devote more screen space to a map or aerial photo image, you can drag the **Active Files** list to the bottom of the screen. Selecting the area at the top of the **Active Files** list where there are three arrows (see Figure 12B) automatically hides or reveals the **Active Files** list.

Figure 12B

> **TIP:** Double-clicking any file in the Active Files list recenters the map on that location.
>
> **TIP:** Having trouble finding an out-of-state vacation spot? Load the states.gpx file that comes with TopoFusion to superimpose state boundaries. That should help.

File Structure

TopoFusion stores data as .gpx files. The default location for these is C:\Program Files\TopoFusion.

The **Active Files** window consists of several panes. On the left is a pane in which you can navigate your hard drive for files, including .gpx, Topo USA .txt, and Maptech .mxf and .txf files. Double-click on a folder to open it and the next pane to the right will show any files that can be displayed in TopoFusion. Select individual files and click **Add File**, or choose **Add All** to add all files shown. Either action will cause the files to show up in the **Active Files** list, the pane to the right.

Remove a file from the **Active Files** list by selecting it and choosing **Remove**. To leave a file in the **Active Files** list but remove it from view on the map, clear the check box next to the file name. Alternatively, you can right-click and then select **Disable File**.

Right-clicking a file also lets you save it using the **Save File** option. Or select **Save As** to create a new file.

Right-click a file and then select **Properties** to view a list of track points or waypoints, or to change the track color.

A few other points to be aware of:

• Each file can contain multiple waypoints or tracks.

• When you close TopoFusion and then restart it, it will show the same files in the Active Files list that were present when it was last shut down.

• You can end up with a lot of files in the Active Files list. One easy way to clear them is to use CTRL or SHIFT to highlight multiple files, then right-click the highlighted files and click **Remove**.

• Remember that you can customize the Active Files list, as discussed in the Configuration section of this chapter. You can also sort based on any column in the active files list by clicking its column header.

• However you configure the directory (see Configuration earlier in this chapter), the directory shown in the Active Files list always defaults to the TopoFusion directory. Because of this, if you wish to create folders to organize your data, I suggest creating them within the TopoFusion folder.

Waypoints and Waypoint Management

To place a waypoint, choose **Mark WayPoint** and click anywhere on the map. This will open the **Waypoint** dialog box, where you can select a file to add the waypoint to, or create a new file for it. This is also where you **Name** the waypoint and select its **Symbol**.

It's often difficult to read waypoint names in many mapping programs, but TopoFusion offers an amazing number of choices when it comes to waypoint font, style, and color. To access these, choose **Options**, then **Preferences**. When the **Options** dialog box opens, select the **Fonts/Colors** tab. This opens the dialog box shown in Figure 12C. Play around with the options here and you will always be able to find a legible combination. Changes here affect all waypoints, which is very helpful when it comes to printing. My personal favorite is to turn off the **White Background**, enable the **Shadow On/Off** feature, and use yellow for the **Text Color** and black for the **Shadow Color**. Users in grassland or desert areas will probably find that other options work better.

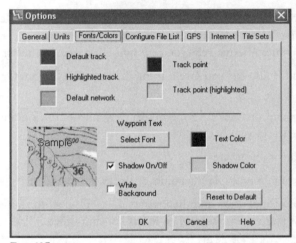

Figure 12C

To edit a waypoint, choose **Mark WayPoint**, move the pointer over the top of any waypoint, right-click it, and select **Edit Waypoint**. Alternatively, you can right-click the waypoint file in the **Active Files** list, select **Properties**, and then choose the **Waypoints** tab. Right-click a waypoint and then select **Edit Waypoint**. You can also select **Delete Points** from here to delete a waypoint.

To move a waypoint on the map, choose **Select Point** and then use it to drag any waypoint to a new location. To delete a waypoint, use the **Select Point** tool to select it, then press the DELETE key. You can also delete a waypoint with the **Mark Waypoint** tool by right-clicking on a waypoint.

> **TIP: Toggle View Status (Waypoints)** lets you show or hide waypoints.

Tracks

We're going to reverse the order here and discuss tracks before routes. TopoFusion has sophisticated track tools, but limited ability to create routes. When you do create routes, you must convert them from tracks. Hence the order in this chapter.

To draw a track on a map, click **Draw Track**. You can now start drawing a track, clicking at each curve, or you can hold down the left mouse button to draw freehand. If you are near the edge of the map, stop drawing momentarily and use the arrow keys to scroll the map. When you're finished drawing the track, right-click it and choose **Save As**. If you do not do this, the track will not be saved. Notice that you also have the option to **Remove Last Segment** or **Clear All Segments**.

> **TIP: Toggle View Status (Tracks)** lets you show or hide tracks on the map.

To download tracks from your GPS, choose **GPS** and then select **GPS Transfer**. In **Select File for Download**, you will be given the option of creating a **New File** or selecting an existing one to add the track to. Selecting **Follow download in map** will allow you to view the track as it is drawn on the map. If no active files are listed, TopoFusion will automatically scroll and zoom to show the entire track.

Once the track is downloaded, TopoFusion provides some sophisticated tools for saving the data. A **Merge/Delete downloaded tracks** dialog box will open, as shown in Figure 12D. A typical track, collected in the field, will be composed of multiple track segments because of loss of satellite coverage. These track segments are listed in this dialog box.

Merge/Delete downloaded tracks

Tracks downloaded from GPS:

Start Time	Duration	Length	Num Points	Source	
Sun Sep 26 10:04:01 2004	0:15:42	1.61 mi	61	Active Log	Remove Selected
Sun Sep 26 10:20:28 2004	0:43:54	4.21 mi	136	Active Log	
Sun Sep 26 11:04:54 2004	0:06:25	0.93 mi	23	Active Log	Merge Selected
Sun Sep 26 11:13:40 2004	0:43:11	3.94 mi	119	Active Log	
Sun Sep 26 11:57:52 2004	0:00:00	0 ft	1	Active Log	Highlight Selected
Sun Sep 26 12:04:34 2004	0:02:47	112 ft	4	Active Log	
Sun Sep 26 12:14:54 2004	0:05:43	0.68 mi	22	Active Log	
Sun Sep 26 12:22:25 2004	0:06:33	0.93 mi	29	Active Log	Save Selected
Sun Sep 26 12:29:37 2004	0:03:25	0.40 mi	10	Active Log	
Sun Sep 26 13:49:38 2004	0:08:48	20 ft	2	Active Log	Save all tracks
					Exit

Figure 12D

There may be times when you wish to delete a certain track segment. Perhaps you just want to record, on a map, areas where you have traveled at least once, and not record a new track each time. Or maybe your trip was "out and back," bringing you over the same area twice. TopoFusion provides tools that help you clean up your maps in this manner. From the **Merge/Delete downloaded tracks** dialog box, select a track segment and then choose **Highlight Selected**. You can select and highlight each segment in the list. You can also pan and zoom the map while doing this. If you find a segment you wish to delete, choose **Remove Selected**. There are advantages to selecting all tracks and then choosing **Merge Selected**. This will connect your entire trip and allow you to visualize it using the **Profile and Playback** feature (which we'll discuss shortly). Finally, you'll be given the option to **Save Selected Tracks** or **Save All Tracks**. Click **Exit** to close the dialog box.

Tracks are made up of connected line segments, which often results in rough approximations along sections of curving trails. TopoFusion's **Spline** function can eliminate some of this jagged appearance. Right-click a track segment and select **Spline/Simplify Track**. In the dialog box shown in Figure 12E, select **Interpolate (Spline)–Add Points**. Make sure you select **Use Nonuniform Parameterization**. This causes interpolation to be based on a two-dimensional model, leaving elevation and time out of the calculations and resulting in more accurate interpolation. The interpolation process adds data points to smooth curves, and you will have to choose the **Number of Points to add**.

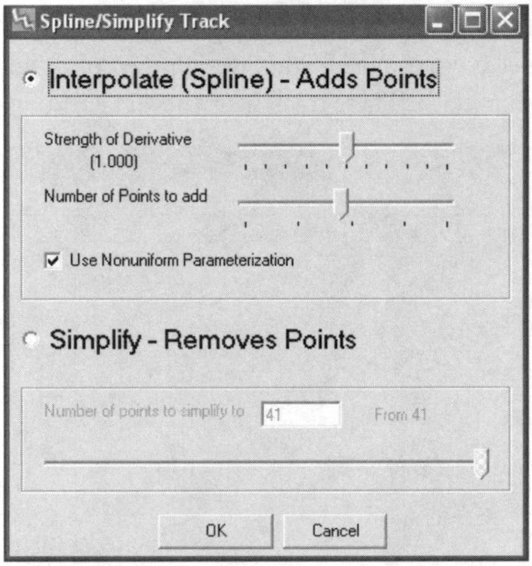

Figure 12E

Several tools are available for managing track points.

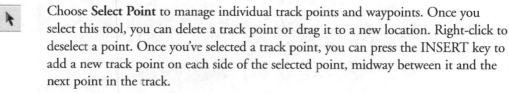

Choose **Select Points** and use this tool to drag a box around multiple track points, which you can then drag to a new location or delete by pressing the DELETE key. Right-clicking will deselect the points and right-clicking while dragging will cancel the operation.

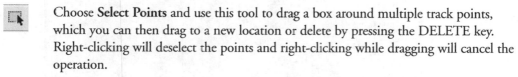

Choose **Select Point** to manage individual track points and waypoints. Once you select this tool, you can delete a track point or drag it to a new location. Right-click to deselect a point. Once you've selected a track point, you can press the INSERT key to add a new track point on each side of the selected point, midway between it and the next point in the track.

Use the **Cut Track** tool to cut an existing segment into two segments. The two new track segments will be retained in the same file as the original segment, which is deleted.

Right-click a track segment to bring up multiple track management options, as shown in Figure 12F. At the top of the menu will be the name of the file containing the track.

Figure 12F

Finally, while viewing tracks, the Active Files list shows a Difficulty Index and Effort Index, both of which are located to the right in the Active Files area, unless you changed their layout when configuring the program. These features let you compare various outings. Information on how they are calculated can be found on the TopoFusion Web site at **www.topofusion.com/stats.php**.

Profile/Playback

One of the more interesting and downright fun features you'll find in TopoFusion is Profile and Playback. Like many mapping programs, TopoFusion can generate elevation profiles. The designers have added a little fun, though, with this feature. Let's try it out:

1. Select the **Profile and Playback** tool and then select any track to display the **Profile** dialog box shown in Figure 12G. Alternatively, you can click **Pan Map**, right-click a track of field-collected data, and then select **Profile (plus Playback)**. The track must be field data, since the playback feature not only depends on three-dimensional data but adds a time element as well.

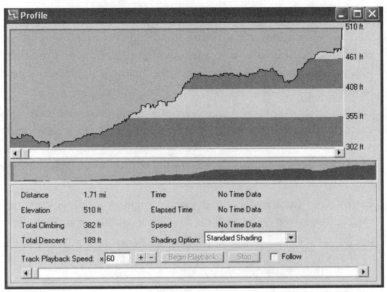

Figure 12G

2. Click **Follow** and, when the track plays, the map will automatically follow it.

 3. Unless you were driving when you collected the track, you will probably want to increase the **Track Playback Speed**.

4. Now select **Begin Playback**, minimize the **Profile** dialog box, and watch the icon follow the route you took.

> **TIP:** To change the icon, select **Options**, then **Preferences**. Choose the **General** tab and then, in the **User Type** area, choose between **No Icon**, **Hiker**, **Cyclist**, and **Equestrian**.

I first used this option to follow a bike ride my wife and I had taken in an area we were just beginning to explore. It turned into a fairly lazy ride as we checked out numerous sidetracks, a plum tree, and a friendly horse. Then we came to a bridge with a nearby rope swing. I didn't realize how long we had dawdled until we returned home and played back the track. It was quite amusing to watch the icon sit in one place for so long!

One last point about the playback feature: TopoFusion has a multitrack playback capability. Does your friend have a GPS on his mountain bike too? Want to see how each of you progressed? Select **Analysis**, then **Multi-Playback**. For more information on using this option, go to **www.topofusion.com/multi.php**.

Before we leave the **Profile** dialog box, we should go over a few other features:

- The **Shading Option** lets you color-code a track according to how fast you were going at the time, or by recorded elevation. If you choose **Vertical Elevation**, you may want to select **Window** on the main map screen, then select **Scale** to see a color-coded elevation key.

- You can zoom in and out on the elevation profile by left-clicking and right-clicking the mouse.

- The slider bar below the elevation profile lets you move along the profile.

- The master profile is located immediately below the slider bar and main profile. For a more detailed examination of a portion of the elevation profile, drag the colored bars to control the area shown in the main profile window.

Creating Trail Networks

Another wonderful track tool available with TopoFusion lets you splice tracks together to create a network of trails. To see how this works, select the **Profile and Playback** tool and then click any track. This brings up the **Profile** dialog box. Now click an adjacent track. The two tracks will be combined, in the order you clicked, to create a new merged track, which will be highlighted on the map and will appear in the **Profile** dialog box.

You can continue adding tracks in succession to build on the trail network. A small blue icon travels the merged track continuously, showing you the direction in which the merged track was created. At some point, you may incorporate a track that was created going in the opposite direction from the rest of the network, which will be made obvious when a straight line connects the merged track with the far end of the newest segment. You can easily resolve this by pressing the R key to reverse the last segment. Alternatively, you can right-click the merged track and then select **Reverse Last Segment.**

Right-clicking the merged network gives other options as well. **Remove Last Segment** does exactly as the name implies, and you can select it repeatedly to remove previous segments. **Clear All Segments** removes them all, eliminating the merged track and allowing you to see the original component segments on the screen.

To save the merged track, right-click it and then select **Save As.**

TIP: Field collected tracks will have elevation data attached. Select **Toggle Elevation Shading** to show or hide color-coded relative elevation differences.

Routes

TopoFusion is designed for data collection and for visualizing trips beforehand and analyzing them after the fact. It is not designed for field use and has minimal features for creating routes.

The designers, however, have provided one tool for creating routes. You can upload tracks as routes, converting track points to waypoints. Because tracks can contain large numbers of points, the designers suggest that you first simplify the route. This may be essential because of the limited number of waypoints that your GPS can accommodate when you send it a route. It helps to know how many waypoints your GPS can accommodate per route; many units are limited to 50 or 100.

 To simplify a track, first click **Pan Map**, then right-click a track and select **Spline/ Simplify Track** to open the dialog box shown in Figure 12E. **Select Simplify– Removes Points** and use the slider bar to decrease the number of track points. As you do so, you will see both the original and simplified track on the map. Select **OK** once you are happy with the results. To avoid losing the original track, go to the **Active Files** list, right-click the track, choose **Save As**, and give the simplified track a new name.

A good alternative for creating routes is to use a program like EasyGPS (see Chapter 6) to create routes from existing waypoints. One advantage of this is that the routes will utilize your own waypoint names.

GPS Interface

To exchange data with your **GPS**, select **GPS**, then **GPS Transfer**. This opens the **GPS Communication** dialog box shown in Figure 12H. The Log Book alluded to in **Add track(s) to log book** will be discussed in the More Tips section at the end of this chapter.

The **Upload Track(s)** options called **to Saved Tracks, to ACTIVE LOG**, and **as Route** are available only for Garmin GPS units.

Printing

TopoFusion does not support map printing, although **www.topofusion.com** lists the feature as in development.

Moving Map

To begin tracking your location in real time, select **GPS**, then **Live Tracking** to open the dialog box shown in Figure 12I. Now select **Start Tracking**. This is a very simple tracking system, with only a couple of options. You can choose to **Center Map on Position** and you can select either **Garmin** or **NMEA/Magellan** as your **GPS Type**.

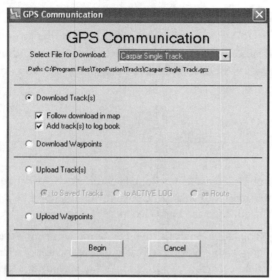

Figure 12H

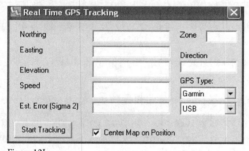

Figure 12I

3-D

As this book was going to press, TopoFusion released version 2.50, automating 3-D imagery. Where you once had to go through a manual download of Digital Elevation Model (DEM) data, you now need only click the 3-D button. 3-D configuration options can be found by clicking **Options** and then clicking **3-D settings**.

Working With Other Programs

TopoFusion saves files to a .gpx format, and can read .gpx files as well. It also reads Maptech's track (.txf) and marker/waypoint (.mxf) file formats. Additionally, it will accept DeLorme Topo USA UTM and lat/lon text (.txt) files. You can also export .jpg and .bmp images.

More Tips

Log Book

TopoFusion's Log Book is a great feature for bikers, runners, or just about anyone who uses a GPS in combination with an athletic pursuit. Note that only field-collected tracks with time data attached can be loaded into the Log Book.

To access the Log Book, select **Analysis**, then **Log Book** to open the screen shown in Figure 12J. This unique feature gives you a calendar-based view of all trips when you download them as field-collected tracks. Let's take a quick look at a few of the buttons:

• **Load File.** This loads the file currently selected in the Active Files list to the Log Book.

• **Center Map on File.** This loads, if necessary, and centers the map on the currently selected Log Book file.

• **Remove File from Log.** This removes only the summary data from the log. TopoFusion still retains the original .gpx file.

• **Add All Loaded Files to Log.** This adds all files in the Active Files list to the Log Book.

Ever wonder how many miles you've racked up on your trips this month or year? Pick the start and end dates using **Select Summary Dates**. A statistical summary will appear in the **Summary Window**. Alternatively, you can enter the dates manually and choose **Compute Summary**. This great feature lets you revisit past trips and analyze your outdoor activities. The data summaries are stored in the TopoFusion directory in a file named TFlog.csv. If you use the Log to record all your trips, be sure to back up this file regularly.

Updates to this book will be posted at www.MakeYourOwnMaps.com. Bookmark and visit often to see what's new in the world of digital mapping.

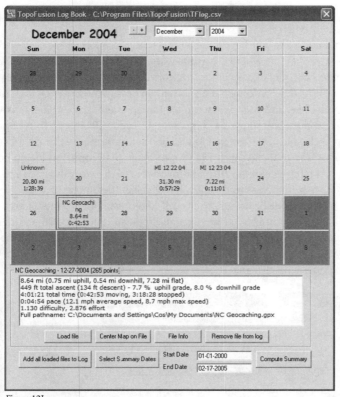

Figure 12J

- TopoFusion provides a simple way to download all topos and aerial photos for a given area. Choose the **Load Maps** tool and drag a rectangle to define an area for downloading. A **Download Maps** dialog box will appear, letting you download, within the defined areas, all scales of topos, aerial photos, or both. You can also use this tool when you get an error message for a downloaded tile, to force it to download again. It can also be used to force the software to look for updated maps for a given area.

- Choose **Window**, then **Image Processing** to alter the brightness, contrast, and sharpness of combination aerial and topo images. Four presets will give you a preview of what you can accomplish here. There are also keyboard shortcuts for these adjustments. The left bracket ([) key makes the topo portion of the image more prominent, while the right bracket (]) key shifts the image in the other direction, making the aerial photo more discernable. The = key increases brightness, while the HYPHEN (-) key decreases it. The 9 key decreases contrast, while the 0 key increases it.

PhotoFusion

PhotoFusion lets you link digital photos to the location where they were shot. You just enter the directory where the images are stored and the time zone your digital camera is set to. Like magic, a camera icon shows up along the track wherever you took a photo. How does it do this? It's all based on timestamps. Your GPS acquires time data from satellites and your digital camera has an internal clock. (First make sure your camera's clock is accurate by comparing it to your GPS clock.) To set up this feature, right-click a file in the **Active Files** list and select **Properties**, or right-click a track with the **Pan Map** tool and select **File Properties**. In the **Properties** dialog box, choose the **Pictures** tab (see Figure 12K) and browse for the directory in which your photos are stored. Next, in the **Set to Time Zone** box, select the time zone your camera is set to. The next field will be automatically calculated, establishing the difference between the time zone you entered and Greenwich Mean Time. Click **OK** and camera icons should appear next to the appropriate tracks. If you receive an error message, see **www.topofusion.com/photofusion.php**. You can even use this feature to produce Web pages with clickable images on your maps!

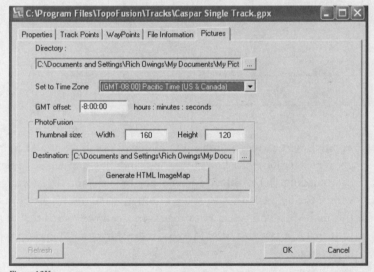

Figure 12K

EXIF Tags

Exchangeable Image File Format (EXIF) is a format used for storing data associated with digital photos. Among the information it contains are time and date stamps. Some photo editors may not preserve EXIF tags; ACDSee is one that does.

USAPhotoMaps (Chapter 5): Urban aerial photo image showing track and waypoint; Angeles National Forest, California. Image courtesy of Doug Cox.

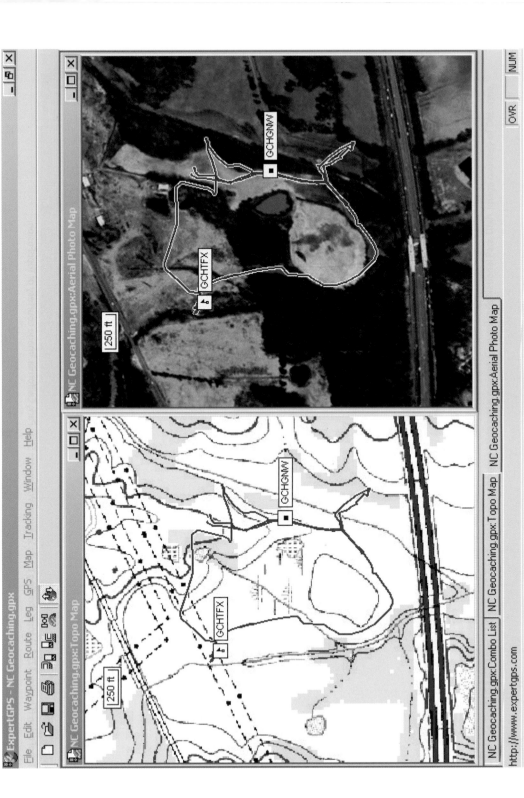

Expert GPS ((Chapter 13):Topo and aerial photo showing track and waypoints from geocaching trip, Cabarrus County, North Carolina. Image courtesy of TopoGrafix.

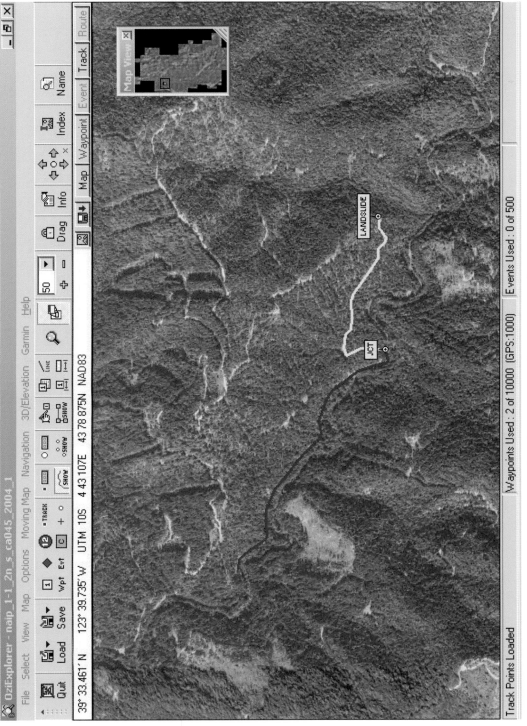

OziExplorer (Chapter 15): MrSID aerial photo showing tracks and waypoints, Mendocino County, California. Image courtesy of OziExplorer.

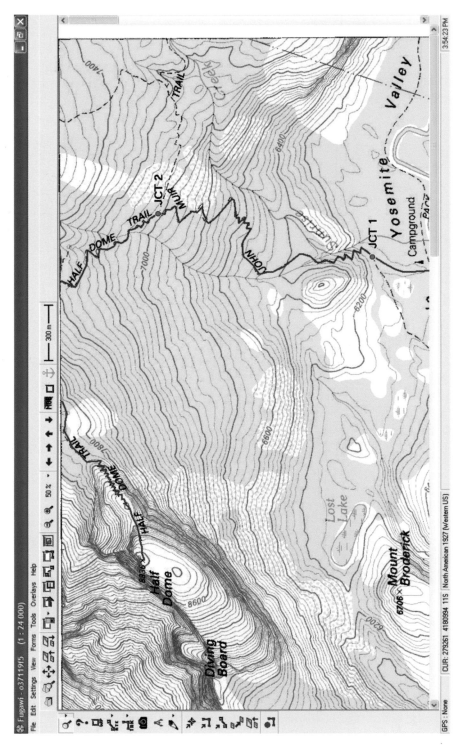

Fugawi GPS Mapping Software (Chapter 16): Topo showing waypoints and track; Yosemite National Park, California. Image courtesy of Fugawi.

Chapter 13 ExpertGPS

Like USAPhotoMaps (Chapter 5) and TopoFusion (Chapter 12), ExpertGPS™ is another program based on Microsoft's TerraServer.

In some ways, ExpertGPS is a hybrid program: in addition to utilizing TerraServer images, it also lets you import several types of georeferenced maps, much like the programs discussed in Section Four.

ExpertGPS also offers some features targeted to geocachers. If you fit into this category, you'll want to take a close look at this program.

Basic Information

COST
• $59.95 for a personal use license

• A $99.95 version lets you import GIS shapefiles

SYSTEM REQUIREMENTS
• Microsoft Windows

GPS COMPATIBILITY
• ExpertGPS works with a wide range of Garmin, Lowrance, and Magellan GPS units, and with some Brunton, Eagle, MLR, and Silva models.

TESTED VERSION
• 1.3.7

CONTACT INFORMATION
TopoGrafix
24 Kirkland Dr
Stow, MA 01775
Info2004@expertgps.com
www.expertgps.com

AVAILABLE OPTIONS
• A GIS Option Pack, available for $39.95, allows you to import and export shapefiles (.shp). See Chapter 23 for additional information on GIS.

• The Yahoo Map Authors group, at **groups.yahoo.com/group/map_authors**, lists ExpertGPS as being discussed on its message board.

Advantages

• A free, 31-day demo version is available.

• It's easy to create a route by clicking waypoints, either on the map or from a list.

• Several features are designed specifically for geocaching.

• You can import calibrated or uncalibrated map images.

• When you place a waypoint, you are automatically taken to the name field—no extra steps are required.

• You can split or join tracks and routes.

• The software includes a **Simplify Track/Route** feature.

• Panning with the **Move Map** tool, combined with scroll wheel zooming, is an excellent way to navigate the map.

Disadvantages

• There is no 3-D capability.

• You cannot toggle between aerial and topo in the same location, though you can view the same location in separate windows, which can be placed side by side.

• The help file is limited.

• Print options are somewhat limited.

• The datum list is limited, though it should meet the needs of most users.

Tutorial/Manual

ExpertGPS would be much more desirable if it had a better help file structure. The software has numerous important features that the help files do not cover. Some features that are otherwise difficult to locate can be found by using the **Search** tab in **Help**.

Installation

Installation is easy. Simply download **SetupExpertGPS.exe** from **www.expertgps.com** and run it.

Configuration

Choose **File**, then **Preferences**, where you will see the following configuration tabs:

• **My GPS Receivers**. Select **Add GPS** to add your model, then choose **Settings** to establish communication settings.

• **Units of Measure**. Choose from **Standard, Nautical**, or **Metric**.

• **Coordinates**. Choose from the options shown in Figure 13A.

• **Map Folder**. Specify the folder in which downloaded map and aerial photo images will be stored.

• **Tracking**. Choose **NMEA–GPS Active** for real-time tracking.

• **Received Waypoints**. Select **Settings** to rename various waypoint symbols to suit your needs.

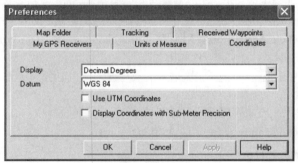

Figure 13A

Getting Started

Go to **www.topografix.com/data.asp** and download the waypoint file for your state. Save it to your desktop, then right-click it and unzip it to the ExpertGPS directory. Select **File**, then **Open** and navigate to the ExpertGPS directory. Open the file, which will have the name of the state with a .loc extension.

This will give you a big list, so it will help to get a little more screen real estate to work with. The screen is divided into three panes. The waypoints are in the upper pane, with the lower pane set aside for routes. The middle pane is used for route waypoints. I'll explain all this in more detail soon. For now, though, drag the separator bars down, shrinking the bottom two windows to give you a little more room in the top one.

Pick a waypoint, right-click it and click **Set Active Point**. Now go to the menus at the top of the screen and select **Map**, then **New Topo Map Window**. (Remember, you have to be online for this to work.) Select **Map**, then **New Aerial Photo Map Window**.

This may result in many more waypoints than you want on your map. For now, one easy way to get rid of them is to select **Map**, then **Show Map Display Options**, opening the **Map Display** dialog box shown in Figure 13B. Set **Symbols** to **Off** and **Text** to **None**. We'll look at other ways to clean things up in the Waypoints section of this chapter.

Figure 13B

TIP: Want to view the same location on an aerial photo and a topo map? You can start with either, but we'll assume you're starting with a topo window. Double-click the center of the window to set an active point. Now select **Map**, then **New Aerial Photo Map Window**. You can resize and drag the windows to place them side by side.

You can move around the map in several ways:

• Click the **Move Map** tool and drag to pan the map.

• Use the **Recenter Map** tool.

• Use the arrow keys.

Zooming in on the map can also be accomplished in multiple ways:

• Use the **Zoom** tool and drag the rectangle anywhere on the map to zoom in.

• Use the mouse scroll wheel.

• Use the plus (+) and minus (-) keys. Pressing the backslash key (\) returns the map to the original scale (1:24,000-scale map or four-meters-per-pixel aerial photo).

• Right-click and click **Zoom** to display the options shown in Figure 13C. **Zoom Reset** returns the map to the original scale.

• Select **Map**, then **Zoom In**, **Zoom Out**, or **Zoom to Original Size**.

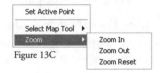

Figure 13C

> **TIP:** A simple way to go to a new location on the map is to select **Map**, point to **Recenter Map**, then choose **Waypoint**. This opens the **Select Waypoint** dialog box shown in Figure 13D, which lists the waypoints in the current **Combo List**.

Figure 13D

Figure 13E

File Structure

ExpertGPS stores its data in .gpx and .loc files. The default location is C:\Program Files\ExpertGPS. All data is managed from the **Combo List** tab. Here you will find all waypoint, route, and track information. To move information between files, select the lines to be moved, choose **Edit**, select **Copy**, and paste the information into another file.

Waypoints and Waypoint Management

To place a waypoint, choose **Add New Waypoint** and click anywhere on the map. This also opens the **Edit Waypoint** dialog box (see Figure 13E), with the cursor in the **Description** field. Any text entered here will also appear in capital letters in the **Waypoint** field. The name in the **Waypoint** field will be the one transferred to your **GPS**, but the **Description** field will show on the screen. If you want the name on the screen to be the same as the one transferred to your GPS, you must use it for the **Description** field. One advantage to this approach is that once you click to place a waypoint, you'll be in the name field. You can always use the **Comment** field for other information.

Setting and Using Active Waypoints

There are many instances when you'll find it useful to set an active waypoint. Select the **Combo List** tab for the current .loc file. Select a waypoint in the waypoint list, right-click it, and select **Set Active Point**. Now scroll right in the list and click the column heading labeled **Distance to Active Point**, sorting the list by distance.

Maybe you just want to rid the map of waypoints outside the area in which you're interested. Set an active waypoint, select **Waypoint**, then select **Find Waypoints**. Choose the **Distance to Point** tab, select **Is Less Than**, and type in a distance, as shown in Figure 13F.

Note that you can also select an active point in the following ways:

• Choose **Waypoint**, then **Set Active Waypoint**.

• From either a map or an aerial photo screen, right-click and select **Set Active Point**. This will establish a point from which you can search or measure distance, without creating a waypoint.

• Right-click an existing waypoint on any screen and select **Set Active Point**.

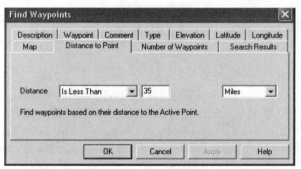

Figure 13F

Updates to this book will be posted at www.MakeYourOwnMaps.com. Bookmark and visit often to see what's new in the world of digital mapping.

Right-click an existing waypoint for the options shown in Figure 13G.

New Waypoint...
Edit Waypoint...
Hide Waypoint
Delete Waypoint

Set Active Point
Clear Active Point
Add Waypoint to Route

Send Waypoint to GPS
Receive Waypoints from GPS

View Waypoint Online
Print Waterproof Topo Map
Project Waypoint

Figure 13G

To search for a waypoint, select **Waypoint**, then **Find Waypoints** to open the dialog box shown in Figure 13H. Select any tab for various ways to perform the search. (You can do this from any screen.) Once you perform the search, all waypoints will disappear, except those meeting the criteria you entered.

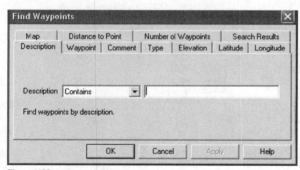

Figure 13H

To go back to the full list, select **Waypoint**, then **Show All Waypoints**.

To save the waypoints with a new file name, select **File**, then **Save As**.

Routes

To create a route, use the **Draw New Route** tool, or press the R key. Click anywhere on the map (or aerial photo screen) to start the route, and continue clicking to add more points. If you click on waypoints, the route will use those names. Otherwise a waypoint will be created wherever you click.

To insert a waypoint, select the **Add Turn to Route** tool and click on the map. The nearest leg will snap to the new route waypoint.

Here are a few other items to be aware of in terms of working with routes:

• You can also create routes from a waypoint list, as described in Chapter 6 on EasyGPS.

• You can reverse routes by selecting **Route**, then **Reverse Route**. Note the other options on the **Route** menu, shown in Figure 13I.

• From the **Combo List** tab, select a route in the **Route List**. Right-click it to bring up the menu shown in Figure 13J. Note that you can combine routes by clicking **Join Route to Active Route**. You can also join tracks this way.

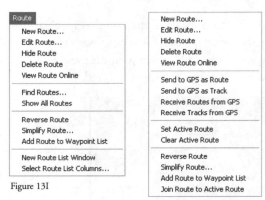

Figure 13I

Figure 13J

Tracks

Select the Track tool using any of the following methods:

• Press the T key.

• Choose the **Draw New Track** tool.

• Select **Map**, point to the **Select Map** tool, and choose the **Track** tool.

Now drag the mouse to draw your track. When you release the mouse button, the **Edit Route** dialog box will appear, allowing you to name the track. No, that's not a typo; click the **Combo List** tab at the bottom left of the screen and note that tracks are stored in the Route List. They have a "T" beside them, while routes have an "R." If you have no desire to name the track, hold down the SHIFT key and release the mouse button when you're finished drawing. ExpertGPS will name the track on the basis of how many track points were used—e.g., TP0001-TP 0195.

To add to an existing track, first choose the **Select** tool using one of the following options:

• Press the S key.

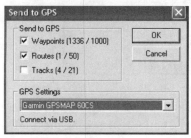

• Choose the **Select** tool.

• Select **Map**, point to the **Select Map** tool, then choose **Select**.

Click a track to make it active. The red track will be highlighted in yellow, giving it an orange appearance. Now switch back to the **Draw New Track** tool and make sure you are close enough to the existing track that the track name shows—otherwise you will create a new track. Now hold the left mouse button down and begin drawing.

You can also split a track (or route) by selecting, the **Cut Route** tool and clicking anywhere along the track.

Finally, it's worth noting that ExpertGPS has a tool that lets you reduce the number of track points. This is especially helpful when you're using your GPS to transfer data from one program to another. Right-click a track in your **Route List** and select **Simplify Route**. In the dialog box that opens, indicate the number of legs (links between track points) to include in the simplified track, then click **OK**. A new track will be created and made active. The old track will not be deleted.

GPS Interface

Select **GPS**, then **Send to GPS**, and ExpertGPS will provide options for sending waypoints, tracks, and routes, as shown in Figure 13K. (Those of you who have multiple GPS units to play with can choose which to use here.) Two numbers appear beside each option. The first is the number of waypoints, tracks, or routes associated with the file; the second is the quantity of each that your GPS is capable of storing.

Figure 13K

To send an individual route or track, right-click it and select the appropriate option, as shown in Figure 13J. Note that you can send these items to your GPS as either routes or tracks. This can come in handy if you want to transfer the data to another software package. From this menu, you can also receive routes and tracks from your GPS.

Another way to send and receive data is to select **GPS** to display the menu shown in Figure 13L. Note that you can also **Turn Off GPS** from here.

Figure 13L

  To send the entire contents of a .loc or .gpx file, select **Send All to GPS**. You can also select **Receive All from GPS**.

Printing

To show a grid, such as UTM, select **Map**, then **Show Map Grid Option**s to open the **Grid** dialog box shown in Figure 13M. You can control what is displayed by selecting **Map**, then **Show Map Display Option**s. There are no options for increasing the size of waypoint or grid labels.

To print, select **Map**, then **Print Map** to open the dialog box shown in Figure 13N.

Figure 13M

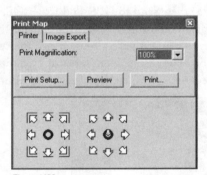

Figure 13N

  To center the map, use **Recenter the Map at the Active Point** or **Set the Active Point at the Center of the Screen**. The only options for resizing the printed map are standardized increments from 25% to 200%. In my experience, 75% produces a readable map. If you reduce a map to 50% you can still read waypoint labels, but grid labels will get pretty small.

You can gain some flexibility by exporting the image. We'll discuss this in Working With Other Programs, later in this chapter.

Moving Map

ExpertGPS supports real-time tracking of your position on a laptop, but only in NMEA mode. More information on NMEA and other real-time tracking tips can be found in Chapter 2. To enable NMEA communication, go to your GPS unit's setup menu and change the interface to NMEA and the baud rate to 4800. You'll also need to change this in ExpertGPS. Select **File**, choose **Preferences**, then select **Tracking** to open the dialog box shown in Figure 13O. Set **Tracking** to **NMEA – GPS Active** and **Baud Rate** to **4800**, then choose the proper port. Click **OK**.

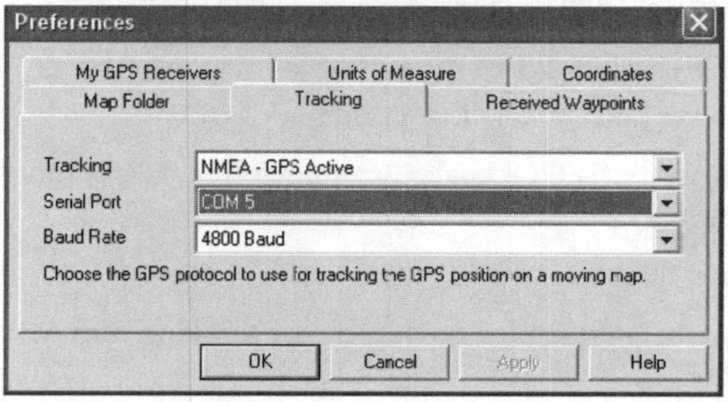

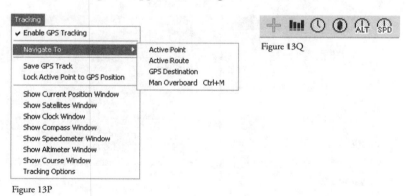

Figure 13O

Now, on the map screen, choose **Enable GPS Tracking**, or choose **Tracking** and select **Enable GPS Tracking**. A yellow circle noting your position will appear, with a line indicating your direction of travel. To navigate to a destination, select **Tracking** and point to **Navigate To**. You will be presented with the choices shown in Figure 13P. Many of these options appear on the right side of the toolbar, as shown in Figure 13Q.

Figure 13P

Figure 13Q

Most of the options in Figure 13P are fairly self-explanatory. **Tracking Options** opens the dialog box shown in Figure 13R. **Record Method** refers to the gathering of track points.

3-D

ExpertGPS provides no options for three-dimensional display. For information on programs that do, see Chapter 21.

Working With Other Programs

ExpertGPS can export and import the following types of data:

• Garmin MapSource (.mps) files

• Maptech's marker (.mxf), route (.rxf), and track (.txf) files

• National Geographic TOPO!'s older .tpg format (note that it cannot utilize the newer .tpo files)

• Lowrance (.usr) files

• .csv files (For more information on this, choose **Working with Microsoft Excel** in **Help Contents**.)

You can get to all these options from the **File** menu. Choose **Import** or **Export**, then choose the appropriate file type using the **Files of Type** or **Save as Type** options.

To export a .bmp, .jpg, or .tif image, choose **Map**, then click **Export Image** to open the **Print Map** dialog box, as shown in Figure 13S. You can increase the **Width** and **Height** to up to 8000, but be careful—this creates a huge image file! You may want to start out with values of 1000.

Figure 13R

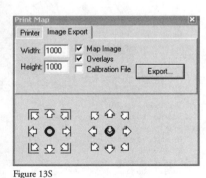

Figure 13S

Importing Other Maps

ExpertGPS can import scanned map images (.jpg, tif, .bmp, .png), and georeferenced maps using OziExplorer .map files and various world files (.jgw, .tfw, .pgw, and .bpw).

Choose **Map,** then **Open Scanned Map Library.** Select **Add** and in the **Files of Type** area, choose the drop-down menu to display file types to import. If you are importing a calibrated map, choose the calibration (world or .map) file first. You will then be asked to locate the image file. You can import only maps created in a supported datum. Though NAD83 is not supported, NAD27 and WGS84 are.

To open a scanned map, select **Map,** then **New Scanned Map Window.** If you are opening a scanned image that is not georeferenced, select **Map,** then **Calibrate Scanned Map.** You can use three calibration points. A set of **Calibration Point Tools** (see Figure 13T) appears on the right side of the toolbar, allowing you to reposition points as you go.

More Tips

• ExpertGPS has many keyboard shortcuts. Choose **Map** and point to **Select Map** tool to display the list shown in Figure 13U.

• To ascertain the age of a map or aerial photo, set a waypoint as active by right-clicking it and then select **Set Active Point.** Now choose **Waypoint** and then select **View Waypoint Online.** Click the Microsoft TerraServer link to see what year the image was created. You can access the aerial photo and the topo map on the TerraServer page.

Figure 13T

Figure 13U

- The **View Waypoint Online** option can also show you geocaches near a certain waypoint. Or click the TopoZone 1:25,000 link to see which 7.5' USGS quad the waypoint is on.

- For more geocaching options, see **Geocaching** under **Help Topics**.

- Right-click any column header in the **Waypoint, Route**, or **Route Waypoint** lists and choose **Select Columns** to customize the display. For example, in the Waypoint List you might add **Sunrise** and **Sunset**. In the Route Waypoint List, **Speed, Elevation**, or **Timestamp** might interest you. While you cannot change the order of columns, you can change their width.

- Choose the **Select** tool, and select a waypoint, route, route waypoint, or track. Then choose the **Move Selected** tool, and drag the selected object to a new location. The tool does not need to be on the object you are moving.

- Select the **Text** tool and click anywhere on the map to place text, opening the **Text Editor** dialog box shown in Figure 13V. Select **Edit Location** to place the text at specific coordinates. Select **New** to open the **Text Style Editor**; this editor, shown in Figure 13W, gives you a great deal of flexibility.

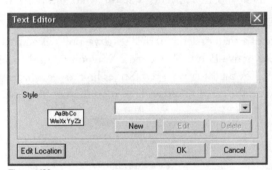

Figure 13V

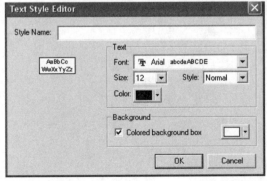

Figure 13W

Section Four Downloading Maps: Free Maps from USGS and Other Sources

Here's where things really start getting fun—not to mention a lot cheaper. The programs in this section allow you to download free maps from all over the world, and import them into mapping programs that will do everything but walk the dog. These programs are perfect for those with a great deal of wanderlust—especially if you'd rather spend your hard-earned money on travel rather than sets of mapping CDs.

The first chapter in this section gets you up to speed on downloading maps. After that we'll look at two software packages that allow you to use topo maps and aerial photos for most of the U.S., downloaded for free from online sources. As long as you have room on your hard drive, you can easily store all your maps there, eliminating the need to shuffle CDs. Both programs offer flexible waypoint display, allow you to link digital photos to maps, and let you transfer maps to a PDA for portable navigation. If you've got a little time, these programs are well worth it, for they put a world of maps a mere click away.

Chapter 14
Maps 201: Downloading Free Maps

Before tackling OziExplorer or Fugawi, you'll need to learn how to download maps. There are some technical things you need to know, and terms you should be familiar with. None of it is too difficult.

> ### Raster or Vector
> As discussed in Chapters 11 and 23, raster images are just that—images. They can be scanned images of topo maps or of aerial photos. Vector graphics, on the other hand, are composed of lines and points. While a vector image won't take up as much disk space, it won't look anything like a standard USGS quad map. This chapter focuses primarily on raster images that you can import into Ozi Explorer or Fugawi. We'll take a detailed look at acquiring and using vector data in Section Six.

Georeferenced Images

Almost all of the maps discussed in this section are georeferenced. This means that attached to the image is data that links the coordinates on your screen (the pixel location) with coordinates in the real world. Sometimes the georeference information is embedded in the image file, and sometimes it is found in an accompanying file, often referred to as a "world file" because it links the image to its location in the real world. Let's take a look at the most common types of georeferenced images available to the digital mapmaker:

• **DRGs (Digital Raster Graphics)**. These are digital, scanned versions of topographic maps. USGS DRGs are scanned at 250 dpi. The images are typically made available in the .tif format. Some are GeoTIFFs, with georeference information (also known as GeoTIFF tags) embedded in the image. Others are paired with a .tfw world file.

> **TIP:** Even though a corresponding .tfw file may be listed, a .tif file may have GeoTIFF tags, making the .tfw file unnecessary in many situations.

- **DOQQ (Digital Orthophoto Quarter Quadrangles).** These are digitized aerial photos. Because of the large file size, each 7.5' USGS quadrangle is broken into four quadrants (NE, NW, SE, and SW). DOQQs are also commonly found as GeoTIFFs or as .tif files with accompanying world files.

- **MrSID (Multi-Resolution Seamless Image Database).** Originally created by LizardTech, this format utilizes highly compressed raster images. Topographic maps and aerial photos are sometimes found in this format.

What Are All Those Numbers?

When you download a DRG or DOQQ, the file names will generally consist of a series of numbers and a couple of letters, known as the Ohio code. For example, the El Capitan, California 7.5' DRG file is named o37119f6.tif. The first letter denotes the scale:

c = 1:250K
f = 1:100K
o = 7.5' quad

The next numbers, 37 and 119, represent the block of latitude and longitude. The following letter (a through h) represents a row within that block, while the final number represents a column (1 through 8) within that block. DOQQs will also have the quarter quadrangle identifier attached (e.g., o37119f6se.tif).

Vector Data

These data formats are discussed in detail in Section Six, but you'll be seeing them mentioned as you start looking for maps to download, so you should know what you can and cannot use in the programs in this section.

- **DLG (Digital Line Graph).** These are data files of public land boundaries, roads, elevation contours, and stream courses. Typical formats include .shp (shapefiles) and .e00 files. You can use OziExplorer to import files from both formats and convert them to tracks or points for display.

- **DEM (Digital Elevation Model).** These datasets provide elevation data every 10 or 30 meters, depending upon the dataset downloaded. They can provide elevation data at the cursor location and allow you to do three-dimensional modeling in programs such as OziExplorer and TopoFusion.

Finding Free Maps Online

With some research, you can usually find free online sources for maps. A great resource for downloading United States DRGs (USGS maps) is maintained by John Galvin at **home.pacbell.net/lgalvin/drgnotes.htm**. Sources are listed for each of the 50 states.

www.gpsy.com/maps lists U.S. and international sources. If you're looking for international maps, the Yahoo OziExplorer discussion board (**groups.yahoo.com/group /OziUsers-L**) is also a good resource. A great deal of international vector data can be found at **data.geocomm.com**. And you'll find an excellent source of scanned maps from around the world (though they are not georeferenced) at **mapy.mk.cvut.cz/index_e.html**.

TIF (Tagged Image File Format) Files

As indicated earlier, these graphics files, when used for maps, often come georeferenced, either through an accompanying world file (.tfw) or through the use of embedded GeoTIFF tags.

For a reason that's far too technical and boring to go into here, Windows sometimes assigns to a downloaded .tif file a four character .tiff extension. If your mapping software is looking for a .tif file, this can cause problems. To remedy this, simply go into **My Computer**, find the appropriate folder, and change the file's extension to .tif. Disregard Windows' apocalyptic warning about making the file unusable. Windows may also add a .txt file extension to a .tfw file. In this case, you'll need to strip the .txt extension from the end of the filename, leaving the .tfw extension.

Zipped Files

When downloading mapping files, you may encounter a couple of unfamiliar file types—.gz and .tar. The .tar file type takes several files and packages them together, while .gz is often used to compress .tar files. To extract the .tar files, you must first "unzip" them.

> **WARNING:** WinZip is a common decompression utility found on many computers. Be careful, though: WinZip's default setup enables **TAR file smart CR/LF conversion**, which will mangle your data when you use it to decompress .gz files. One option is to disable this feature. Another is to use a different program for decompressing files. I prefer WinRAR, a trial version of which is available at **www.rarlab.com/download.htm**.

To unzip a compressed file with WinRAR, right-click it to open the menu shown in Figure 14A. Choose **Extract Here** to extract files to the current folder or select **Extract Files** to choose a different location. If you select the latter option, the software will create a folder with the name of the extracted file.

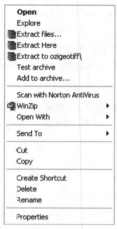

Figure 14A

Projection Files

When you import a map into your software, you may have to enter some technical information, even if it's a georeferenced map. Often you can find this information on the Web site from which you downloaded the maps, or in an accompanying projection (.prj) file. You don't need to understand all these technical terms; you just need to know where to find the values and where to enter them. Most of the items you may need to enter are covered below (datums are discussed in Chapter 4):

• **Map Projection.** This is the system used to project a two-dimensional image of a three-dimensional object: the earth. Projections vary in how much they preserve or distort shape, area, distance, and direction. Examples include the Albers Equal Area and Lambert Conformal Conic projections. If you want to learn more about common projections, a good starting point can be found at **biology.usgs.gov/geotech/documents/datum.html**.

• **False Easting and Northing.** These are values added to all "x" and "y" values for a map projection. They are often used to eliminate negative numbers.

• **Standard Parallel.** OziExplorer refers to this as Latitude 1 and 2. It is defined as the line of latitude in a conic or cylindrical projection at which the surface of the Earth intersects with the cone or cylinder. The map is free from distortion along this parallel.

Clear as mud, huh? Don't worry; just be sure that you are using the right format. If your projection file uses decimal degrees and shows the standard parallel as 40.5, and your mapping program uses degrees, minutes, and seconds, you would need to convert it to 40° 30' 0."

- **Central Meridian**. The central meridian is the line of longitude at the center of a map projection, generally used as the basis for constructing the projection. The key thing to know here is that a negative number indicates "west." In other words, when a projection file shows the central meridian as -120 and your software uses cardinal directions, enter the central meridian as 120 W.

- **Origin Latitude**. One more nebulous definition and we're done: The origin latitude is the latitude chosen as the origin of rectangular coordinate for a map projection.

Manual Calibration

Map images that are not georeferenced, or that are scanned or captured in some fashion, must be manually calibrated. The programs discussed in the next two chapters allow manual calibration of image files, as does ExpertGPS (see Chapter 13).

To calibrate an image, click on a point on the map and enter its coordinates. Road or grid line (e.g., lat/lon or UTM) intersections are good choices, but any location you can clearly identify, and for which you know the coordinates, is fine. Ideally you will do this for at least three points on the map. They should not be located in a straight line. One method is to use another program, such as USAPhotoMaps or TopoFusion, to establish a temporary waypoint for, and thus the coordinates, for these locations.

You may occasionally come across maps in image formats such as .jpg that you wish to incorporate into your system. You may also come across images online that, using a basic graphics program, can be converted to .jpg or .bmp files. A popular freeware conversion program is IrfanView, available at **www.irfanview.com**.

> ### Creating Tracks From JPEGs
> I recently learned that a local university had acquired a piece of land near me to use as an ecological reserve. I have up-to-date boundary files of all public lands in my area and I wanted to add this one. I found a jpeg online, captured it, and imported it into OziExplorer. Since road intersections and stream confluences were identified on the jpeg, I was able to calibrate the map. I traced the boundary as a track file and then overlaid it onto a USGS quad. Since the boundary followed streams, roads, ridgetops, and section lines, I was able to improve the accuracy at that point and accomplish my goal.

Image Stitching

Most GPS users will at some point experience a wilderness trip that falls right at the intersection of four quads. If you were to buy paper maps for this trip, you would have to buy four. But what if you want to make your own map? The answer is to stitch images together. If you're an OziExplorer user, rejoice: A new utility for this purpose, called MapMerge, is available at **www.oziexplorer.com**. Once you're at the site, click the **Optional Extras** link.

If you don't have OziExplorer, you're stuck with a more manual approach. Some of the better manual stitching options:

• Global Mapper **www.globalmapper.com**

• PanaVue **www.panavue.com/index.htm**

• WinChips **www.geogr.ku.dk/chips/WinChips.htm**

More Tips

• Think about how you name your map files. Calling a map Half Dome will make it easier to find than if you use the USGS default name—o37119f5.tif.

• Be aware that bitmap (.bmp) image files are huge and can dramatically slow your system's performance.

> Updates to this book will be posted at www.MakeYourOwnMaps.com. Bookmark and visit often to see what's new in the world of digital mapping.

Chapter 15 OziExplorer

OziExplorer™ is a package that seems to have it all—and the price is right, too. Separate demonstration and trial versions allow you to explore nearly all the software's features without charge, and you can use the software in demo mode for as long as you like. But if you start using Ozi regularly, you'll probably want to hand over $85 for the registered version, which allows full use of its rich features.

Ozi is a nickname for Australia—fitting since the software was designed Down Under by Des Newman, who continues to offer frequent improvements to the program. Ozi lets you use maps in a wide range of formats, downloaded from online sources. There is even a module for your PocketPC and one that lets you create three-dimensional images from topo maps or aerial photos.

Before we get started, I want to note that OziExplorer is packed with features. Because of space limitations, it is impossible to cover them all here. Nevertheless, I have tried to devote some space to all but the most esoteric.

Basic Information

COST
• The separate demonstration and trial versions are free. $85 buys the registered version, which allows use of the full range of features.

SYSTEM REQUIREMENTS
• Microsoft Windows 95, 98, ME, NT 4.0, 2000, or XP

GPS COMPATIBILITY
• OziExplorer works with Magellan, Garmin, Lowrance, Eagle, Brunton, Silva, and MLR GPS units.

TESTED VERSION
• 3.95.4

CONTACT INFORMATION
info@oziexplorer.com
www.oziexplorer.com

- OziExplorer3D™ adds three-dimensional capabilities. An evaluation version is available for free, while the full version is $30. For more information, see the 3-D section of this chapter.

- OziExplorerCE™ allows you to export Ozi maps to a PocketPC and use them to track your position in real time. As with Ozi3D, an evaluation version is available for free, while the full version is $30. For more information on OziCE, see Chapter 22.

- The following utilities and optional extras are available for free from **www.oziexplorer.com**:

- Img2Ozf conversion utility

- Map Merge for OziExplorer utility

- MrSid image loading support file

- Maptech maps and chart support files

- GeoTIFF support file

- Maptech PCX and RML chart support files

- ECW image loading support files

- Magellan POI manager symbols

- MGRS grid support

- Example of user-defined moving map pointer

- Example index maps (World, Australia, Canada)

- World Cities names database for use in name search

- OziExplorer File Format Converter

- OziSounder

- .tif file utilities

- OziMC

INTERNET RESOURCES

- For a great message board that has answers to nearly any Ozi-related problem you can imagine, go to **groups.yahoo.com/group/OziUsers-L**. The board focuses on the main OziExplorer package.

- Another very active and helpful board, **groups.yahoo.com/group/Ozi-UsersCE**, focuses on OziExplorerCE, the software package for Pocket PCs.

- You may find some answers on Yahoo's Ozi3D users' board at **groups.yahoo.com/group/Ozi-Users3D**, but this board is not very active. Most Ozi3D questions are addressed on the main OziExplorer message board.

Advantages

- Free demo versions are available.

- OziExplorer lets you import many different types of map formats, including .tif, .bmp, .jpg, .ecw, .sid, and .png.

- OziExplorer is the only major mapping program discussed here that allows you to import GIS shapefiles without paying for another module. See Chapter 23 for more information on this subject.

- Pocket PC and 3-D versions are available.

- OziExplorer lets you manipulate the location of waypoint labels, which is very helpful when multiple waypoints appear in close proximity to each other.

- You can click on existing waypoints to form a route.

- The software features sophisticated track management tools, including the ability to split and join tracks.

- A comment tool allows you to place notes on the map.

- The extensive list of datums may benefit international users.

Disadvantages

- There is a fairly steep learning curve—but that's what this book is for. Read on and you'll be up to speed in no time. Be forewarned, though; this is a deep program and you'll probably be learning things about it for months.

Tutorial/Manual

- OziExplorer, Ozi3D, and OziCE are all supplied with excellent tutorials. I highly recommend that you begin with this useful tool.

- The help file is incredibly thorough. One of the best ways to develop expertise with Ozi is to actually read the entire thing! This is a deep program that can do amazing things. There is a learning curve but, as I said, this chapter will help make it as short as possible.

- To print the entire help file as a reference, first open the help file. In the left-hand pane, select the **Contents** tab. Choose the first item, **OziExplorer Help**. It doesn't matter if it is expanded or collapsed. Right-click it and then select **Print**, then choose **Print the selected heading and all subtopics**.

Installation

Download Ozi at **www.oziexplorer.com**. Two versions are supplied in the download file—a shareware/demo version and a trial version. Generally, you will want to use the shareware/demo version, labeled simply as OziExplorer. The trial version will allow you to try out almost all of the more advanced features not available in the demo version. The trial version closes after one hour of use.

Configuration

Choose **File**, then **Configuration** to open the dialog box shown in Figure 15A. This is where you will set various options for OziExplorer. If there is something you don't understand, click the **Help** button on each tab to find detailed information about the choices available on that tab. Let's take a closer look at each tab:

• **System** (see Figure 15A). Here you can tell OziExplorer how to behave **At Startup.** You may find it convenient to select **Load Last Map,** otherwise you can leave the default settings alone.

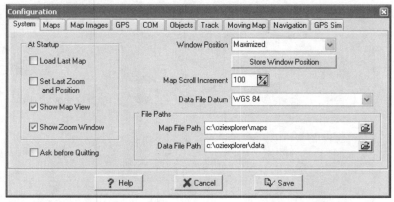

Figure 15A

• **Maps** (see Figure 15B). This is one of the more immediately important configuration tabs. This is where you will set your units. Note that you are provided with an **Alternate Grid** option—I suggest selecting **UTM.** Select your **Country or Region.** This will ensure that when you enter latitude and longitude, you'll be in the right hemisphere. That's why **USA (NW)** is labeled the way it is—north latitude, west longitude. For **Distance Calcs**, choose **Ellipsoid** if you use a Garmin GPS and **Spherical** for Magellan, Lowrance, and Eagle. (If you want to know why, it's all in the help files!)

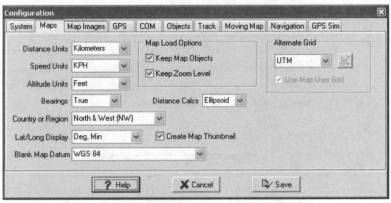

Figure 15B

• **Map Images** (see Figure 15C). Map images are the maps that you import into Ozi. They may be .tif or .jpg files, among others. This tab allows you to customize storage locations.

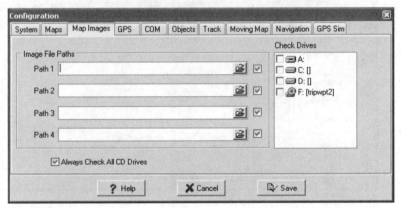

Figure 15C

• **GPS** (see Figure 15D). Select your **GPS Make** and **Model**. Ozi should automatically select the correct **GPS Symbol Set**. Check the **GPS Parameters** against your manual and change any that are incorrect. Don't change the **GPS Upload/Download Datum** from **WGS84** without good reason. Read the section on datums in Chapter 4 before making any changes here. Leave the **GPS NMEA Output Datum** set to **WGS84** unless you are using it with a moving map set to another datum.

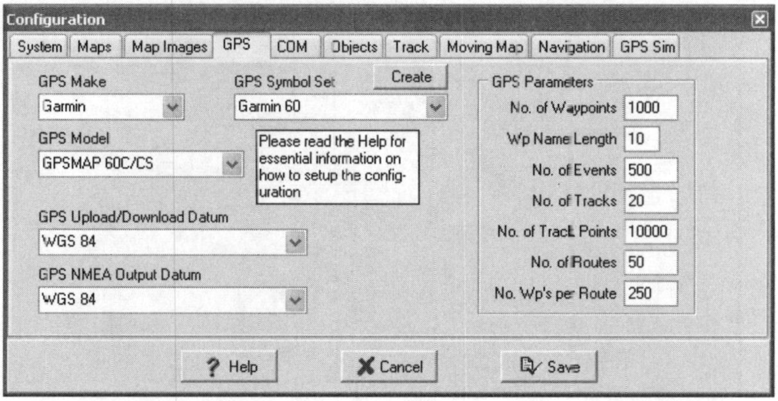

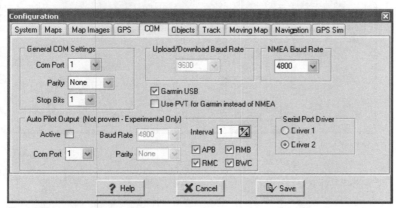

Figure 15D

• **COM** (see Figure 15E). Check your GPS manual for the correct settings here. If you have a **Garmin USB** model, you must select this option. If you use a USB-to-serial converter, and have communication problems, try selecting **Serial Port Driver 1**. Detailed information on connecting many GPS models can be found in the help files.

Figure 15E

• **Objects**. The only option here is **Route Line Width**.

• **Track** (see Figure 15F). Specify the **Default Track Color** and **Default Track Width**. **Track Control** determines the **Initial Size** of the **Track Control** dialog box when it is first opened. I tend to work with a lot of tracks, so I prefer to see the **Toolbar + All Tracks**.

• **Moving Map** (Figure 15CC), **Navigation** (Figure 15G), and **GPS Sim**. Yes, Ozi supports real-time tracking. For more information on configuration options for this feature, see the Moving Map section of this chapter.

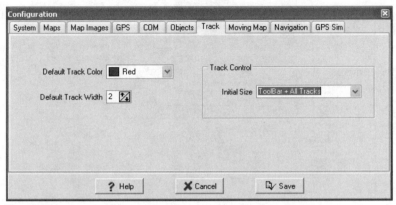

Figure 15F

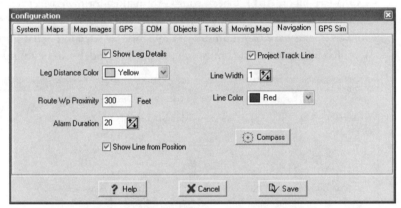

Figure 15G

Getting Started

Importing Maps

Once you've gone through the Ozi tutorial, you're ready to import a map.

There are two ways you might first consider getting maps into Ozi. My preferred method is to import a map, perhaps a DRG file downloaded from the Internet, as discussed in the preceding chapter. I'll walk you through this process momentarily.

Alternatively, you can import maps as graphics files (.bmp, .jpg, .tif, .png, .kap, .ecw, and .sid)—but you must manually calibrate these files, giving the latitude and longitude (or UTM coordinates) for at least two different points. Though this process may be easier to understand, it is faster in the end to use maps that are georeferenced, since these have the coordinates for the map embedded in an accompanying file. Here's a step-by-step approach:

Sample Import

1. Download OziExplorer.

2. Go to **www.oziexplorer.com** and click the **Optional Extras** link. Scroll to the GeoTIFF Support File and click on the link to download **oziGeoTIFF.zip**. Once it downloads, unzip it and place it in the OziExplorer folder. This file will automatically calibrate the map. We'll discuss manual calibration shortly.

3. Now go to **casil.ucdavis.edu/casil/gis.ca.gov/drg/7.5_minute_series_albers_nad27_untrimmed/37119/**.

4. Scroll to the **Half Dome** link, **o37119f5.tif**. Right-click on the .tif file, choose **Save As**, and save it to your **OziExplorer/Maps** directory. Leave the Web page open. We'll return there shortly.

5. For a not-so-helpful technical reason, Windows may change the .tif file extension to .tiff. If this happens, right-click the file and select **Rename**, then remove an "f" to make the three-character .tif extension. Click anywhere else on the screen and ignore (choose **Yes**) the ominous Windows warning shown in Figure 15H.

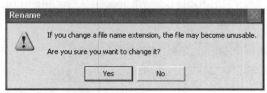

Figure 15H

6. Now start the trial version of OziExplorer.

7. Choose **File**, point to **Import Map**, and choose **Single DRG Map**, as shown in Figure 15I.

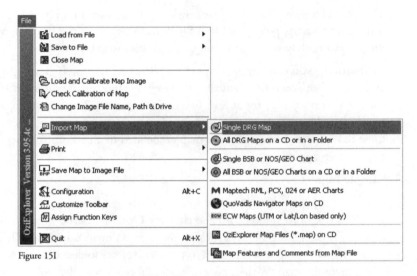

Figure 15I

8. When you see the **USGS DRG File Import** dialog box shown in Figure 15J, click **OK**, locate the image (now labeled **o37119f5.tif**), and select **Open**.

Figure 15J

9. When the next **USGS DRG File Import** dialog box, shown in Figure 15K, appears, click **OK**. A **Save Map File** dialog box will appear, defaulting to the OziExplorer/ Maps folder. Choose **Save**.

Figure 15K

10. The next dialog box, shown in Figure 15L, will appear. Click **OK** and there's your map! Hang on to it; we'll use this same map later when we try out OziExplorer3D.

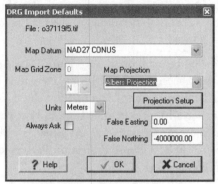

Figure 15L

Changing Projection Parameters

Notice that the map has a collar. (Map collars are discussed in Chapter 4.) Let's look at what happens if you download a trimmed version of an adjacent map, sans collar. This next tutorial will also demonstrate how to manually change some parameters, should that become necessary (it will, sooner or later, when you're downloading maps).

1. Go to **casil.ucdavis.edu/casil/gis.ca.gov/drg/7.5_minute_series_albers_nad27_ trimmed/37119/**. Note that at the top of the page it says Albers (the projection) and NAD27 (the datum).

2. This time, scroll down to the **El Capitan** links. Right-click **o37119f6.tif**, choose **Save As**, and save to your **OziExplorer/Maps** directory. Leave the Web page open.

3. Once again, if Windows changed the .tif file extension to .tiff , right-click it, choose **Rename**, and remove an f, changing the extension to .tif.

> **TIP:** You don't need the accompanying .tfw file here, since this is a GeoTIFF file and Ozi will automatically extract the reference point and scale. There may be times where you do need the .tfw file, though, such as when the GeoTIFF tags are missing or corrupted. Be aware that, here too, Windows may very well change the file extension from .tfw to .tfw.txt. In this case, just strip the .txt extension from the end.

4. Select **File**, point to **Import Map**, and choose **Single DRG Map**, as shown in Figure 15I.

5. Choose **OK** when you see the **USGS DRG File Import** dialog box shown in Figure 15J. Locate the image, now labeled **o37119f6.tif**, and click **Open**.

6. When the **USGS DRG File Import** dialog box shown in Figure 15K appears, choose **OK**. A **Save Map File** dialog will appear, defaulting to the **OziExplorer/Maps** folder. Choose **Save**.

7. A **DRG Import Defaults** dialog box will open (see Figure 15L). Some of the fields in this dialog may be incorrect, because a GeoTIFF tag is missing from the file—a fairly common occurrence. To further complicate matters, the dialog fields default to the ones used in the last successful import. The bottom line: you need to check the dialog fields against the projection parameters. As a matter of fact, this is the first of two places you need to check. Choose **Projection Parameters** to see the other dialog box, shown in Figure 15M.

Figure 15M

8. Remember the Web page we left open way back in Step 1? Go back there and click on the link labeled **CaSIL Projection Information**. Example 1's GeoTIFF header information is shown in Table 1, which includes a key showing where to find all the projection information needed for these two dialog boxes.

9. Make whatever changes are necessary. Make sure that you include the negative sign for the **False Northing**, and use West for the **Central Meridian**.

10. Choose **OK** and look at the dialog box that opens, as shown in Figure 15N. This warning refers to the fact that there are two files associated with this map: the .map file, where the projection information is stored, and the .tif image file. If you move the image file, Ozi will not know where to look for it. We'll talk about this more in the section on File Management.

11. Choose **OK** again and you've got another map!

Table 1. Projection data

```
Example 1. Geotiff header information
   Geotiff_Information:
      Version: 1
      Key_Revision: 1.0
      Tagged_Information:
         End_Of_Tags.
      Keyed_Information:
         GTModelTypeGeoKey (Short,1): ModelTypeProjected
         GTRasterTypeGeoKey (Short,1): RasterPixelIsArea
         GeographicTypeGeoKey (Short,1): GCS_NAD27 Map Datum
         ProjectedCSTypeGeoKey (Short,1): User-Defined
         PCSCitationGeoKey (Ascii,38): "Albers Equal Area North American 1927" Map Projection
         ProjectionGeoKey (Short,1): User-Defined
         ProjCoordTransGeoKey (Short,1): CT_AlbersEqualArea
         ProjLinearUnitsGeoKey (Short,1): Linear_Meter Units
         ProjStdParallel1GeoKey (Double,1): 34 Latitude 1
         ProjStdParallel2GeoKey (Double,1): 40.5 Latitude 2
         ProjNatOriginLongGeoKey (Double,1): -120 Central Meridian
         ProjNatOriginLatGeoKey (Double,1): 0 Origin Latitude
         ProjFalseEastingGeoKey (Double,1): 0 False Easting
         ProjFalseNorthingGeoKey (Double,1): -4000000 False Northing
         End_Of_Keys.
End_Of_Geotiff.
```

Figure 15N

The point of this exercise was to show you how to find and use projection information. Projection files sometimes carry a .prj extension. If you're going to be downloading maps to use in OziExplorer, it's essential that you know how to do this.

Now that you've got a map or two under your belt, I'm sure you can't wait to try and get maps for your favorite outdoor locations. Here are some general tips on downloading maps for use in OziExplorer:

- A great online resource for DRG maps for the entire United States is **home.pacbell. net/lgalvin/drgnotes.htm**. If you haven't yet read Chapter 14, do so before going any further. You'll find advice for additional sources of online map files there.

- I suggest going to **www.oziexplorer.com**, clicking on **Optional Extras**, then downloading and installing the **MrSID dll** file. This file is required for using MrSID images.

- The **Import Map menu** shown in Figure 15O can look pretty confusing. The box on page 194, What Are All These Acronyms?, offers a quick tour of the options.

- If you cannot locate the proper DRG file on your hard disk using the **Single DRG Map** option, try **All DRG Maps on a CD or in a Folder** (see Figure 15O). And remember, for more detailed information on downloading maps, including sources, see Chapter 14.

- The map datum should always be the datum the map was originally drawn in, with one possible exception: If you are manually calibrating a map, and getting coordinates from a map in another datum, you're probably better off using the datum of the reference map. Better yet, avoid this situation entirely.

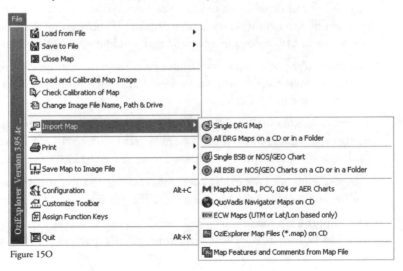

Figure 15O

Calibrating Scanned Map Images

If all this seems overwhelming, you can always import a scanned map image, though you will have to manually calibrate the map by picking two or more locations and entering the coordinates for those points.

Though you can scan your own maps, I suggest finding other sources of high-quality scanned images. If you have one of the programs discussed in Section Two, you can export maps from many of them. The shareware version of Ozi supports .bmp files, while the registered version accepts .tif, .jpg, .png, and other formats.

1. To get started, select **File**, then **Load and Calibrate Map Image**.

2. Select the image file to import and select **Open**.

3. The image file will open, along with the panel shown in Figure 15P. On the **Setup** tab, enter the **Map Datum** and **Projection**.

4. Choose the **Point 1** tab. Click a point on the map for which you know the coordinates. A series of red concentric circles will appear around that point.

Figure 15P

5. Enter the coordinates. Remember that you can change the coordinate format on the **Configuration** menu. You can also select **WP** to import the coordinates from a waypoint. Other mapping programs discussed in this book, such as USAPhotoMaps and TopoFusion, are a good source of accurate coordinates.

6. Choose the **Point 2** tab and repeat the process. It is best to place the two calibration points near opposite corners of the map image. Click **Help** for more information on calibration.

7. Choose **Save** to finish.

Navigating the Map

The first thing you'll notice when you open a map is the smaller **Map View** window. This shows the entire map at a smaller scale. You can do several things with the **Map View** window:

• Click anywhere in the window or drag the red rectangle in the window to a new location, to be taken there on the main map screen.

• Grab a corner and drag to change the size.

• Grab the title bar to drag the **Map View** window to a new location.

• You can close the **Map Window** and reopen it at any time by choosing **View**, pointing to **Show**, and choosing **Map View**.

• You can also opt not to display the **Map View** at startup by choosing **File**, then **Configuration**, then clearing the **Show Map View** check box.

You can also navigate the main map screen as follows:

• Use the arrow keys.

• Click any point on the map, then press the left mouse button while dragging it to reposition the map within the window.

• Use the scroll bars. Note that scroll bars may not show for all types of map images.

• Use a mouse scroll wheel.

• Double-click a point on the map to recenter the map at that location.

To zoom the map:

• Use the drop-down **Zoom Range** box or the **Zoom In** and **Zoom Out** buttons.

- Right-click any point on the map and choose one of the zoom options shown in Figure 15Q.

- Use the PAGE UP and PAGE DOWN keys.

| Close Menu |
| Refresh Screen |
| Zoom Full Map |
| Zoom 50% |
| Zoom 100% |
| Zoom 200% |
| Find Map at Cursor |
| Show Compass at Cursor |
| Set Waypoint at Position ▶ |
| Hide ▶ |
| UnHide ▶ |
| Grid Line Setup |
| Configuration |
| Print ▶ |
| Close map |

Figure 15Q

To load maps:

Load

- Choose **Load**, then select **Load Map File** or point to **Open Recent Maps** to display a list of the last twenty maps viewed.

- Locate the **Map Find** button on the right side of Ozi's toolbar. This excellent feature is designed to help you find other maps at the current location or find maps of areas north, south, east, or west of the current map.

Index

- Choose **Show the Index Map** to open an Index Map window. The default index map is a world map, so the scale is difficult to work with. But there is value in exploring this feature. Use the scroll bars and zoom buttons to navigate the map. Move the pointer over an area for which you have multiple maps, perhaps your home state. You will see a list of available maps for that area. Click on the map to open a dialog box labeled **Maps Available for Cursor Position**. For information on creating your own custom index map, search for **Index Map** in Ozi's help files. Though the help file warns against using too large a map, I was able to load and use a map of the entire United States without having to resize it.

File Structure

Shown below are file extensions Ozi uses:

- **.wpt** Waypoints
- **.plt** Tracks
- **.rte** Routes
- **.map** Map files

Remember that each map file (.map) is linked to a corresponding image file, which could be .tif, .bmp, .jpg, and so on. By default, Ozi places .map files in the **OziExplorer/Maps** directory. It's up to you to decide where to place the image files, though it's simplest to place them in the same directory. Use the **Configuration Map Images** tab to customize where Ozi searches for image files. The default location for waypoints, tracks, and route files is the **OziExplorer/Data** directory.

The key is to make the setup useful for you; a good directory structure is very helpful. For example, in the **OziExplorer/Maps** directory, you could create folders for a certain state's .tif files. You could have separate data folders for tracks and waypoints. It's up to you.

Think also about how you name files. A list of downloaded DRG files with nothing but numbers to identify them isn't as helpful as having the quad name. For example, you could name the DRG we downloaded earlier as CA Half Dome 24K, indicating that it is a 1:24,000-scale California quad named Half Dome. The ideal time to do this is before you calibrate the maps. Just be sure to give the same name to both the .tif and .tfw files. The only time this will cause problems is if the georeferencing information has been stripped from the .tif file, in which case you will need to enter the UTM zone when importing the map image.

When importing DRGs with an accompanying .fgd file, by default Ozi will name the .map file with the quad name. Use caution, though, as many .fgd files have incorrect georeferencing information.

> **NOTE:** Once Ozi has created a corresponding .map file for an image, the .tfw file is no longer needed; you can delete it.

Once you get involved in digital mapping, your collection of map files is likely to grow by leaps and bounds, in ways that you may not anticpate. Fortunately, a feature in Ozi makes it easy to reorganize things. Select **File**, then **Change Image File Name, Path, and Drive**. This opens the dialog box shown in Figure 15R, which provides the following options:

- **Change Map Image File for Current Map**. This allows you to change the location and name of the image for the currently loaded .map file.

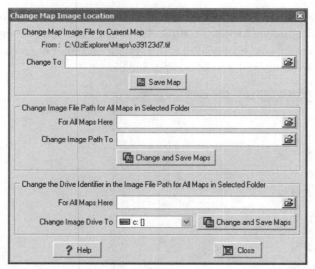

Figure 15R

- **Change Image File Path for All Maps in Selected Folder.** This allows you to change the location of images for all maps in a selected folder.

- **Change the Drive Identifier in the Image File Path for All Maps in Selected Folder.** This changes only the drive Ozi uses to find images.

Waypoints and Waypoint Management

To create a waypoint, select **Wpt.** Now click anywhere on the map to place a waypoint. The waypoint is automatically numbered; if you want to name it, right-click on the waypoint and then choose **Properties** to open the dialog box shown in Figure 15S. Here you can also change display properties, including the **Pointer Direction**, which changes the placement of the waypoint label on the map. A word of explanation here: Selecting **Top** as the pointer direction means that the pointer attached to the waypoint is aimed at the top of the label. Therefore, the label itself is at the bottom of the waypoint. (Must be a Down Under thing!)

> ### Zoom Window
> In the upper-left-hand corner of the screen is a small window with crosshairs. This is called the **Zoom Window.** Notice that wherever you move the pointer, a zoomed-in view of your location appears in the **Zoom Window.** This is an excellent tool for accurately placing waypoints. You can use your mouse to drag the **Zoom Window** anywhere on the screen.

Choose **Save** in the **Waypoint Properties** dialog box (see Figure 15S) to close the dialog box and save whatever changes you made. Important note: To make any changes permanent, you must save the waypoint in a waypoint file. You can save a group of waypoints as a waypoint file in several ways, including:

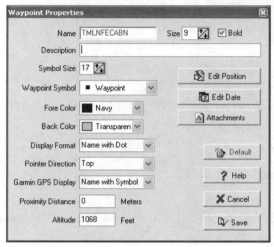

Figure 15S

1. Choose **Save**, then choose **Save Waypoints to File**.

2. Choose **File**, point to **Save to File**, then choose **Save Waypoints to File**.

3. Choose **Waypoint**, one of the **Quick Save** buttons on the right side of the tool bar (see Figure 15T).

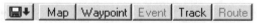

Figure 15T

> **TIP: QUICK SAVE BUTTONS** On the right of the tool bar is a set of **Quick Save** buttons labeled **Map, Waypoint, Event, Track,** and **Route**. When the button text is dimmed, there is no file loaded. When the text is black, a file is loaded but it has not been modified. When the text is red, the file has been modified but not saved. Click the button to save the file using the existing filename. If the data is new, a dialog box will appear, prompting you for a filename.
>
> Click **Save All Files** to save all changes to the currently loaded map, waypoint, event, track, and route files.

Load

Loading saved waypoint files is simple. Choose **Load,** then **Load Waypoints from File.**

Here are some other tips on working with waypoints:

Load

• Need to combine two waypoint files? After loading the first file, select **Load,** then **Append Waypoints from File.** If you want to give the file a new name, save it using method 1 or 2 above. To save it under the name of the first file, simply click the **Waypoint Quick Save** button.

• Not sure if a saved waypoint file has waypoints for the map you are viewing? Choose **Load,** then **Append Visible Waypoints from File.** You can then save the waypoint to a new file, or to the current file as just described.

• To display waypoints in a table or list form, from the **View** menu point to **Lists,** and select **Waypoint List.** This will open the dialog box shown in Figure 15U. Waypoint management is excellent in this program. I especially like the **Select if Not on Map** feature. Say I have a large waypoint file that exceeds the 500 held by my GPS. I can open the waypoint file, select the waypoints not found on the map, and delete them. Now my GPS can import all the waypoints on the map. Other nice **Waypoint List** features include the ability to change the **Datum** for waypoints and the **Find Map for Selected Waypoint** function. Choose **Show Help** to learn more about the available options.

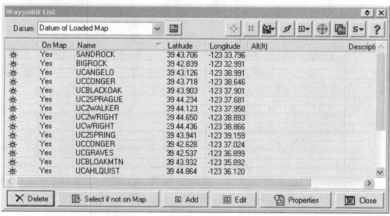

Figure 15U

• To remove all waypoints from the map, choose **Map** and then select **Clear All Waypoints from Map.**

• Finally, remember that you can use the **Waypoint Properties** dialog box (see Figure 15S) to alter the waypoint display in a number of ways. To bring up this dialog box, right-click on a waypoint and select **Properties.** Alternatively, from the **Waypoint List,** select a waypoint and then choose **Properties.**

Routes

It's easy to create routes either by selecting waypoints from a list or clicking on waypoints. To get started, load a waypoint file as described in the previous section, then select **Show/Hide the Route Editor**. Alternatively, from the **View** menu, choose **Route Editor**. The **Route Editor** (see Figure 15V) has a list of available route numbers, determined by the number of routes accommodated by your GPS and as set in the **Configuration** files. There are two ways to create routes with the **Route Editor**:

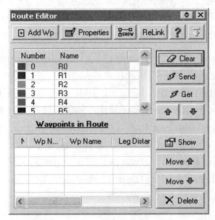

Figure 15V

1. The easiest way is to choose a route number and then select **Add Wp**. Click a waypoint on the map to add it to the route. If you can't see the waypoint you wish to add, drag the **Route Editor** out of the way or scroll the map.

2. Alternatively, select a route number and then select **Properties**. The **Route Properties** dialog box will appear (see Figure 15W). From here you can name the route and begin selecting waypoints. Unfortunately, once this dialog box is open, you cannot scroll the map to see additional waypoints, so I prefer the method discussed in the previous paragraph. This method would work well, though, if you had a numerical list of waypoints to follow.

> **NOTE:** You can create routes only from pre-existing waypoints. There is no way to click the map and create a waypoint as you are forming the route.

You can save route files by choosing **Save**, then **Save Routes to File**. Alternatively, choose **Route** on the **Quick Save** toolbar (see Figure 15T).

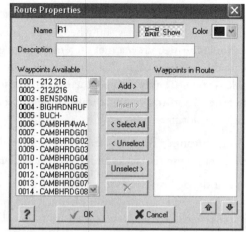

Figure 15W

Here are a few other tips for working with routes in OziExplorer:

• You can easily modify routes from either the **Route Editor** or the **Route Properties** dialog box. Both have tools to delete waypoints and to move them up or down in the list.

• From the main Ozi toolbar, select **Show/Hide Route Plot** to show or hide the line connecting route waypoints.

• GPS manufacturers differ in how they handle routes exported to GPS units. For example, some models require waypoints to be loaded to your GPS before you upload the route. I suggest reading Ozi's help section on this subject, paying close attention to your particular brand of GPS. Choose **Help** and then **Help Contents**. Now choose **Routes**, then **Working with Routes**.

• Also look to the help files for other critical information about sending routes to your GPS. For example, errors may occur in a route if you are working with a different waypoint file than the one in which you originally created the route, or when waypoints have been edited since you created the route.

• The **ReLink** button in the **Route Editor** is designed to cure some of these ills. If you change a waypoint's geographic location, or if you sort waypoints, click **ReLink** to relink the waypoints in the route file with those stored in the waypoint file. Relinking does not work if you change the names of any waypoints, a task to attend to before you construct your route.

Tracks

The Track feature in OziExplorer not only shows you where you've been with your GPS; it also gives you the simplest way to draw a trail on a map. To begin, choose **Manually Create Track Points** from the toolbar. You can then click from point to point on the map, creating a track as you go. Unfortunately there is no way to draw a track freehand. Click away and create a short track with at least a dozen points. We'll come back and work with it shortly, exploring various options.

Let's take a look at an important feature, **Track Control**. Choose **Show/Hide Track Control** or, from the **View** menu, point to **Tracks** and select **Track Control**.

This opens the **Track Control** dialog box (see Figure 15X). You'll see that the track you created is in the first position. You can load multiple track files onto an Ozi map, but Track 1 is always the active track. Tracks downloaded from your GPS go into the Track 1 position; if you want to upload a track into your GPS, it must be in this position. Track 1 is also the only one you can draw using the **Manually Create Track Points** button.

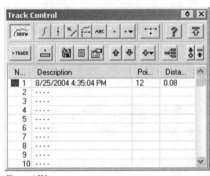

Figure 15X

Let's take a look at the various ways you can save tracks:

1. Choose **Save**, then **Save Track to File**.

2. Choose **File**, **Save to File**, and then **Save Track to File**.

3. Choose the **Track Quick Save** button (see Figure 15T).

4. Select a track in the **Track Control** box, then select **Save the Selected Track**.

Now save the track you drew using method 4 above, and name it "test." Notice that when you select Track 1 in the **Track Control** box, you can see the individual track points at each place you clicked to create the track file.

Manipulating tracks in Ozi can be a little awkward, but only until you get to know the **Track Control** options. Let's take a quick tour:

- As you move your pointer over **Track Control** buttons, you'll see pop-up labels. Click the one labeled **use mouse to draw a box around track points. All points within the box are made Active.**

- Let's pretend you placed the last track point in the wrong location. Select that point by dragging a box around it with the mouse. Notice that it turns red, indicating it is "active," while the others remain white.

- If you just need to move the active track point, depress the SHIFT key and drag the point to a new location.

- But what if you want to delete the track point? Here are two ways to do this:

  –Move the pointer over it until the cross hairs turn into a hand, then right-click and click **Delete.**

  –In the **Track Control** box, choose the button labeled **More Options for active Track Points.** Now choose **Delete Active Track Points.**

- Now let's take a look at how to insert a track point. Make some track points active, as previously described. Click the button labeled **Insert Track Point after Selected Active Point. Hold down ALT key and press left mouse button.** Let's do just that: move the pointer over an active track point, hold down the ALT key, and click to insert a new track point immediately to the right of the point you clicked. The new track point will be blue. Note that this track point will be inserted after the one you clicked. Now all you have to do is hold down the SHIFT key and drag this track point to the desired location.

The track features are a very important and useful part of Ozi. I suggest going through all the buttons in the **Track Control** box, as well as the options found under the **View** menu when you point to **Tracks**. Master these and the following tips, and you'll be a power user in no time:

- Remember that Track 1 is the only track with which you can do many things, including activating and manipulating points.

- Select the Track 2 position in the **Track Control** box. Now click **More Options** and choose **Move Selected Track to Track 1.** You can now draw a second track on the map, and you know how to move tracks into this critical position. If you have tracks loaded, and want to download a track from your GPS, just move a blank track into the Track 1 position.

- From the **Load** menu, you can select **Append Track from File**, allowing you to add a saved track onto Track 1.

- Track **Distance** is shown in the last column in the **Track Control** box. If you want to figure out how long a trail is, this is the place.

 - Need to work on a track that is right next to other tracks? No problem. Make sure the track you want to work on is in the Track 1 position, then click the button, labeled **Use mouse to draw a box around a track point. All points in the same track section are made active.** Drawing a box around only one point makes every point in the entire track section active.

- This is a good place to mention track sections. You can have multiple, non-continuous sections as part of the same track. Your GPS does this when it isn't receiving data from enough satellites to track your location. When your GPS starts tracking again, it's working on the same track, but on a different section of it.

- Right-clicking an active track point will bring up a menu (see Figure 15Y) with options to **Delete** a track point and **Delete & Split track**. When you take the latter action, it will delete the active waypoint and split the track into two separate sections. The new sections will start from the adjacent track points—so if your track points are far apart, the new track sections will have some distance between them.

Figure 15Y

 - You can also split a track from the **Track Control** box using the button labeled **Split Track 1 into separate Tracks for each Track Section**. Remember, tracks downloaded from your GPS may be composed of several non-contiguous sections. This feature segments those sections into separate tracks.

 - Want to change the color of a given track? Click **Selected Track Properties**. Here you can change the **Color** and line **Width** of any loaded track. The **Fill Color** option applies only to polygons, areas completely enclosed by a track.

- From the **Track Control** box, choosing **More Options** will give you access to a number of features including the **Track Move Control.** (You can also find this feature from the **View** menu by pointing to **Tracks**, then selecting **Track Move Control**.) If you import a track in a datum other than that of the map, it will likely be located incorrectly on the map. This feature allows you to move a track until it is in the proper location on the map. I have found this feature to be useful when importing large GIS boundary files. (See Chapter 23 for more information on GIS.)

- The **Track Profile** feature allows you to view an elevation profile for a track, if elevation data is included for each track point. Tracks downloaded from many Garmin receivers contain this data. To get to **Track Profile,** go to the **Track Control** box, then select **More Options**, and **Track Profile**. Alternatively, use the **View** menu, point to **Tracks**, and choose **Track Profile**.

- Be sure to read the information in the help files on how tracks are uploaded from Ozi to your GPS. Some GPS brands will append (add) the track to an existing one. Others will replace the existing track. To view this information, select **Help**, then **Help Contents**. Choose **Tracks**, then **Working with Tracks**.

GPS Interface

When you configure Ozi for your model of GPS receiver, Ozi lists the brand at the head of a customized drop-down menu. As a result, different options may appear on the menu according to the brand and model you're using. See Figure 15Z for a sample Garmin menu.

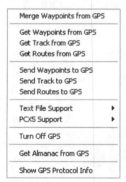

Figure 15Z

Printing

Before you print, consider whether or not you wish to show a grid on the map. Choose **Map**, then **Grid Line Setup** to open the **Grid Configuration** dialog box shown in Figure 15AA. Here you'll see two tabs, **Lat/Lon** and **Other Grid**. These allow you to control grid display options. The latter can be used to show a UTM grid. To establish the type of grid used on the **Other Grid** tab, select **File**, then **Configuration**. Now choose the **Maps** tab and, in the **Alternate Grid** box, select the type of grid you wish to use. Remember that the grid will be printed only if it is displayed on the map as you set up the print job.

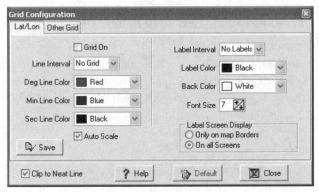

Figure 15AA

To print a map, from the **File** menu point to **Print**, and choose **Print Map Image**. This will bring up the **Print Map** dialog box (see Figure 15BB). This dialog box lists the six print options.

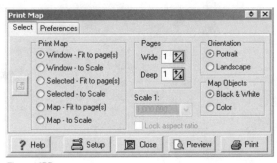

Figure 15BB

If you choose one of the two **Selected** options (**Selected–Fit to pages** or **Selected–to Scale**), you can then choose **Show Map to Select Area**, which will bring up a miniaturized version of the entire map file you are working with. You can then drag a box around the area to be printed.

Print Map options are as follows:

• **Window–Fit to page(s)**. This option prints only the area shown on the screen, fitting it to the page(s). Use the Zoom control on the main map screen to define the area to be printed. The map's aspect ratio will be preserved.

• **Window–to Scale**. This also prints just the area shown on the screen. Instead of fitting it to the page, though, you select the scale (e.g., 1:24,000) at which it is to be printed.

• **Selected–Fit to page(s)**. This option allows you to select an area of the screen to be printed, fitting it to the printed page(s). The map's aspect ratio will be preserved.

• **Selected–to Scale**. This also prints just the area you have defined. You then choose the scale at which it will be printed.

• **Map–Fit to page(s)**. This option prints the entire map, fitting it to the page(s). The map's aspect ratio will be preserved.

• **Map–to Scale**. This option also prints the entire map, to whatever scale you define.

Any time you use one of the **Fit to pages** options, use the **Pages** box to select or enter the maximum number of pages to be printed.

For the **to Scale** options, use the **Scale 1:** box to enter or select a scale. You can enter any scale you wish; you are not restricted to the scales in the drop-down menu.

Be aware that the last option, **Map–to Scale**, could result in a very large print job. You can stop printing by pressing the ESC key while you're in the Ozi window, though the response may not be instantaneous.

You may want to consider selecting **Black & White** in the **Map Objects** box. This will affect waypoints, events, map features, and comments, and may make them easier to read. It will not affect route, track, or grid colors.

If your printer has a preview option, I always recommend enabling it when printing maps. Choose **Setup** and explore your printer settings. You will often have to click a button labeled **Properties** or **Preferences** to reach a preview option.

Finally, choose the **Preferences** tab in the **Print Map** dialog box to experiment with **Track Line**, **Route Line**, and **Grid Label** widths. You can select or enter a number into any of these boxes.

Moving Map

OziExplorer provides real-time GPS support for tracking your actual position on your laptop. (See Chapter 22 for information on moving maps for PDAs, including information on OziExplorerCE.)

Because of the added features available in NMEA mode, you may wish to change your data transfer settings when you use Ozi for real-time tracking.

Some helpful options for moving map use are found in the configuration setup. In the **File** menu, choose **Configuration**, then select the **Moving Map** tab (see Figure 15CC). You can set the following options:

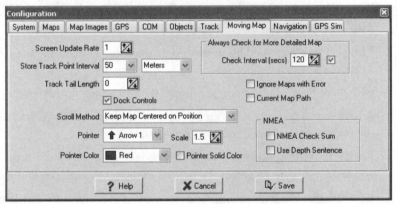

Figure 15CC

- **Screen Update Rate**. This controls how often your position is updated, in seconds. Setting the rate too low can affect performance on slower laptops.

- **Store Track Point Interval**. This tells Ozi how often to record a track point.

- **Track Tail Length.** This controls how many trailing track points are displayed, helping you see where you've been. Setting it to zero will display all points collected. This is another setting that can significantly affect performance, so it pays to be conservative.

- **Dock Controls**. Check this to keep the **Moving Map** and **Navigation** windows on the right side of the screen. Leave it unchecked to move the windows around the screen.

- **Scroll Method**. Your options here are **Keep Map Centered on Position**, **Center When Near Window Edge**, and **Show More Map in Heading Direction**.

- **Pointer**. This controls the type symbol used in tracking your position; you can also choose the **Pointer Color**. The pointer can be an outline or you can select **Pointer Solid Color**. **Scale** controls the size of the moving map pointer. (A larger pointer takes longer to redraw at every screen update; this can also affect performance.)

- **Always Check for More Detailed Map.** This is useful if you have maps of multiple scales. I suggest leaving this box checked.

- **Ignore Maps with Error.** This keeps Ozi from trying to load a blank map when an image file cannot be found.

- **Current Map Path.** If this is checked, Ozi will look there for the next map as you travel along. If you leave **Current Map Path** unchecked, Ozi will use your configured map file path.

- **NMEA Check Sum.** Leave this checked.

- **Use Depth Sentence.** There is no advantage to checking this unless you are on water instead of land.

Now, while you're still in the **Configuration** dialog box, choose the **Navigation** tab (see Figure 15G) to access more moving map options:

- Check **Show Leg Details** to show the distance and bearing to the next waypoint when following a route.

- You can also set alarms to be triggered as you near waypoints along a route. Enter the desired number in feet of the **Route Wp Proximity** and the **Alarm Duration** in seconds.

- **Show Line from Position** draws a line from your current position to the next waypoint in a route.

- **Project Track Line**, on the other hand, draws a line from your current position straight ahead in the direction you are currently traveling. You can change the **Projected Line Color** and **Projected Line Width**; widths greater than 1 point will be drawn as solid and those less than 1 point will be dashed.

- Select **Compass** to configure the compass rose.

Now close the **Configuration** dialog box and, on the main OziExplorer screen, select **Moving Map**, then **Moving Map Control** to open the dialog box (see Figure 15DD). Note the following moving map controls:

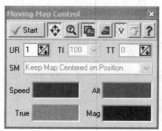

Figure 15DD

• **Start/Stop.** This starts and stops NMEA communication, if your GPS transfer format is set to NMEA.

 • **Automatically Scroll Map to Keep Position in View.** Self-explanatory.

 • **Find Maps at GPS Position.** This searches the Map File path (settings for this option are controlled on the **Configuration** window's **System** tab).

 • **Check for More Detailed Map.** When this button is depressed, Ozi searches for more detailed maps at the interval specified on the **Moving Map Configuration** tab.

 • **Moving Map Looks for Maps Only in the Folder of the Currently Loaded Map.** Unless this button is depressed, Ozi will search the Map File path and its subfolders.

 • **Ignore NMEA Valid Data Flag.** This is only an issue when in simulator mode. (Choose **Help** for more information.)

 • **Reduce/Expand Control Window.**

The following sections of the **Moving Map Control** (see Figure 15DD) cannot be modified in the shareware versions of Ozi:

• **UR.** This is the screen update rate, in seconds.

• **TI (Track Interval).** This is the minimum interval in the units set in the Moving Map Configuration. Set it to zero to disable track data collection in Ozi.

• **TT (Track Tail).** This is the number of track points displayed. High settings will slow down the screen refresh rate. Set it to zero to display all points collected.

• **SM (Scroll Method).** Self-explanatory.

Finally, the **Speed** and **Alt** (altitude) are displayed in the units specified on OziExplorer's **Maps Configuration** tab.

We should also look at a few features on the main screen's Moving Map menu:

• **Show GPS Fix Data.** This provides information on satellite acquisition, if you are using the NMEA transfer format.

• **Anchor Alarm.** This is strictly for marine use.

• **NMEA Simulator.** Use this to experiment with moving map features indoors, without a GPS. See **Moving Map** menu **Help** for details.

• **Log Track to Memory/Map.** This logs the track file to Track 1 and displays it on the map.

• **Log Track to File.** This logs the track to the default file mmTrack.plt, or to the file specified in...

• **Change Track Log File.** This lets you specify a new file for the track log.

- **Clear Track Log File**. This erases the file specified above. If you keep using the same file, it gets bigger and bigger. Erase it between trips (after copying it to a new location if you wish to save it).

- **Range Rings Setup**. Select this to open the **Range Rings Setup** dialog shown in Figure 15EE. Use this feature to draw concentric circles around your current position.

Figure 15EE

Figure 15FF

- **Show Regional Map Window.** This allows you to load a larger-scale map of the region into a smaller window. Right-clicking the regional map window provides additional options. (Search for Regional Map in the help files for more details.)

Now let's try having Ozi direct us somewhere. On the main OziExplorer map screen, select **Navigation**. Point to **Navigate To** and you'll see options for **Along a Route** or **Waypoint from a List**. You also have the option to **View Waypoint Proximity Zones**.

From the **Navigation** menu, select **Navigation Control**. This opens a pane on the right of the screen, shown in Figure 15FF. You must load a set of waypoints, and optionally load a route, before you can use the navigation features. You can load these from the **Navigation** menu or from the **Navigation Control**.

Choose **Navigate Along a Route** from the latter, and you'll be presented with a **Reverse Route** option in the **Set Active Route** dialog.

One other tip: On the main Ozi screen, choose **Options** for **Night Vision** color. Also **Set Intensity** options. The latter changes the screen brightness.

3-D

OziExplorer3D is a great add on package that easily converts maps and aerial photos to 3-D images.

Here's a quick guide to get you started:

1. Download the OziExplorer3D evaluation version from **www.oziexplorer.com.** It has some minor limitations, but you'll get a good feel for what it can do. Close all programs and run the setup file to install Ozi3D.

2. Start Ozi3D. Select **File,** then **Configuration** and, on the **System** tab shown in Figure 15GG, change the **Default Height Factor** to 1.0. This way the elevation won't be exaggerated (and since we're going to go back and use the Half Dome quad from Yosemite Valley, it seems unnecessary to enhance it). You can leave Ozi3D open or close it.

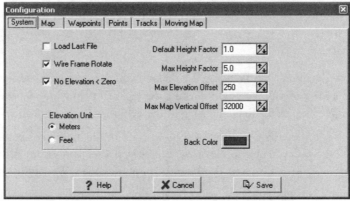

Figure 15GG

3. Now open the OziExplorer Trial Version (or just Ozi if you've ponied up the $85) and you'll see a new menu option on the top of the screen labeled **3D/Elevation.** Select this and then choose **Elevation Configuration.** On the **System** tab, check **Use Elevation Data.** Now select the **DEM File Paths** tab and, on the right side of the **USA DEM 24K** line, check the **Active** box as shown in Figure 15HH. This tells OziExplorer to look there for elevation data. If you'd like, you can go ahead and create a specialized directory such as c:\oziexplorer\elevation data\usadem24k. While in this dialog box, choose **Help** for more information on configuring 3-D options. Be sure to select **Save** to close the **Elevation Configuration** dialog box.

4. Go to **www.geocomm.com** and sign up for a free account. This is where we'll get our elevation data. If you haven't used this Web site yet, it's got tons of free maps and data.

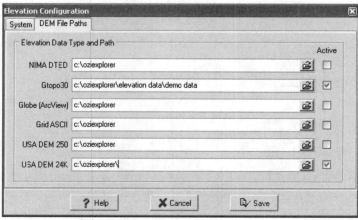

Figure 15HH

5. Log in and choose the **GIS Data** tab on top, then select **Download Data** on the left side of the next screen. Scroll to the U.S. map and select California (**CA**). Select **Countywide Data** and then choose **Mariposa**. Choose **Digital Elevation Models (DEM)–24K**.

6. Scroll to **Half Dome** and then click the green **Normal Downloads** button for a free download. (There is a small charge for ordering the data on CD.) Now choose the 30-meter file labeled **1662926.DEM.SDTS.TAR.GZ** and save it to the Ozi directory you established for USA DEM 24K data.

7. From the Windows **Start** button, point to **All Programs** and then to **OziExplorer**. Now select **OziUnGzip** and choose **Select File**. Navigate to the file you just downloaded. Choose **Open**; you'll see a brief DOS window, and then a small window where you can click **OK**. Close the OziUnGzip program window. What happened there, briefly: OziUnGzip unzipped the .gz file, extracted SDTS files from the .tar file, converted the SDTS file to a DEM file, and deleted the SDTS and .tar files. The DEM file was sent to the directory that the compressed file was in; that's why it is essential that you download that file to the correct directory. There's more detail on this process in the Ozi3D help files.

Load

8. Now close the trial version of OziExplorer and restart it. When Ozi starts, it looks for new elevation data in the paths specified in Step 3. Choose **Load**, point to **Open Recent Maps**, and select the Half Dome map you imported earlier.

Figure 15II

9. Now select **3D/Elevation**, then **3D Map Control**, to open the dialog box shown in Figure 15II.

10. Choose **Draw Box to Set Limit of 3D Map**. Using your pointer, do just that by dragging a box on the screen. I understand the temptation to look at Half Dome, but the first time out let's take a look at some gentler terrain. This is especially true if you don't have the full Ozi. The trial version limits 3-D views so that you can't zoom below 100% to cover more area.

11. Now select **Create the 3D Map**. Ozi3D will open, and you'll need to choose OK on the **Evaluation Version** box and close the **Help** screen. If all has gone well, you'll have a very cool 3-D image.

Ozi3D is a deep program in its own right, as you can probably tell from a quick look at all the icons on the toolbar. Space limitations do not allow description of all its features, but here are some basics to get you started:

• Drag the 3-D image with the left mouse button to spin it around a point at the center of your screen. You can pull the image down for an overhead view or view it as if from the ground, or from any point in between. You can also rotate the image with the arrow keys.

• Notice that when you move it, the image switches to a wire grid. Pretty cool, huh?

• Zoom the image with a mouse scroll wheel or with the PAGE UP and PAGE DOWN keys.

• Use the right mouse button to drag the image on the screen, allowing the center rotation point to shift to a different part of the image.

• For more information on Ozi3D, read the help file, especially the tutorial. And be sure to check out the **Configuration** options.

Updates to this book will be posted at www.MakeYourOwnMaps.com.
Bookmark and visit often to see what's new in the world of digital mapping.

Working With Other Programs

In this chapter, we've looked at:

- The various types of maps that can be imported and used in Ozi (see "What Are All Those Acronyms?" on page 194).

- Importing and calibrating scanned map images such as .tif, .bmp, .jpg, and .png.

- The native file formats (.map, .wpt, .rte, .plt) Ozi uses. (See the File Structure section of this chapter for more information on file formats.)

Beyond these file types, Ozi allows you to import and export data in a wide range of formats:

Importing Data

- To import waypoints in a text (.txt) file format, choose **Load**, then select **Import Waypoints from Text File.**

- Click **Load** and point to **Import** for the import options shown in Figure 15JJ.

- Click **Load** and point to **Import ESRI Shape File** to import points, polylines, or polygons in .shp format. Note that ArcInfo .e00 files are imported via the menu shown in Figure 15JJ.

- You can also get to all of the above options by choosing **File** and pointing to **Load from File.**

```
Track from Text File
From MapInfo MIF Files
From MapGen Vector Files
From ArcInfo E00 Files
From IGC Track Files
From Compe-Gps Track Files
```

Figure 15JJ

Exporting Data

- To export waypoints in a text (.txt) file format, select **Save**, then **Export Waypoints to Text File.**

- Choose **Save** and point to **Export Track** for the options to export a track **To Text File** or **To IGC Track File.**

- Choose **Save** and point to **Export to ESRI Shape File** to export **Points**, export **Waypoints to Points**, or export **Tracks to Polylines.**

- You can also get to all of the above options by choosing **File** and pointing to **Save to File.**

- Choose **File** and then point to **Save Map to Image File** to save the map image as a color or black-and-white .bmp or .png file.

For more information on moving data between programs, see Chapter 26.

More Tips

- You can attach waypoint, route, and other files to a map, so that they are loaded whenever a map is opened. Select **File**, then **Check Calibration of Map**. Now select **Options** to choose files to attach to the map.

- You can customize the User Toolbar with buttons for tasks that you perform frequently. Select **View**, point to **Show**, then choose **User Toolbar**. The toolbar will be displayed just below the **Main Toolbar**. Select **Customize Toolbar** to choose which buttons to display.

- Map Comments and Map Features can add depth to your map and provide additional information. Map Comments are text boxes that can be used to place additional information directly on the map. To place them, choose **Position & Set Map Comments on Map**.

- Map Features can include a link to a digital photo, with the photo visible in the **Map Feature Properties** dialog box. To place Map Features, choose **Position & Set Map Features on Map**. Right-click on a map feature and select **Properties** to attach photo links, change symbols, and so on.

- If waypoints or other objects appear on top of each other, or too close together to read, right-click them and select **Hide**. To make them reappear, right-click anywhere on the map and select **Unhide**, then pick the items you wish to reveal. You can also hide groups of objects this way—right-click anywhere on the map other than on an object, select **Hide**, and choose the category you wish to hide.

- For a number of keyboard shortcuts see **Hints, Tips & FAQs** in the help section.

- OziExplorer is updated frequently. Check the Web site at **www.oziexplorer.com** on a regular basis to ensure that you have the latest improvements to the program.

Chapter 16 Fugawi GPS Mapping Software

Fugawi GPS Mapping Software™ is similar to OziExplorer. And while it has a few drawbacks in terms of supported file types and lack of 3-D capabilities, Fugawi publishes extensive maps for Canada, its home base, and for far-flung places from Iceland to Nepal.

Basic Information

COST
- $99 U.S., $149 Canadian

- Comes packaged with street maps for the entire U.S. and a set of nautical planning charts

- A 30-day demonstration version is available from **www.fugawi.com**.

  –One-hour time limit until restart required.

  –No printing, map export, or transfer of navigation data.

  –Limit of three maps, four waypoints, two routes, and two tracks.

  –No PDA support.

SYSTEM REQUIREMENTS
- Microsoft Windows 98, 2000, ME, XP, or NT 4.0

- Pentium processor or better

- 64 MB of RAM

- 100 MB of free hard disk space

- CD-ROM drive

GPS COMPATIBILITY
- Any GPS receiver with NMEA 0183 V2 output

TESTED VERSION
- 3.1.4.635

Northport Systems, Inc.
95 St. Clair Ave. West, Suite 1406
Toronto, Ontario M4V 1N6 Canada
416.920.9300
support@fugawi.com
www.fugawi.com

AVAILABLE OPTIONS

• Fugawi offers an impressive array of topographic, street, and marine maps for locations around the world. See **www.fugawi.com/docs/mapframe.html** for details.

INTERNET RESOURCES

• The Yahoo Map Authors group, at **groups.yahoo.com/group/map_authors**, lists Fugawi as a product discussed on its message board.

Advantages

• A free demo version is available.

• Importing maps is a breeze.

• You can easily organize maps and data (waypoints, etc.) into file folders you manage from within the program.

• The Zoom Mode tool is a convenient way to navigate maps.

• You can construct routes from existing waypoints.

• Fugawi is packaged with street maps and geographic names for the entire U.S.

• It contains excellent moving map features, including integrated Palm and PocketPC PDA use.

• Fugawi includes features designed specifically for geocaching.

• You can manipulate the location of waypoint labels, which is very helpful when multiple waypoints appear in close proximity.

• A **Reduce Track** option allows you to decrease the number of points in a given track, which can make it easier to transfer tracks to your GPS without them being truncated.

• You can split tracks.

Disadvantages

• The demo carries some significant limitations.

• There is no 3-D option, though one is planned for Version 4, slated for release in March 2005.

- You cannot import .sid or .shp files into Fugawi.

- As with OziExplorer, there is a fairly steep learning curve, but that's what this book is for. Read on and you'll be up to speed in no time.

Tutorial/Manual

Fugawi 3 GPS Mapping Software comes with a hard-copy manual and extensive help files. Context-sensitive help is available from many dialog boxes.

TIP: Select **Help**, then **Contents** to open the **Contents** dialog box shown in Figure 16A. Click on the **Contents** button at the top, opening yet another set of Contents (see Figure 16B) with different topics.

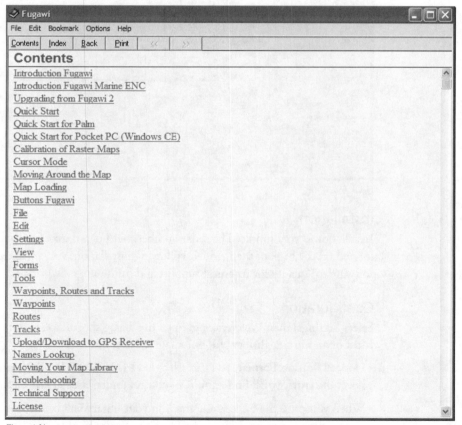

Figure 16A

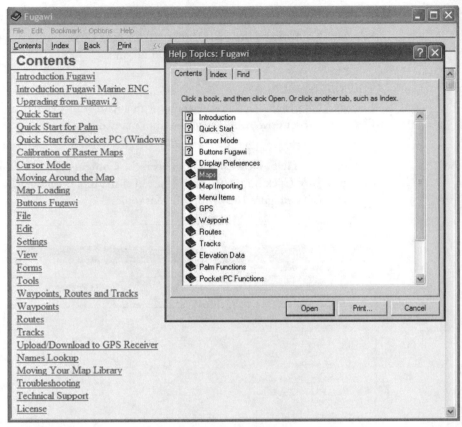

Figure 16B

Installation

Installation is very simple. The serial number that Fugawi asks for upon installation is located on the back of the manual. Following installation, you are asked to register the software to "qualify for technical support and future upgrade pricing."

Configuration

Select **Settings**, then **Preferences** to open the dialog shown box shown in Figure 16C. Most items are straightforward, but a few warrant more discussion:

• Under **Location Format**, you can select **UTM**, **NAD27**, **WGS84**, or **User**. If you select the latter, you'll find additional choices under **User UTM datum**.

• When you press the F2 key, any maps in your library will be outlined. Outline color and thickness are controlled in the **Outline Display** section.

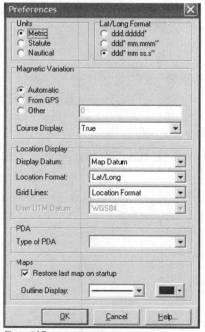

Figure 16C

Figure 16D

• Note that selecting **Help** provides context-sensitive help.

Select **Settings**, then **Geocaching** to open the dialog shown in Figure 16D, with the following options:

• **Geocaching waypoint (LOC) files**. This associates LOC files with Fugawi.

• **Assert associations when Fugawi starts**. This overwrites LOC associations assigned to other programs. I suggest clearing this check box unless Fugawi is the only mapping or waypoint management program you use.

• **Waypoint Download Location**. This section allows you to select a specific location for downloads from the **www.geocaching.com** Web site.

Select **Settings**, then **GPS** to open the GPS dialog box. Here are some of the options you'll find there:

• **Settings**. Here you can **Change Port** and choose from a wide range of icons to **Display** your position when tracking it in real time. Check **Course Projection** to project your track at the current speed and heading for up to the next 86,400 seconds (24 hours).

• **Model**. Here you set your **GPS Model** and chose the type of waypoint **Icons** your GPS supports.

Select **Settings**, then **Route** to open the dialog box shown in Figure 16E, with the following options:

- **Display**. Set the appearance of lines and points here.

- **Labels**. Here you can label route points and set their background appearance.

- **Drawing Crosstrack Errors**. This smoothes routes that have been drawn freehand. A small number will generate a route that more accurately reflects the line drawn, yet also results in a larger number of route points.

- **Navigation Proximity**. This sets how far ahead of a waypoint you wish to receive a turn warning.

- **Arrival Notification**. This controls how you are notified upon reaching the proximity zone, referred to by Fugawi as the "arrival circle."

Figure 16E

Figure 16F

Select **Settings**, then **Track** to open the dialog shown in Figure 16F, with the following options:

- Track **Recording** can be **Enabled**, and you can set the time **Interval** for recording track points as well as the **Min Dist** and **Max Dist** apart.

Choose **Settings**, then **Waypoints** to open the Waypoint dialog box, which has the following options:

• Choose the waypoint **Icon.**

• Set the **Position** for the waypoint label, and choose the **Background** and **Background Color** and the **Font** and **Font Color.**

Here are some other items in the **Settings** menu that you may want to take a look at:

• **Libraries.** These are used to configure directory locations for maps, waypoints, routes, tracks, and elevations.

• **Palm.** This opens a **Palm Library** dialog box that provides additional configuration options.

• **Drawing.** This allows you to configure **Line Width** and **Color.**

• **Map.** Point to **Options** and then select **Image Cache** to increase dedicated memory, which can improve panning.

• **Lock Toolbar.** This prevents the toolbar from being moved.

• **Live Scrollbar.** This allows the map image to be updated while scrolling.

Getting Started

Though Fugawi comes with street maps, and others are available for purchase, the real power of this program becomes evident once you begin downloading maps from the Internet. To get off to a good start, let's walk through the downloading and importing of a USGS map—the 7.5' Mount Shasta (California) quad:

1. First, let's create a directory for the map fields we will be downloading. This can be located anywhere. I'm going to call mine 24K DRGs and place it on the desktop for now.

2. Now go to John Galvin's excellent DRG map resource at **home.pacbell.net/lgalvin/ drgnotes.htm** and scroll down to the California section.

3. Click the first link under California, but take a moment to read the information associated with it. This tells us that the projection is Teale Albers and that the datum is NAD27. Now click the link **casil.ucdavis.edu/casil/.**

4. Click the **drgs** link above the directory list, which will take you to **casil.ucdavis.edu/ casil/gis.ca.gov/drg.**

5. Scroll down and click the link labeled **7.5 minute series albers nad27 trimmed,** which will take you to **casil.ucdavis.edu/casil/gis.ca.gov/drg/7.5_minute_series_ albers_nad27_trimmed.**

6. Scroll to the folder **41122** and select it.

7. Scroll to find the two Mount Shasta files, **o41122d2.tif** and **o41122d2.tfw**. Right-click them and select **Save Target As** to save them to the **Map Library** folder. The path for the Map Library, unless you changed it, is C:\Program Files\Common Files\Fugawi\Map Library.

> **TIP:** For a not-so-helpful reason, Windows may change the file extensions on these two files! Once you've downloaded the files, if Windows changed the .tif file extension to .tiff, right-click on the file, select **Rename**, and remove an f, changing the extension back to .tif. Click anywhere else on the screen and ignore the ominous Windows warning shown in Figure 16G (select **Yes**).
>
> If Windows added a .txt file extension to the .tfw file, right-click on the file, select **Rename**, and remove the .txt, leaving the file extension as .tfw. Click anywhere else on the screen and ignore the Windows warning as before.

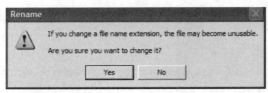

Figure 16G

8. In Fugawi, select **File**, point to **Import**, and select **DRG/ChartTiff/JPR** to open an **Import** dialog box.

9. Navigate to the directory you downloaded to and select it to open the **TIFF/TFW Grid** window.

10. In the **Map Grid** field, select **Teale Albers**. Select **Scale** and enter **24000**. Unless you are very organized, uncheck the box **Use this grid and datum for all maps in directory**. The **TIFF/TFW Grid** window should appear as the one shown in Figure 16H. Notice that the **Datum** is correctly listed as North American 1927 (Western US). Click **OK**.

11. Select the file **o41122d2.tif** in the **Import DRG/ChartTiff/JPR Charts** dialog and click on **OK**.

12. Select **Open Map**. In the **Open Map** dialog box, choose **DRG** and then choose **o41122d2**, as shown in Figure 16I. Click **OK**. That's it; you've imported your first map into Fugawi!

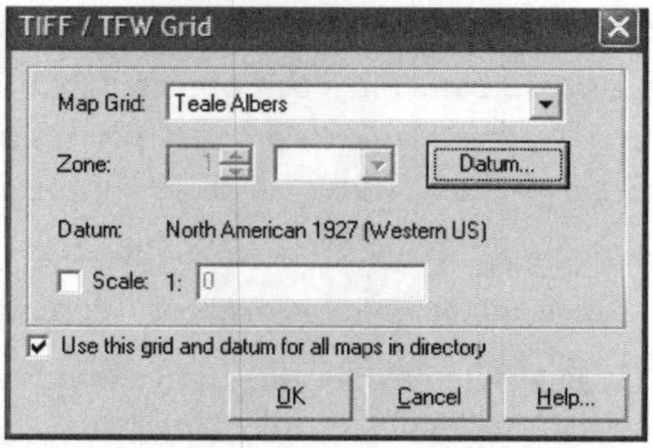

Figure 16H

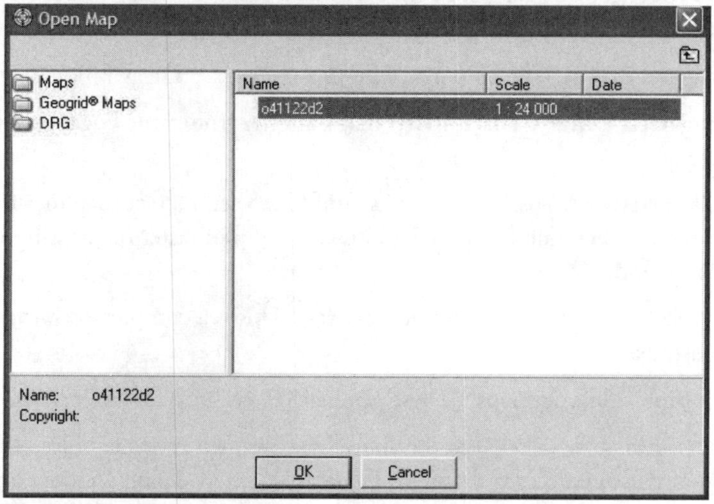

Figure 16I

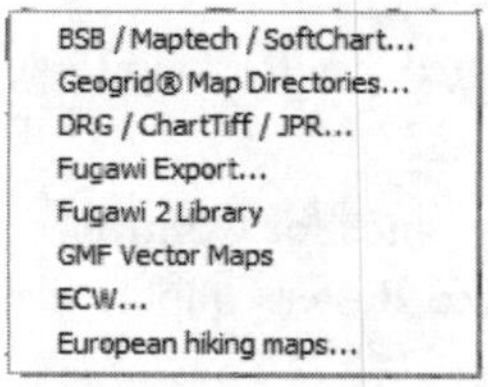

BSB / Maptech / SoftChart...
Geogrid® Map Directories...
DRG / ChartTiff / JPR...
Fugawi Export...
Fugawi 2 Library
GMF Vector Maps
ECW...
European hiking maps...

Figure 16J

Importing Other Map Formats

Let's take a look at the range of map formats that can be imported into Fugawi. Select **File**, and then point to **Import** to display the menu shown in Figure 16J. Here are the choices you're presented with:

- **BSB/MapTech/SoftChart***.BSB is a marine chart format licensed to MapTech by NOAA. Information for each map is stored in a pair of files, a .bsb file and an accompanying .kap file. (To import any other MapTech product, you must copy the entire CD.) SoftCharts are also marine products, with each chart comprised of a pair of files, a .geo and a .nos file.

- **Geogrid Map Directories***. These are topographic maps of Germany and Austria.

- **DRG/ChartTiff/JPR***. DRG maps were used for our sample import. This is a primary USGS format, commonly available in the U.S. and relatively easy to find for free online. See Chapter 14 for information on Internet sources for these maps. ChartTiff maps are commercial products (available from **www.charttiff.com**), some of which utilize an accompanying georeference file with a .jpr file extension.

- **Fugawi Export.** This imports .fxf (Fugawi 2), .fx3 (Fugawi 3), and .fx4 formats.

- **Fugawi 2 Library.** This imports maps directly from your Fugawi 2 library, if one is present.

- **GMF Vector Maps.** This imports .gmf files, vector street map files for Europe and Canada. These can be layered and used on top of raster maps using Fugawi's Overlays command.

- **ECW (Enhanced Compressed Wavelet).** This is a compressed format common in Australia.

- **European hiking maps***. These generally carry .gmp file extensions.

Items with an asterisk (*) in the above list have their own help files. When you click on any of these choices, as shown in Figure 16J, a new dialog window opens to allow you to locate the files. The **Help** button in this dialog provides additional information for the file format you are importing.

Additionally, the following formats can be imported. See the help topic "Map Importing" for more information.

- **CIB/CADRG.** This is a military format. CIB stands for Controlled Image Base, while CADRG represents a Compressed Arc Digitized Raster Graphic file. Select a .toc file to import these formats.

- **ADRG.** Arc Digitized Raster Graphic is another military format. Select a .thf file to import this format.

TIP: Copy maps to your hard disk if possible. Performance will be much better than if you work with maps stored on CDs.

Calibrating Map Images

Map images that do not carry georeferencing information must be calibrated (typically these are scanned images or images captured off the Internet). Fugawi supports the following image formats: .tif, .jpg, .bmp, .gif, .png, and .pcx. To import a map image for calibration:

1. Select **File**, then **Calibrate Map**.

2. Select the image to import from the **Open Map Image** dialog box and choose **Open**.

3. In the **Map Information** dialog (see Figure 16K), enter a **Name** for your map. Now select the **Projection**, **Datum**, and **Scale**. Fugawi's help files state "If you do not know the projection, choose the Equidistant Cylindrical projection, and Fugawi will make a mathematical approximation of the true map projection. On a large scale map, the errors from using the wrong projection will be small." Unfortunately no such broad advice can be given regarding selection of the proper datum. Don't worry about the **Advanced** button. Click **OK**.

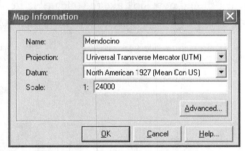

Figure 16K

4. Enter any required information in the **Projection Parameters** dialog. (See Chapter 14 for more information on the fields shown here.) Click **OK**.

5. Use the scroll bars or page navigation tools (see Figure 16L) to move around the map. Use the **Reference Point Mode** tool to select several calibration points. Double-click a known location on the map. Once you do this, a zoom window will appear in the **Reference Points** panel (see Figure 16M). Move the pointer over the zoom window and click your reference point again for more accurate placement.

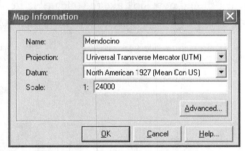

Figure 16L

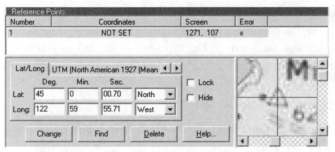

Figure 16M

6. Enter the latitude and longitude (or UTM coordinates) of the point in the **Reference Points** panel and click **Change**.

7. Now repeat Steps 5 and 6 two more times for reference points two and three. Make sure that your three reference points are widely spaced and are not in a single line.

8. Your **Calibration Checklist** should now look like the one in Figure 16N. Click **Next** and use the **Boundary Points Mode** tool to select the four corners of the map.

9. Click **Save** and name the map.

Figure 16N

> **TIP:** The Calibration window has its own menus and buttons. There is also a separate calibration help file.

Navigating the Map

To move around the map, you can:

- Use the scroll bars.

- Use the **Page Left**, **Page Right**, **Page Up**, and **Page Down** buttons (see Figure 16L).

- Use the **Zoom Mode** tool to click anywhere on the map and center the map at that location.

• Click the arrow adjacent to the **Zoom Mode** tool. Click **Grab,** as shown in Figure 16O. Use this tool to pan the map.

Figure 16O

• Use your arrow keys. Using SHIFT + an arrow key will move the map one full screen. Using CTRL + an arrow key will move the map one-half screen.

• Use the PAGE UP and PAGE DOWN keys.

• Use your mouse scroll wheel.

• Click **Overview** to open the Overview window showing the entire map (see Figure 16P). You can either click on a new location or drag the red rectangle to a new location.

Figure 16P

To zoom the map:

• Use the **Zoom Mode** tool to drag a rectangle around an area to be zoomed in on.

• While in **Zoom Mode,** right-click to zoom out.

• Use the **Zoom In** and **Zoom Out** tools.

• Use the **Set Zoom** button.

• Use the plus (+) and minus (-) keys.

You can load maps in several ways, too:

• Select **Open Map**.

• Select **File**, then **Open**.

• Select **Forms**, then **Map Library**.

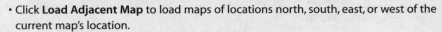

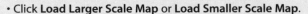

File Structure

Fugawi has a user-friendly interface for file management. It uses file folders, just like Windows. The difference is that these folders are readily accessible and visible within the Fugawi 3 program. Find map files in the map libraries by clicking on **Open Map**, as discussed earlier in this chapter.

> **TIP:** Fugawi recommends that you organize map folders by scale. Select **Forms**, then **Map Library** to reorganize you map folders.

Waypoints, routes, and tracks are also managed through libraries of folders. Each will be discussed in detail in the following sections. You can access these libraries by selecting **Forms** then choosing the appropriate item in the **Forms** menu, or via one of these toolbar buttons:

- **Display Waypoint Window**
- **Display Route Window**
- **Display GPS Track Window**

Windows folder locations are as follows:

- The default location for routes folders and tracks folders is C:\Program Files\Common Files\Fugawi\Map Library. Georeference information for maps is also stored here. Waypoints are stored in the same folder as .wpt files.

- Images for maps that you have imported are stored in the original image directory. If you change their location, when you try to open a map you'll see an exclamation point in a yellow circle in the **Open Map** dialog, as shown in Figure 16Q. Double-click the file to change the file path where Fugawi looks for the image.

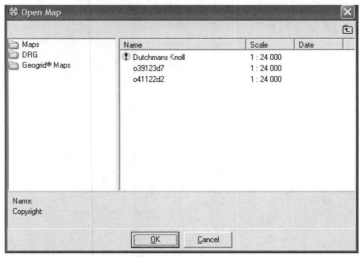

Figure 16Q

> **TIP:** When you're in any library dialog, you can select and drag items and folders to new locations. You can also **Rename** and **Delete** folders.

> **TIP:** Want to move all your files to a new computer? Copy the C:\Program Files\Common Files\Fugawi\Map Library to your new computer and move all map image files as well. You'll have to go through the process we just discussed to reassign the directory location for map images.

Waypoints and Waypoint Management

To place a waypoint, select **Waypoint Mode**. Then either double-click at the desired point on the map or press ALT while single-clicking. Fugawi automatically assigns new waypoints a number. Unfortunately, the only way to change the name is to go through the multi-step editing process described below. Waypoints are saved automatically.

To edit a waypoint, open the **Waypoints** dialog shown in Figure 16R using one of the following methods:

• Select **Display Waypoint Window**.

• Double-click on an existing waypoint.

• Select **Forms**, then **Waypoints**.

• Press CTRL + W.

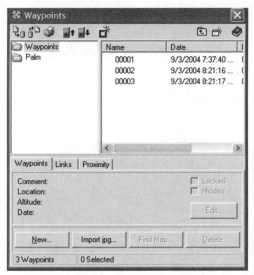

Figure 16R

The folder tree on the left side of the **Waypoints** dialog box allows you to manage your waypoint folders. Select a folder to show the waypoints in it. You can right-click a folder and select **New Folder** to create a subfolder.

To edit a waypoint, from the **Waypoints** dialog box (Figure 16R) select a waypoint and choose **Edit**, or right-click a waypoint and choose **Edit**. This will open the **Edit Waypoint** dialog shown in Figure 16S, where you can change the **Name**. The **Comment** field allows you to add a note that can be transferred to your GPS (up to the number of characters accepted by your unit). Comments will show on the Fugawi map when the pointer is placed over a waypoint. You can also add a **Description**, although you won't be able to transfer it to your GPS. Choose the **Icon** tab to change the waypoint symbol. Choose the **Caption** tab to change waypoint label attributes, including the label **Position** (a very helpful feature).

Let's go back and take a closer look at the Waypoints dialog box (Figure 16R). Select a waypoint and choose **Hidden** to hide it on the map. Choose **Locked** to prevent it from being moved. Choose **Find Map** to show all maps with the selected waypoint. Choose **Delete** to delete the waypoint.

The buttons at the top of the Waypoints dialog box (see Figure 16R) do the following:

- **Import Waypoints** and **Export Waypoints**. These functions are discussed under Working With Other Programs.

- **Print**. Select this to open the **Print Waypoints** dialog, where you can choose which fields to print.

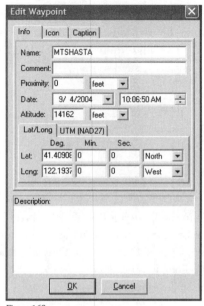

Figure 16S

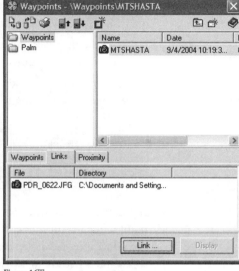

Figure 16T

- **Upload to GPS**. Select any waypoints you wish to send and then click here. Alternatively, click here first and then select **All** to send all waypoints in the folder.

- **Download from GPS**. This downloads waypoints to the current folder. (To download waypoints to a new folder you create, use **New Waypoint Folder**, below).

- **New Waypoint**. Click here to create a waypoint by entering coordinates.

- **Go To Parent**. This goes one step up the directory tree from the current directory.

- **New Waypoint Folder**. This creates a new waypoint folder within the current folder.

- **Help**. This opens the Waypoints section of the help files.

Photo Waypoints

You can link digital photos or sound files to a waypoint. Select a waypoint and choose the **Links** tab in the Waypoints dialog box (Figure 16R). Click the **Link** button and locate the image or sound file you wish to attach to the waypoint. Notice the camera icon adjacent to the waypoint, as shown in Figure 16T, letting you know that a file is attached.

Click **Photo Waypoints** on the cursor mode bar, and only waypoints with a photo or sound file attached will be displayed. Double-click one of those waypoints while you're in **Photo Waypoint** mode to open the image or play the sound.

Routes

To create a route on the map, choose **Route Mode**. Now click at the beginning of your route on the map, and you'll see the **Drawing Route** dialog box (see Figure 16U). Continue clicking at turns, laying out the desired route.

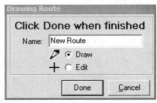

Figure 16U

If you make an error, choose **Edit** in the **Drawing Route** dialog box. To move a route point while in edit mode, click on or near it once and release the mouse button, and then drag it to the desired location. Choose **Draw** on the **Drawing Route** dialog box when you are ready to add more points. If you wish to start over, choose **Cancel**. When you're finished, **Name** the route and click **Done**.

> **TIP:** While in Route mode, you can right-click to toggle between the **Draw** and **Edit** functions.

Rather than click at each route point, you can also hold down the mouse button and draw a route freehand. When you release the mouse button, the freehand route will be converted to a series of straight segments. See the Configuration section of this chapter for information on **Route Settings** for **Drawing Crosstrack Error**, which affects the accuracy of the conversion and the number of route points generated. When creating routes in this manner, be aware that GPS receivers have an upper limit on the number of points that can be used to construct a route. Often this number is 50 or even lower.

To construct a route from existing waypoints:

1. Choose **Display Route Window**.

2. Choose **New Route**.

3. Choose **Route Details**.

4. Choose **Display Waypoint Window**.

5. Drag waypoints from the **Waypoint Window** and drop them in the **Route Window**.

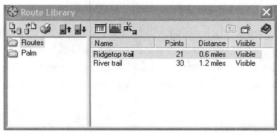

Figure 16V

Routes are managed in much the same way as waypoints. Route files and other features are managed from the **Route Library** dialog box (Figure 16V), which can be opened in any of several ways:

• Choose **Display Route Window**.

• Choose **Forms,** then select **Routes**.

• Press CTRL + R.

The buttons at the top of the **Route Library** dialog are similar in function to the ones in the **Waypoints** dialog. There are a few, however, that warrant further discussion:

• **Import Route File** and **Export Route File**. These functions are discussed under Working With Other Programs.

• **Route Details**. Select a route, then click here to open a new dialog window showing route details.

– Within this window, choose **Display Options**, to select the color and scale for route **Lines** and **Points**.

– **Invert Route** reverses the route direction. This dialog also allows you to shift the position of points within the route.

• From the **Route Library** or **Route Detail** dialogs, choose **Trail Profile** to create an elevation profile of a route. We'll explore how to do this after we look at creating tracks.

> **TIP: Center Route Selection** centers the map screen on the current route.

> Updates to this book will be posted at www.MakeYourOwnMaps.com.
> Bookmark and visit often to see what's new in the world of digital mapping.

Tracks

To begin drawing a track, click **Track Mode**. This allows you to draw just like in route mode—either click to "connect the dots" or hold the mouse button down and draw a track freehand. The **Drawing Track** dialog (see Figure 16W) works just like the **Drawing Route** dialog. If you wish to name the track, it's easiest to do so before clicking **Done**.

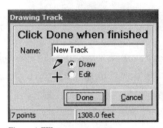

Figure 16W

Track management works in much the same way as it does for waypoints and routes. Track files and other features are managed from the **Track Library** dialog (see Figure 16X), which can be opened several ways:

• Choose **Display GPS Track Window**.

• Select **Forms**, then **Tracks**.

• Press CTRL + T.

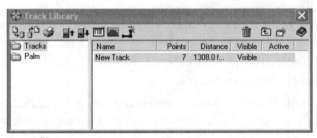

Figure 16X

The buttons at the top of the **Track Library** dialog are similar in function to the ones in the **Route Library** dialog.

Double-click a track in the **Track Library** to open a dialog showing point-by-point track details, as seen in Figure 16Y. There are a couple of noteworthy features here:

• **Reduce Track** allows you to simplify a track, reducing the number of points. Click here to open a dialog that allows you to specify the allowable error.

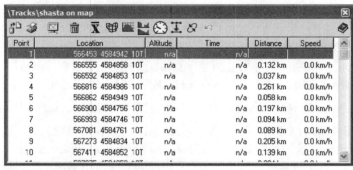

Figure 16Y

• If you aren't happy with the results, click **Undo Reduction**.

• To split a track, select a point, then right-click on it and choose **Start New Segment**. The connection with the preceding point will be deleted. Right-click again and choose **Join Segments** to reconnect them.

> **TIP: Center Track Selection** centers the map screen on the current track.

Elevation Profiles

Fugawi allows you to create elevation profiles for tracks and routes. Let's give it a try. If you don't have it open, choose **Open Map** and load the Mount Shasta quad (o41122d2).

Now we need to acquire elevation data. The help files present several ways to accomplish this; we'll use the Shuttle Radar Topography Mission (SRTM) format.

1. Go to **ftp://e0mss21u.ecs.nasa.gov/srtm**, and open the **North America 3 arcsec** folder. The file names represent the southwest corner of the dataset, which covers a full degree of latitude and longitude.

2. Let's look at the southwest corner of our Mount Shasta map. The coordinates are 41° 22.5034' N and 122° 14.9974' W. Drag your pointer across the map from south to north. Notice that the latitude coordinates (on the bottom left corner below the map) get larger. Now do the same for longitude, noticing that the numbers increase going east to west. The file we are looking for, which will include the area of the map, is **N41W123.hgt.zip**. Scroll down the Web page, select the file, and save it to your desktop. Note that if we had selected N41W122, we would have data for an area to the east of the Mount Shasta quad.

3. Unzip **N41W123.hgt.zip**. You can use WinZip or WinRAR (which will work better if you ever need to unzip a .gz file). You can get a free demo version of WinRAR at **www.rarlab.com**.

4. Once you've unzipped the file, go back to Fugawi and select **Forms**, then **Elevation Library** (see Figure 16Z). Select **HGT SRTM 3 Second** in the drop-down box.

5. Choose **Import Elevation Files**. Locate **N41W123.hgt** and click on **OK**.

6. An **Import DEM Files** dialog opens. Select the **N41W123** file and choose **Import Selected**. Select the imported file in the **Elevation Library** dialog, which should now look like the one in Figure 16Z. Close the **Elevation Library** dialog.

7. Create a track on the Mount Shasta map, as described earlier. There are no trails on the map near the summit, but there are plenty on the northern portion of the map. Trace one of these, or just draw an imaginary one freehand.

8. Now open the **Track Library** dialog box and select the track you drew, as shown in Figure 16AA.

9. Choose **Plot Profile**, creating a **Trail Profile** similar to the one in Figure 16BB.

GPS Interface

To transfer data with your GPS, click one of the following:

• **Display Waypoint Window**

• **Display Route Window**

• **Display GPS Track Window**

You can also perform these functions by choosing **Forms**, then selecting the appropriate item in the **Forms** menu.

From any of the above dialog windows, choose **Upload to GPS** or **Download from GPS**. When transferring data to your GPS, select the folder or individual item within a folder that you wish to transfer. When transferring data from your GPS, open the folder in which you want the data to reside, or create a new one for this purpose.

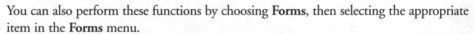

TIP: If you're using the Lowrance iFinder GPS series, read the help section on transferring data to and from an MMC card. To access this section, open help, select **Index**, then **Find**, type **Lowrance**, and select **Lowrance Data Exchange**.

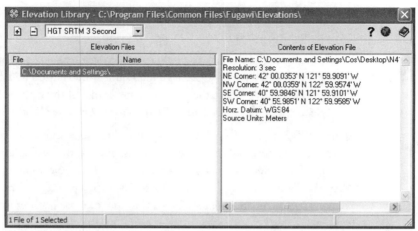

Figure 16Z

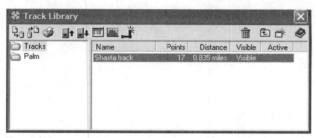

Figure 16AA

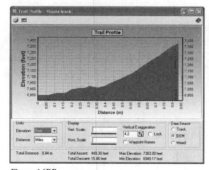

Figure 16BB

Printing

Fugawi provides two ways to select an area to print:

1. To select a portion of the map to print, zoom as necessary to see the entire area you wish to print. Choose the arrow adjacent to the **Zoom Mode** button and choose **Select**, as shown in Figure 16O. Place the pointer in any corner of the map and drag it to form a rectangle, defining the selected area. Right-click and choose **Clear Selection** to cancel.

2. Alternatively, you can define the area to be printed so as to include certain waypoints, tracks, and routes found on the map. Choose **Forms**, then **Selection** to open the **Selection Elements** dialog box shown in Figure 16CC. Now choose **Display Waypoint Window**, **Display Route Window**, or **Display GPS Track** to open the waypoint, route, or track library. Next, drag any of these features into the **Selection Elements** dialog box. Any features not found on the current map will be ignored. Use **Delete Selected Elements** or **Clear All**, if desired.

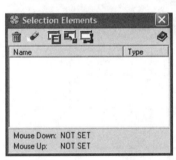

Figure 16CC

Grid Line Setup

Before finalizing your print job, make sure you have your grid lines set if you wish to display any. To set the **Location Format** (UTM vs. Lat/Lon), choose **Settings**, then **Preferences**. Make sure you set **Units** to **Metric** if you are using UTM. Now press F4 or click on **View** and select **Grid Lines**.

Once you have selected the area to print and decided whether or not to display a grid, click **File** and then click **Print**, opening the **Print Map** dialog shown in Figure 16DD.

• **Scale** choices allow you to **Fit to page** or **Print to scale**. Fugawi will not allow you to print a map that exceeds one page in size.

• **Map Detail** reduces the level of detail for older printers with low memory capacity.

Figure 16DD

- **Waypoint Scaling** allows you to change the size of waypoints on the printed map. The number you enter multiplies the size—2 doubles the waypoint size and 0.5 halves it.

- Takes you to **Printer Setup**.

- Choose **Print Map**. If you have a grid showing, a **Grid Spacing** dialog will open.

Moving Map

Fugawi maps can be transferred to a Pocket PC or Palm for portable real-time navigation. See Chapter 22 for more information on this and other PDA applications. In the U.S., Fugawi comes packaged with street maps for the entire country.

To begin tracking your position, click **Center GPS**.

Here are some tips for using Fugawi to track your position in real time:

- From the **Settings** menu, **GPS**, **Route**, and **Track** influence real-time tracking. More information is available in the Configuration section of this chapter.

- Choose **Track Record** to begin logging your track.

- Choose **Autoload** to have Fugawi automatically switch to the appropriate map when your position moves off the current one. If you wish to view maps other than one showing your present location, you'll need to disable this feature temporarily.

- You can apply the **Autoload** feature selectively. Select **Forms**, then **Map Library**, and place a check mark next to folders you wish to enable for autoloading.

- Choose **Auto Scale**, and Fugawi will load the largest scale map available when you move off the current map. Check marks placed in the **Map Library** apply to this feature as well.

- Choose **Display Navigation Window**. The **Navigation** tab displays information about the next waypoint, current route, and current information being received from your GPS. The **Route** tab is used to manage route navigation. Click **Select** to load a route for navigation, choose **Goto** to begin navigating the route, and choose **Clear** to end navigation along the route.

- To create a waypoint at your current location, choose **New Waypoint**.

- Choose **View** to select from **Day, Dusk,** or **Night Display**.

- Choose **View**, then **Map Orientation** for the options shown in Figure 16EE. You can toggle between **Map Up** (which is usually north) and any other orientation by pressing F8. **Tolerance** allows you to select the amount of deviation before the screen is redrawn. A smaller number may slow computer performance. **Min. Interval** is the minimum time between screen redraws.

Figure 16EE

Finally, click **Display GPS Window** for a number of important moving map options:

- The **Position** tab provides information about your current position.

- The **Log** tab reads out NMEA sentences.

- The **Satellites** tab shows the current configuration of satellites and their signal strength.

- On the **Settings** tab, you can **Change Port**, choose to show a **Course Projection** (from your current position estimating where you will be in a given length of time at your current speed), and select your position **Display** icon and color.

- The **Model** tab allows you to change your GPS **Model** and the type of **Icons** it uses. You must select icons supported by your receiver.

- The **Out** tab is a concern only if you are connecting to an external device such as an autopilot.

3-D

Fugawi has no three-dimensional capability, though I have been told this will be featured in Version 4. For more information on 3-D mapping, see Chapter 21.

Working With Other Programs

To import or export data, choose **Display Waypoint Window**, **Display Route Window**, or **Display GPS Track Window**.

From the appropriate dialog, select:

- **Import Waypoints.** Use this to import waypoints from a Fugawi waypoint file, Lowrance .usr file, Garmin PCX file, or text (ASCII) file.

- **Export Waypoints.** Choose this to export to a Fugawi .wpt file, an ASCII .txt file, .lwr or .usr Lowrance files, or a .shp shapefile.

- **Import Route File.** Use this to import routes in Fugawi 2 or Fugawi 3 (.rte) format, Lowrance (.usr) files, or as text (.txt) files.

- **Export Route File.** Use this to export routes in Fugawi 3 format (.rte), shapefiles (.shp), Lowrance (.usr) files, or as text files (.txt). See the "Route Export" section of the help files for more information.

- **Import Track File** and **Export Track File.** Use these to import and export the same file types as for routes (above). The only difference is that Fugawi tracks carry a .trk file extension.

> **TIP:** Fugawi allows you to customize the fields imported and exported in waypoint, track, and route ASCII text files. This can make it easier to share data between programs. For more information on this process, choose **Help**, then **Contents**. Select **Index** and type **Input Fields**. You can find additional information on transferring specific types of data in the help files under Waypoints, Routes, or Tracks.

> Updates to this book will be posted at www.MakeYourOwnMaps.com.
> Bookmark and visit often to see what's new in the world of digital mapping.

More Tips

The following items are found under the **Tools** menu:

- **Destination.** This allows you to enter your coordinates, a waypoint, or a current GPS position as a starting point, then establish a distance and bearing to travel.

- **Magnetic Variation.** This calculates the magnetic variation for any given coordinates.

- **Simulator.** This allows you to follow the route of your choice through a simulated NMEA data stream.

- **Sunrise/Sunset.** This allows you to calculate these times for any date and set of coordinates.

- Want to place notes on the map? Though Fugawi offers no note tool, you can use waypoints for this purpose, since there is great flexibility in waypoint font, color, and position.

> **TIP:** Want to create your own position or waypoint icon? Waypoint icons should be a .bmp image of 28 x 28 pixels, though the icon itself should be no larger than 24 x 24 within the image area. A current position icon should be 65 x 65, keeping in mind that the position image must be able to rotate within the 65 x 65 area. The icon should point upward; your position will be the center of the 65 x 65 area. Icons should be placed in c:\Program Files\CommonFiles\Fugawi\Icons. Thanks to Doug Adomatis (**www.travelbygps.com**) for this great tip.

Section Five GPS-Based Maps

The programs we'll look at in this section are designed to work on certain types of GPS receivers. The lower-end receivers typically cannot display any but the most rudimentary of maps. To display detailed maps that can show contour lines, you'll need a more sophisticated receiver and a program such as those in this section. The three programs covered here are proprietary; each works only with its particular brand of GPS. For example, Garmin's MapSource maps cannot be displayed on a Magellan GPS.

There are many commonalities between these programs. Each displays vector maps, which are composed of lines and points, rather than raster maps, which are image files. (For more information about the difference between vector and raster maps, see Chapter 23.) All of these programs have limited functionality—none can display aerial photos or 3-D images. While you can manage waypoints and routes with them, their primary advantage is that they can transfer detailed maps to your GPS.

Despite their commonalties, there are some differences in the programs' level of detail in terms of contour intervals. Garmin's MapSource United States Topo maps appear to be based on 1:100K data, which means that the contour lines appear about 130-140 feet apart. The other programs in this section display contour intervals of 50 feet.

Chapter 17 Garmin MapSource
United States Topo

MapSource® is a family of Garmin® products that work with selected Garmin units. If you want to display MapSource maps, you must have a compatible Garmin unit.

MapSource refers to the underlying program, and United States Topo is a map package designed to work with it. It can display 1:100,000-scale topographic maps for the entire U.S. US Topo 24K (see the box on page 251) covers national parks at a 1:24,000 scale.

MapSource also has products designed for automotive and marine navigation. You can access multiple MapSource map packages from the same MapSource screen, and your GPS can switch from one to another where coverage overlaps. You cannot, however, layer them on top of each other to view them as transparent layers.

For the sake of space, I'll usually refer to this software as US Topo.

Basic Information

COST

• $116.65 for United States Topo

• $116.65 for US Topo 24K, National Parks (East or West)

• No demonstration version is available, but you can see an image just as it will appear on your GPS by going to **www.garmin.com/cartography** and selecting the appropriate product in the **MapSource Map Viewer**.

SYSTEM REQUIREMENTS

• Microsoft Windows 95, 98, 2000, NT 4.0, ME, or XP

• Pentium processor

• 16 MB of RAM (minimum)

• 20 MB of hard disk space (compact installation)

• CD-ROM drive

• 256-color display adapter and monitor (24-bit color recommended)

• Mouse or other pointing device

GPS COMPATIBILITY
- cf Que 1620

- eMap

- eTrex Legend, LegendC, Vista, and VistaC

- GPS 12MAP, 18 Automotive Bundles, III Plus, and V

- GPSMAP 162, 168 Sounder, 172C, 176, 178C Sounder, 196, 276C, 295, 296, 3006C, 3010C, 60C, 60CS, 76, 76C, 76CS, 76S, 96, and 96C

- IQue 3200 and 3600

- NavTalk and NavTalk GSM

- Quest

- Rino 120 and 130

TESTED VERSION
- 6.3

CONTACT INFORMATION
Garmin International, Inc.
1200 East 151st Street
Olathe, KS 66062
www.garmin.com
www.garmin.com/support (technical support)

- Telephone support is available Monday through Friday from 8:00 a.m. to 5:00 p.m. CST at 1.800.800.1020

AVAILABLE OPTIONS
- A Canadian version based on 1:50,000- and 1:250,000-scale data is available.

- MapSource software packages are available for urban navigation (City Select and MetroGuide, including international versions), marine and boating use (Blue Chart, Minnesota LakeMaster, and U.S. Recreational Lakes with Fishing Hot Spots), and WorldMap.

US Topo 24K
United States Topo is designed to display on a GPS screen at a 1:100,000 scale. Garmin's US Topo 24K covers some U.S. National Parks at a 1:24,000 scale, and is available in Eastern, Central, and Western U.S. packages.

• The Yahoo Map Authors group, at **groups.yahoo.com/group/map_authors**, lists MapSource as a product discussed on its message board. This group tends to focus on creating their own maps for use in MapSource, using programs that will be discussed in Chapter 25.

• More basic questions might be better addressed by a Yahoo Garmin users group, such as one of those mentioned in Chapter 2.

Advantages

• Well-designed route tools allow you to click on existing waypoints to form a route.

• You can set the software to automatically turn off your GPS unit following transfer.

• You can e-mail a MapSource file to other MapSource users, though they must have the same or a later version of MapSource.

• Covers all 50 states.

• The Zoom tool offers a convenient way to navigate maps.

• When you place a waypoint, you are automatically taken to the name field—no extra steps are required.

Disadvantages

• Contours are based on 1:100K data, resulting in contour intervals, of 130 to 140 feet or more.

• You cannot draw tracks or alter the way tracks are displayed on the map.

• The only way to change existing waypoints to a different symbol is to do so one at a time.

Tutorial/Manual

MapSource comes with a user's manual, and the program has a good help file.

US Topo also comes with a tutorial, though it's a little hard to find. Select **File**, then **Open**, and then select **Import MPS File**. Look in the **Garmin** folder on your hard disk drive and select **MapSource tour.mps**. The file contains 13 waypoints and one route. You'll need to use the U.S. East disk to view the maps associated with the tutorial.

Installation

> **TIP:** Want to avoid having to load the CD each time you run MapSource? Here's a simple way to store the software's maps on your hard disk:
>
> 1. Before you install the software, create a folder on your hard disk and copy the CDs, including the setup CD, to that folder. I created a folder named Garmin, which is what the setup CD would have done anyway.
>
> 2. Now insert the first disk into your computer's CD-ROM drive. If it goes into setup mode, select **Cancel** and quit the setup.
>
> 3. **Use My Computer** or **Windows Explorer** to located the CD-ROM drive. Right-click it, then select **Open** or **Explore**.
>
> 4. Now you're going to copy the contents of the disk into the Garmin folder you created. Select **Edit**, then **Select all**. Right-click on one of the selected items and select **Copy**.
>
> 5. Find the Garmin folder, right-click on it, and select **Paste**.
>
> 6. Repeat Steps 3 through 5 for any additional disks in the set.
>
> 7. Finally, shut down all other Windows programs, open the Garmin folder, and run the setup.exe file from your hard disk. That's all there is to it. No more messing with CDs!

The manual refers to three types of installations: non-autorouting, autorouting, and the Setup CD, which is the type done with US Topo. Autorouting is for programs for automotive use, such as City Select.

The setup CD will instruct you to exit all Windows programs; you must then scroll to the bottom of the license agreement to select the **Yes** button.

Next comes a potentially difficult area for those who own GPS receivers with a USB interface. You'll see a message reading, "Your Garmin GPS may require a software update to work correctly... Would you like to check your GPS now?" If you select **Yes**, a dialog box will pop up with a **Port** list, but it shows only COM1 through COM4, with no USB port. If your GPS isn't detected, don't worry; just skip this part.

A **Typical** installation will be the only choice given on the next screen. After that, the program will install and you will be ready to start MapSource. I suggest going to **www.garmin.com/cartography** and selecting **Software Updates** to download and install the latest MapSource update. Once the update is installed, MapSource should recognize GPS units with USB connections without any trouble.

Configuration

Select **View** and point to **Show Toolbars**. Select **Show All Toolbars**. You can drag a toolbar to a new location by grabbing an open area on it.

If you have a compatible Garmin GPS receiver and have installed the latest US Topo update, the program should automatically recognize it, so setting up your GPS is not a problem. For more information, see "GPS Interface" later in this chapter.

To begin configuring other aspects of US Topo, select **Edit**, then **Preferences**. The **Preferences** dialog box will open, displaying the following tabs:

- **Display**. The **Map Detail** slider adjusts the amount of detail shown on the map on the computer screen. It does not affect how much data is sent to your GPS. **Services** and **Light Sectors** settings do not affect the map display in US Topo, nor do **Spot Soundings** or **Terrain Shading**. Select **Change Map Font** to change the fonts for all text on the map.

- **Units**. This tab is shown in Figure 17A. Most choices are straightforward, though **Heading** offers some choices you may not see in other programs. The **Automatic** setting will calculate the magnetic variation for the area you are viewing, while **User** allows you to enter the magnetic variation yourself. **Cardinal Direction** uses letters such as N, SE, and so on. **Depth** and **Temperature** are of use only to nautical navigators.

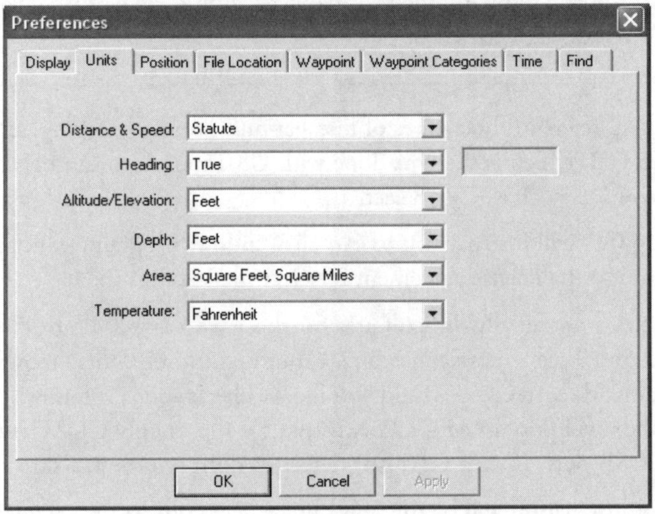

Figure 17A

- **Position.** Here you can set the **Grid** and **Datum**.

- **File Location.** This allows you to set a default location for MapSource files, importing PCX5 data and exporting .txt and .dxf files. We'll cover these formats in Working With Other Programs later in this chapter.

- **Waypoint.** This tab is shown in Figure 17B. Here you can limit the number of characters in waypoints created by the program. I suggest you set this to the limit your GPS receiver can handle. You can also create your own default choices for a waypoint **Name Prefix**, **Symbol**, and what to **Display**. These choices apply only to waypoints created in US Topo.

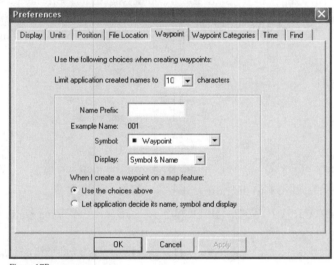

Figure 17B

- **Waypoints Categories.** This tab allows you to create searchable categories for waypoints. These categories can be searched from the **Waypoints** data tab on the left side of your screen.

- **Time.** Here you can choose to use the local time zone set on your computer or **Use an offset from** UTC. You remember UTC, don't you? We covered it way back in Chapter 4.

- **Find.** This tab allows you to customize Find searches.

Getting Started

Insert a MapSource disk into your CD-ROM drive and start the program. When you restart MapSource it will return to the location you last viewed, if you are using the same disk as before.

On the left side of the screen are a group of data tabs, labeled **Maps**, **Tracks**, **Routes**, **Waypoints**, and **GPS**. We'll come back to these shortly, but I want to call your attention to the **Select a Product** drop-down menu above the data tabs (see Figure 17C). This box contains a list of all MapSource products that you own. For example, the US Topo set shows up as four items in the list (see Figure 17D). You must select a new product when you move to a different region or to a different MapSource software product. Notice the item that says My Maps. This will appear only if you're using some of the programs discussed in Chapter 25—but yes, you can make your own maps for a Garmin GPS.

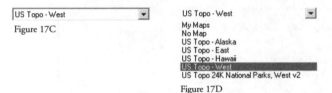

Figure 17C

Figure 17D

MapSource offers several ways to move around the map screen:

- Use the **Hand** tool to drag the map to a new location.

- Use the PAGE UP and PAGE DOWN keys to move the screen a full screen length up or down.

- Use the arrow keys to move the screen any direction. Use CTRL + an arrow key to move a full screen width or length.

- Use the scroll bars at the right and bottom of the map screen.

- Use your mouse scroll wheel to move the map screen up and down.

To zoom the map:

- Use the **Zoom** tool to drag a rectangle around an area and zoom in on it. When the **Zoom** tool is enabled, you can zoom in on a point on the map by left-clicking it; zoom out by right-clicking. You can also activate the **Zoom** tool by pressing the Z key.

- Use the **Select a Map Scale** box (see Figure 17E). The selected scale is shown in the lower right portion of the map screen.

Figure 17E

- Use **Zoom In** and **Zoom Out** to change the map scale one step at a time, along the scale found in the **Select a Map Scale** box.

- Use the plus sign (+) key to zoom in and the minus sign (-) key to zoom out.

Finally, right-clicking a map feature brings up a menu that presents additional options (see Figure 17F). If you select multiple features in the map area you chose, you'll see a menu allowing you to choose between them, as shown in Figure 17G.

Figure 17F

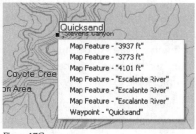

Figure 17G

File Structure

Let's take another look at the data tabs on the left side of the screen (see Figure 17H).

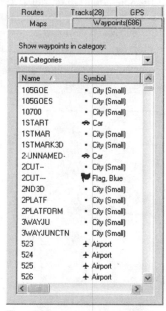

Figure 17H

The **GPS** tab is for real-time tracking, which we'll discuss in the Moving Map section of this chapter.

Map sets, waypoints, routes, and tracks are stored by MapSource as .gdb files. Each tab shows the number of waypoints, tracks, and so on, in the currently loaded file (see Figure 17H). The default location for .gdb files is C:\Garmin.

Selecting Maps to Transfer to Your GPS

Select the **Map** tool, then either drag a rectangle to define the area you want to transfer or simply click on a location. Either way, you'll see an area on the map screen turn pink, defining the area to be transferred. If you move your pointer to the edge of this area, you'll see the border delineated by a yellow rectangle (see Figure 17I). Garmin predetermines the extent of a rectangle around a given point.

When you click on a map, it is placed on the **Maps** tab. You can select multiple maps to transfer to your GPS, even maps from multiple products. You cannot overlay maps on your GPS, however: Selecting San Francisco maps from US Topo and MapSource City Select North America, for example, will not allow you to see the features from both on your GPS at the same time.

MapSource automatically generates a default map set name based upon the (typically 1:100,000) USGS quadrangle name(s) for the selected map or maps. You can give the map set a custom name by selecting **Map Set Name** at the bottom of the **Maps** tab to open the dialog box shown in Figure 17J. Clear the box labeled **Autoname the map set**, enter the name of your choice in the **Map Set Name** box, and click **OK**.

To delete a map from the **Maps** tab, right-click it and then select **Delete Map**.

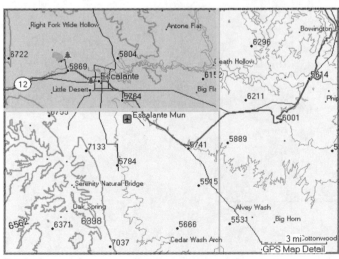

Figure 17I

Figure 17J

Click **Save** to save map sets, waypoints, routes, and tracks to a Garmin GPS Database File (.gdb for short). Open existing files using **Open**, then select **Open GDB File**. To create a new, blank .gdb file, click **New**.

Let's take a quick tour of the data tabs. First, grab the splitter bar that separates the map screen from the data tabs and drag it to the right, so you can see all of the columns associated with a data tab. You can sort on any column by clicking the column header, or change the order in which the columns appear by dragging a column header to a new location. Figure 17K shows some of the available columns on the Waypoint tab.

See the Tip titled Cut, Copy, and Paste in the following section for information on how to move data between files.

Figure 17K

Waypoints and Waypoint Management

To create waypoints, select the **Waypoint** tool and click anywhere on the map, which will also open the **Waypoint Properties** dialog box (see Figure 17L). If the full set of options is not shown on your screen, click **More Details**. Let's look at a few of the options:

• You can choose from a wide array of symbols including everything from Alien Contact to Skull and Crossbones. Of course, there are more standard choices, too, including Trailhead and Boat Ramp.

• If you know the elevation, you can uncheck **Unknown** and enter the **Altitude**.

• Some Garmin GPS units can signal a **Proximity** alarm when you get within a certain distance of a given waypoint.

• You can add a **Link** to a digital photo on your computer, or to a Web site.

• Establishing waypoint **Categories** is discussed in the Configuration section of this chapter. You can sort waypoints by categories from the **Waypoints** tab.

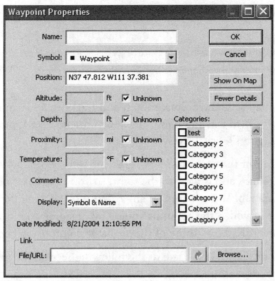

Figure 17L

Right-click a waypoint to bring up the menu shown in Figure 17M.

Figure 17M

> **TIP: CUT, COPY, AND PASTE** It's not often you'll see these commands used in mapping programs, but they are present throughout MapSource products, where **Cut**, **Copy** and **Paste** work just like they do in any Windows-compatible software. Let's say you have several hundred waypoints in one .gdb file, and you want to work only with those starting with a certain prefix. Select them, click **Copy**, then **New**, to open a blank .gdb file. Select the **Waypoints** Tab and click **Paste**. For those of you who will move on to more advanced mapping pursuits, this is a good way to extract your data for movement to a text editor or spreadsheet.

Routes

MapSource makes it exceptionally easy to create routes from existing waypoints. Just select the **Route** tool, then click a waypoint to begin a route. Continue clicking in order, linking waypoints to form the route. When you're finished, press ESC to complete the route. The route will be automatically named using the beginning and ending waypoints.

You can also create routes by clicking on any location on the map. MapSource creates a waypoint each time you click and names waypoints on the basis of map features, spot elevations, and so on.

You can mix these methods, creating waypoints as you go and also clicking on pre-existing ones. You can even go back and change waypoint names.

Right-click a route leg (the line connecting two waypoints) or a route on the **Route Tab**, and select **Route Properties** to open the dialog box shown in Figure 17N. Let's take a look at some of the options found here, on the **Via Points** tab:

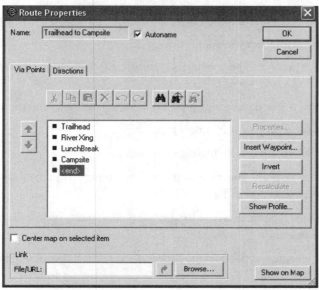

Figure 17N

- To give the route a different name, clear the check box labeled **Autoname.**

- To change the order of waypoints in the route, highlight the waypoint you wish to move and click the **Move Up** or **Move Down** buttons.

- You can also **Invert** (reverse) a route.

- The **Find** features allow you to find and insert locations into the route.

> **NOTE: NO AUTOROUTING** The **Recalculate** button on the **Route Properties** dialog box is useful only for MapSource programs such as City Select that support automatic routing along roads. Autorouting is not available in US Topo, but it is found in US Topo 24K.

To insert a waypoint into a route:

1. Use the **Selection** tool and click the route, which will turn yellow when selected.

2. Click on the leg where you wish to insert the waypoint. The pointer now has a plus sign (+) next to it. If you decide you want to cancel the operation at this point, press the ESC key.

3. Drag the leg to either an existing waypoint or a point on the map and click there.

To extend a route:

1. Use the **Selection** tool to highlight the route.

2. Click the first or last waypoint in the route.

3. Move the pointer to an existing waypoint, or to any point on the map, and click there.

4. Repeat Step 3 as desired and press the ESC key to finish the route.

To move a route waypoint to a new location:

1. Use the **Selection** tool to highlight the route.

2. Click the waypoint you wish to move. The pointer will now show an arrow and waypoint marker, as in Figure 17O.

3. Move the waypoint to a new location and click there, or just drag it and release the mouse button.

To remove a route waypoint, right-click it, then select **Remove Waypoint from Route**.

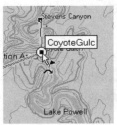

Figure 17O

> **TIP:** You can perform all of the above route editing (inserting waypoints, extending a route, and so on) from the **Route Properties** dialog.

Using the **Selection** or **Route** tool, right-click a route to bring up the menu shown in Figure 17P. Among the choices available is **Show Selected Route on Map**. This is useful when you can see only a portion of the route. Click here to zoom and see the entire route. You can also choose **Delete Route** from here to delete the entire route.

Insert Route Section
Duplicate Route
Invert Route
Recalculate Route
New Waypoint...
Begin Route
Begin Measurement
Find Nearest Places...
Cut
Copy
Paste
Delete Route
Show Selected Route On Map
Route Properties...

Figure 17P

Tracks

You can transfer tracks between your GPS unit and MapSource. Tracks downloaded from your GPS are displayed as a series of connected dots. You cannot draw tracks on the map freehand, nor can you alter the display of tracks on the map screen. This limits your abilities to customize the display on your GPS. If you know of trails that are not shown on MapSource, you can use a program such as USAPhotoMaps to create a track, move it to your GPS, and display it on the map. This is also what the programs in Chapters 24 and 25 are designed to do—allow you to customize your maps.

This rudimentary track display and lack of ability to draw tracks is one reason why MapSource is not the best program for printing a map for use in the field. Many of the programs covered in previous sections of this book are much better suited for this task.

GPS Interface

To transfer data to your GPS, choose **Transfer**, then **Send To Device**. This will open the dialog box shown in Figure 17Q. Your GPS device will not be shown, nor will you see any options for transfer, unless your GPS unit is connected and turned on. Should you forget to connect and turn on your GPS before you open the **Send To Device** dialog box, choose **Find Device** once you have done so.

Figure 17Q

Once you're connected and powered up, you'll see options to transfer any data shown on the data tabs in the currently opened .gdb file. For example, if the only data in the .gdb file is waypoints, that will be the only item shown as available for transfer in the **Send To Device** dialog box. Note also that everything on a data tab will be transferred. You cannot highlight individual items for transfer.

Check the desired boxes under **What To Send** and then select **Send**, and the dialog box shown in Figure 17R will open. Note the check box labeled **Turn off GPS after each transfer**. This is a nice feature; I can't tell you how many times I've come home after an outing, downloaded my track, and immediately started saving it, modifying it, or playing it back and forgotten to turn off my GPS until hours later.

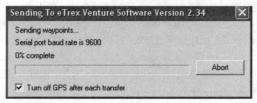

Figure 17R

TIP: MapSource erases all existing maps on your GPS when you transfer new ones, so you'll need to create a .gdb file containing all the maps you want on your GPS.

To transfer data from your GPS to MapSource, choose **Transfer**, then **Receive From Device**. The remainder of the process works like it does for sending data. Before transferring data, consider whether you want it to go into an existing .gdb file or a new one.

Printing

MapSource print options limit you to printing only the current map view. To check this feature out, select **File**, then **Print Preview**. Click **Zoom In** once to get a view approximating the size the image will be when it comes off your printer. Click **Close** to close the print preview window. Clicking the **X** in the upper right corner will close the MapSource program, not just the print preview window.

Many of the programs covered in previous sections of this book are much better suited for printing. You should always go into the field with a compass and a good paper map. Never rely entirely on your GPS.

Moving Map

MapSource US Topo products support real-time tracking of your location. First, check your data transfer format. If you have a more recent receiver, choose the **Garmin** option. If this is not available, choose **NMEA**.

Select Device...

To open the dialog shown in Figure 17S, click the **GPS** tab and choose **Select Device**. Enter the proper settings and click **OK**.

Figure 17S

Start Tracking

Figure 17T

Now choose **Start Tracking**. The **GPS** tab should appear (see Figure 17T). Note the options **Keep vehicle visible on map** and **Record track**. To stop recording, uncheck **Record track**. The track will be saved automatically and the file name displayed in the **Tracks** tab.

Filter...

Click **Filter** to display the **Track Filter** dialog shown in Figure 17U. Selecting **None** records a new track point every second. **Time** and **Distance** are self-explanatory. **Automatic** adds points as necessary to fit the actual path of travel; you can fine-tune this setting to capture **Fewer points** or **More points**.

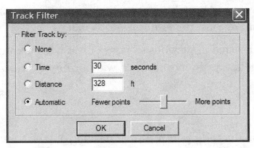

Figure 17U

3-D

MapSource does not support three-dimensional display. For a list of programs that do, see Chapter 21.

Working With Other Programs

MapSource can import .mps files, a format used before MapSource Version 6.0 that has been replaced by the .gdb format. To import a .mps file, click **Open**, then select **Import MPS File**.

Garmin also used to use a DOS-based program called PCX5. File types used in PCX5 software include .wpt (waypoints), .rte (routes), .trk (tracks), and .grm, which is a map format. You can import these file types by choosing **File**, then **Import**.

To export MapSource data as .mps files, select **File**, then **Save As**. You can export data as .txt (tab-delimited text, useful for exporting to text editors and spreadsheets) and .dxf files (an AutoCAD vector format) by choosing **File**, then **Export**.

> **TIP:** The **File Location** tab on the **Preferences** dialog box allows you to set a default location for MapSource files, importing PCX5 data and exporting .txt and .dxf files.

More Tips

• Want to make sure your computer's clock is as accurate as the one on your GPS, which is updated by the atomic clocks on satellites? Connect your GPS, turn it on, select **Utilities**, and then choose **Set PC Clock**.

Chapter 18 Magellan MapSend Topo for the U.S.

Like the other programs in this section, Magellan® MapSend is specific to one company's products. It too has its advantages and disadvantages but, like the others, it's the only game in town!

Basic Information

COST
• $149.99

• No demonstration version is available, but you can see an image just as it will appear on your GPS by going to **www.magellangps.com/en/products/software.asp**. Scroll to **MapSend Topo in the US** and select **Preview**.

SYSTEM REQUIREMENTS
• Microsoft Windows 95, 98, or NT 4.0 or higher

• Pentium 100 MHz or higher processor

• 32 MB of RAM

• 80 MB of free hard disk space

• VGA video card

• Serial COM port

• 8X or faster CD-ROM drive

• Mouse

• Magellan PC cable

GPS COMPATIBILITY
• Magellan Meridian® series, SporTrak® Color, SporTrak Pro, SporTrak Pro Marine, SporTrak Map, SporTrak Topo, MAP 330, or MAP 330M

TESTED VERSION
• 4.20d

CONTACT INFORMATION
Magellan
960 Overland Court
San Dimas, CA 91773
800.669.4477
800.707.9971 (support)
www.magellangps.com

AVAILABLE OPTIONS

• MapSend Topo for the US is one of a family of Magellan MapSend products that includes autorouting-capable street maps, marine, and topographic applications for locations including Canada, Europe, and South Africa. A worldwide base map is also available. For more information, go to **https://www.magellangps.com/en/products/software.asp**.

INTERNET RESOURCES

• MapSend has its own Yahoo discussion group, at **groups.yahoo.com/group/Mapsend**.

Advantages

• You can install maps onto your hard disk.

• You can display contour intervals every 50 feet.

• The Zoom In tool makes for easy navigation.

• MapSend offers the best-quality printed map of any program in its class. Unfortunately, UTM display is not an option.

Disadvantages

• You cannot split tracks.

• You cannot display UTM coordinates on your screen or on the printed map, nor can you enter waypoints in UTM format.

Tutorial/Manual

MapSend has an excellent help file. Two additional features you should be aware of:

• Context-sensitive cursor tips show up on the status bar at the bottom of the screen.

• For context-sensitive help, click **What's this**, then click any object on the screen.

Installation

Installation is straightforward. There are two installation options:

1. **Full.** With this installation, you'll never have to load the CD again, as all maps are written to the hard disk. This will make the program run a little faster. The only downside is that it takes 700 MB of hard disk space. In an age of 100+ GB hard disks, this may not be an issue.

2. **Typical.** Though this compact installation requires only 80 MB of hard disk space, it comes with two downsides. You will need to load the CD each time you run the program and, because the software is accessing maps from the CD, it will run a bit more slowly than it would if you were running the full installation.

Configuration

Choose **Options** to display the menu shown in Figure 18A. Most items are fairly self-explanatory, but a few warrant further discussion:

• **Window Size Locked.** When this is unchecked, you can drag the separator bars to change the size of the windows on the right side of the screen.

• **Points of Interest.** Open the **POI Display Properties** window to select which POIs are displayed on the map.

• **Show Quick Info.** This switches cursor tips, shown on the status bar at the bottom of the screen, on or off.

• **Show Map.** This shows or hides some map details.

• **Color Track by Speed.** This changes the display color of tracks based on speed.

Figure 18A

Getting Started

You can pan or move about the map with any of the following methods:

- Select **Pan** and drag the map to a new location.

- Click anywhere on the **Overview Map** window, in the upper left portion of the screen, to move in the main **Map Window**. If it is not visible, choose **View**, then **Overview Map**.

- Click within the map window, then use the arrow keys.

- Most keyboards place several keys together that are typically used for page navigation. MapSend uses these in an interesting way: Use the PAGE UP key to move NE, the PAGE DOWN key to move SE, the END key to move SW, and the HOME key to move NW.

You can also zoom in on the map in multiple ways:

- Click **Zoom In**, then drag a rectangle to zoom and pan at the same time. Or simply click the map to zoom in at that location. **Zoom Out** is used the same way.

- Use the plus sign (+) and minus sign (-) keys. Your numeric keypad keys will zoom in smaller increments than the other plus (+) and minus (-) keyboard keys. On your keyboard, you don't have to press SHIFT; equal (=) works the same as plus (+).

- Click the arrow in the **Set Scale** box (see Figure 18B) and then choose **Zoom to**, opening the **Set Scale** dialog shown in Figure 18C. Enter the desired scale and click **OK**.

Figure 18B   Figure 18C

TIP: For zooming out on a large scale, try one of the following:

- Select **Tools**, then **USA** or **World Map**.

- Select the **Map Scale** box, which defaults to **Set Scale**, for a variety of options.

- Click the arrow beside **Go To** for additional options.

File Structure

Magellan saves routes and waypoints as .wpt files and tracks as .trk files. It saves map regions as .rgn files and GPS logs as .gps files. The default directory for this data is C:\Program Files\Magellan\MapSend Topo US\DOCS.

To save a file, select **File**, then **Save Waypoints**, **Save Track**, or **Save GPS Log**.

Waypoints and Waypoint Management

To create a waypoint on the map, press the F5 key or click **Place Waypoints**. This opens the **Routes and Waypoints** dialog shown in Figure 18D. In the **Next** area of this dialog, select the desired symbol; underneath the symbols type the **Name of Waypoint to be placed next**. Now click on the map to place the waypoint.

Figure 18D

If you click to place the waypoint first, you can go back and change the name using one of two methods:

1. Select the name in the **Table of Waypoints** (located in the lower half of the **Routes and Waypoints** dialog box).

2. Select a waypoint in the **Table of Waypoints**. Next, in the **Waypoint Form** (located in the upper right portion of the **Routes and Waypoints** dialog box), change the name in the **Name of the currently selected waypoint field**.

You cannot change a symbol by clicking on it, since symbols are in the **Next** area. Instead, in the **Waypoint Form,** click on the drop-down **Icon of the currently selected waypoint** box.

> **TIP:** Choose **Options**, then **Show Waypoint Labels** to show or hide waypoint labels on the map.

Notice that in the **Table of Waypoints,** a check box is found next to each waypoint. Right-click a waypoint to display the menu shown in Figure 18E, which includes the following options:

• **View**. This centers the map on the waypoint.

• **New Waypoint**. This creates a waypoint at 0° latitude and 0° longitude.

• **Delete**. This deletes the selected waypoint.

• **Delete Unmarked**. This deletes any waypoints not checked.

• **Delete Unused**. This deletes any waypoints not used in routes.

Figure 18E

> ## Using Columns in the Table of Waypoints
> You can customize and use the columns in the **Table of Waypoints** in a number of ways:
>
> • Select a column header to sort waypoints based on that column. This can come in handy if you want to sort based on name.
>
> • Change the order of columns by dragging a column header.
>
> • Select the right side of any column header to resize it to fit the contents of the column.
>
> • You can also resize columns by dragging the right border of the column header.

Routes

To create a route, click on **Build Route**. The **Routes and Waypoints** dialog will open and a name will automatically be assigned to the route. If you want to change the route name, click it, pause, and then click again. Regardless, the route name in your GPS will be based on the starting and ending waypoints.

Once you select **Build Route**, you can start clicking on waypoints in the desired order to form the route. Notice that a thick gray line connects the waypoints in the route. When you're finished, right-click the route and the gray line will become thin. Note that you cannot click on an area without a waypoint to create a route waypoint.

To edit a route, in the **Tree of Routes** (see Figure 18F), select the route you wish to edit. Right-click it, then choose **Build Route**. The line connecting the waypoints will thicken. You can now add waypoints to the route in one of two ways:

1. Click waypoints on the map to add them to the end of the route.

2. Drag a waypoint from the **Waypoint Table** or **Tree of Routes** to any location in the Tree of Routes. As you drag over the list, waypoints in the route will be highlighted. The waypoint you are moving will be placed immediately before the highlighted waypoint. To place a waypoint at the end of a route, drag it onto the route name.

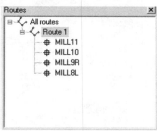

Figure 18F

To stop editing, do one of the following:

• Click **Build Route**.

• Right-click the map.

• Select **Waypoints**, then **Edit Route/Waypoint**.

Tracks

You cannot draw tracks on the screen, but you can download them from your GPS and edit them.

> **TIP:** A downloaded track is temporarily named DOWNLOADED. If you want to retain tracks after shutting down **MapSend**, you must save them. To do so, select **Tracks**, then **Save to File**; or select **File**, then **Save Track**. Either way, the **Save Tracks** dialog shown in Figure 18G will appear. Select **Save** and name the file.

Figure 18G

Choose **Tracks**, then **Control Center** to open the dialog shown in Figure 18H. Most work with tracks can be done from here.

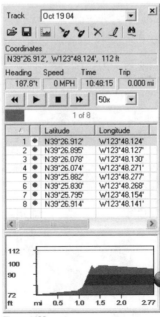

Figure 18H

From the **Control Center**, choose **Load from File** to open and display a saved track. Select the desired track and **Open** it.

Choose **Clear** to remove a track from the current set. This does not delete saved tracks from your hard disk.

To edit a track, from the **Control Center** click **Edit**. This causes track points to be displayed. You can select a point or points for editing by dragging a rectangle around them. If you wish to select multiple points that are not adjacent to each other, press and hold the SHIFT key while selecting. Once you've selected points, you can:

• Move the cursor over the selected points until it changes to the symbol shown in Figure 18J, then drag the points to a new location.

Figure 18J

• Press DELETE to delete them.

When you're finished editing, click **Edit** again.

Click **Save to File** to save the modified track.

The other buttons near the top of the **Control Center** function as follows:

• **Profile** displays an elevation profile and associated data.

• **Show** zooms the map to display the entire selected track.

• **Upload to GPS** and **Download from GPS** allow you to transfer tracks. Unfortunately, the arrow points up for downloading and down for uploading (just pay attention to the direction of the arrow in relation to the GPS and you'll be fine).

GPS Interface

To transfer waypoints, routes, or tracks to or from your GPS, click the arrow on the right side of **Upload Regions**, displaying the menu shown in Figure 18K. You can also select the **Waypoints** and **Tracks** menus for transfer options.

```
Download Waypoints/Routes
Upload Waypoints/Routes
Download Track
Upload Track...
Upload Regions...        Ctrl+U
```

Figure 18K

WARNING!

There is a risk of data loss when you transfer data to or from your GPS. When you transfer data to your GPS, all existing data on it (including previously transferred maps) will be erased. When you transfer data from your GPS to MapSend, any data in the program that has not been saved will be deleted.

Transferring Maps to Your GPS

First you need to save the region you wish to transfer:

1. Click **Draw New Region** or select **Regions**, then **New**. You can press the ESC key to cancel. The estimated size of the region is shown on the status bar. Remember that this is only an estimate and the file that is transferred may actually be larger.

2. Right-click anywhere on the map, click **Cut Region**, or select **Regions** then **Cut Region**.

3. Name the map set and click **OK**. The name will appear in the **Saved Regions** list to the right of the screen.

Next, mark the regions(s) to be transferred by placing a check box next to them in the **Saved Regions** list (see Figure 18L). Notice the boxes with the letters **T** and **P** by the region names. **T** stands for topographic, while **P** represents points of interest (POI). You can click these letters to include or not include that data in the transfer.

You're now ready to send the maps to your GPS.

View	Select	Mark	Remove
	Name	Size	Date
☑**T**	**P** Canyonlands NP	162 Kb	10/19
☑**T**	**P** San Rafael Swell	204 Kb	10/19

| Upload limit | 2 rgns | Selected: | 0 | 0 Kb |
| | | Marked: | 2 | 386 Kb |

Figure 18L

Click **Upload Regions** (or select **Regions**, then **Upload to GPS**) to open the **Upload Wizard** dialog box shown in Figure 18M. If your GPS is a Meridian, Magellan recommends uploading to an SD card, since it is much quicker than transfer over a serial cable. The help file says that an 8 MB map can take up to 20 minutes to upload, while a larger map can take a couple of hours. Note the **Store on Hard Drive** option for storing maps to be transferred at a later date.

> **TIP:** Right-click a region in the **Saved Regions** list to display the menu shown in Figure 18N, which includes the following options:
>
> • **View**. This centers the region in the map window.
>
> • **Remove**. This removes the region from the **Saved Regions** list, but not from your hard disk.
>
> • **Delete file(s)**. This command deletes the stored region from your hard disk.
>
> • **Edit Region**. This allows you to redefine a region's boundaries.

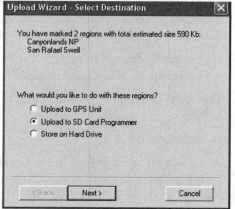

Figure 18M

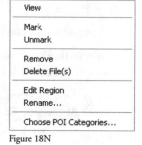

Figure 18N

Printing

To set options for printing, click **Print Preview** (or select **File**, then **Print Preview**). From the preview window, select **Options** to open the **Print Options** dialog box shown in Figure 18O. Here you can make changes to what is seen on the screen, which is what will be printed. The slider bar at the top of the screen affects the scale, but not the level of detail shown on the map. It gives you some fine control over the area to be printed. Clicking **Zoom In** once approximates the size of a printed page. Once you are satisfied with the displayed image, click **Print**.

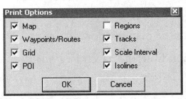

Figure 18O

Moving Map

Select **GPS log**, then **Start** to begin tracking your position in real time. Also found on the **GPS log** menu are the options below, shown in Figure 18P:

• **Show**. This displays the current GPS log file (track) on the map.

• **Automatic Pan**. Select this to constantly display your position as it is updated by your GPS. You will not be able to manually pan while this is enabled.

• **Go to Last Position**. This displays the location of your last GPS fix. You can only do this if **Automatic Pan** is disabled.

• **Clear**. This deletes the current GPS log file.

• **Save to File**. Use this to save log files for later playback in the **Control Center**. Click **Load from File** to load files for playback.

Figure 18P

3-D

MapSend, like the other programs in this section, offers no 3-D display. As this book was going to press, Magellan released a new software package, MapSend Topo 3D USA, which can display 3-D images on your computer, but not on your GPS.

Working With Other Programs

You can import waypoints, routes, and tracks from an Excel (.xls) file and export them as .xls or ASCII .txt files. Select **Waypoints** (for waypoints and routes) or **Tracks** and then select **Import** or **Export**. For more information on importing data, search for **Data Format Requirements for Import Files** in the help files.

More Tips

- Selecting **View**, then **Full Screen** will eliminate the toolbar and allow you to close any windows on the right side of the screen.

- You can display elevation profiles for roads, routes, tracks, and GPS logs. From the help file's **Contents** tab select **Vertical Profiles** for more information.

- Select **View**, then **Legend** to see a key to MapSend's symbols.

- For keyboard shortcuts, in **Help**, choose the **Index** tab and enter **Shortcut Keys**.

- Select **Search** to search by address, name, or coordinates.

> Updates to this book will be posted at www.MakeYourOwnMaps.com. Bookmark and visit often to see what's new in the world of digital mapping.

Chapter 19 Lowrance MapCreate USA Topo

MapCreate™ USA Topo is one of a series of Lowrance® MapCreate products. The version of MapCreate that I tested is designed solely for use with MMC/SD cards.

There is a long history of technology exchange between Lowrance, Brunton, and Eagle, all of which make GPS receivers. They each sell products branded as MapCreate, and much of the information in this chapter may apply to the Brunton and Eagle versions of this product.

Basic Information

COST
• $99.95

SYSTEM REQUIREMENTS
• Microsoft Windows 98 or later

• Pentium 133 MHz or faster

• 64 MB of RAM (128 MB recommended)

• 200 MB of free hard disk space

• High-color (16-bit) display

• CD-ROM drive

GPS COMPATIBILITY
• Compatible with Lowrance models LCX-104C, LCX-19C, LCX-18C, LCX-16, LCX-15, LMS-320, LMS-320DF, LMS-240, GlobalMap® 7000C, GlobalMap® 6000C, GlobalMap® 5000C, GlobalMap® 4000M, GlobalMap® 3200, GlobalMap® 3000MT, GlobalMap® 2400, and iFINDER®

TESTED VERSION
• 6.3

CONTACT INFORMATION
Lowrance
12000 East Skelly Drive
Tulsa, Oklahoma 74128
1.800.324.1356
www.lowrance.com

• A Canadian Topo version is available, as are U.S. and Canadian products designed for marine and automotive use.

INTERNET RESOURCES

• The Yahoo Map Authors group, at **groups.yahoo.com/group/map_authors**, lists MapCreate as a product discussed on its message board.

• You might also want to try the Yahoo iFinder GPS group, at **groups.yahoo.com/group/ifinder_gps**.

Advantages

• You can click on existing waypoints to form a route.

• The software displays contour intervals every 50 feet.

• You can transfer irregularly shaped maps to your GPS.

• **Undo/Redo** buttons make it easy to correct mistakes.

• The **Zoom Area Tool** makes for easy navigation.

• **Cut, Copy,** and **Paste** commands are included.

Disadvantages

• You can't use SHIFT with **Cut, Copy,** or **Paste.**

• You are limited to five MMC/SD cards.

• You must load a CD into your computer to start the program, even if the maps reside on your hard disk.

• The program cannot display UTM coordinates.

• You cannot name routes. They are assigned generic names (e.g., Rte 001*).

• There are no programs available that allow you to move shapefiles into MapCreate beyond Version 4. Shapefiles can be converted to tracks for display, however. See Chapter 24 for more on this.

Tutorial/Manual

The help file opens in your Web browser. Each time you click **Help**, a new browser window will open—but it shouldn't take you long to learn not to do that!

The help file is relatively complete, even if the layout isn't the most user friendly. To search, select **Edit**, then **Find** in your browser.

Installation

- Load Disk 1 to begin the installation process. Note that it says you are installing "MapCreate USA Hunting with Topo." If this is a surprise, don't worry; you didn't buy the wrong software. MapCreate USA Topo comes with a hunting database.

- You will be asked to disable any antivirus software. Don't forget to enable it when you're finished!

- You will then be asked to insert the rest of the disks in order, with the copying of large-scale map files from each one taking several minutes.

- Finally, you will be asked to install the card reader software and restart your computer.

Configuration

Select **View**, then **Map Display Options** for settings on the following tabs:

- **Zoom**. Here you can select **Zoom Range Units**. Choose from **Miles**, **Nautical Miles**, **Kilometers**, or **Mercator Meters**. You can also control how far the map will zoom with one click.

- **Position Format**. Choose from the options shown in Figure 19A. Notice that UTM is not an option.

- **Display**. On this tab, you can select what **GPS Data** is shown on the master map. You can also select a **Default Symbol** for waypoints.

- **Map Borders**. We'll discuss this tab when we get to GPS Interface.

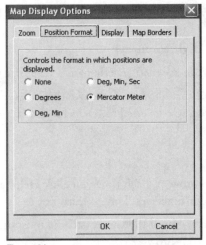

Figure 19A

Getting Started

Each time you start MapCreate, you'll have to insert one of the regional CDs, though the CD can be removed once the program is up and running.

MapCreate uses a series of windows for management of map data. Select **View** to open or close the **Map Category Options** window or the windows showing the **Waypoint**, **Route**, **Icon**, or **Trail Lists**. You can drag and resize windows, and you can select **Window**, then **Auto Arrange** to return to the default arrangement.

> ### Map Categories
> All **Map Category Options** with a plus sign (+) next to them can be expanded to view and select from subcategories. Only those categories that are checked can be transferred to your GPS.

Choose **View**, then point to **Toolbars** to display the menu shown in Figure 19B. Note that you can have only one **Create Map** toolbar showing at any one time.

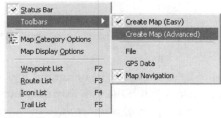

Figure 19B

You can move around the map using any of the following methods:

• Click **Center Map** and click anywhere on the map to recenter it at that location.

• Move your pointer to the edge of the map screen until an arrow appears, then click to move in that direction. Each click will move the map approximately one-third of the screen.

• Use one the four **Move** buttons (see Figure 19C) on the **Map Navigation** tool bar to move the map approximately one-third of a screen with each click.

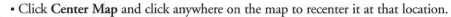

Figure 19C

• Click **Full Map** to show a map of the entire U.S.

You can zoom the map using any of the following methods:

- Use the **Zoom Area** tool to drag a box around an area to zoom in on.

- Click **Zoom In** or **Zoom Out**.

- Click **Z-In** or **Z-Out**, located at the lower left corner of the screen.

- Click the **Zoom Range** box at the lower right corner of the screen. The number represents the approximate width of the screen in miles. Click inside the box to scroll with your mouse wheel.

TIP: Click **Back** or **Forward** to view the map screen at other scales and locations you have viewed.

Finally, a **Pop-up Tool Tip Box** shows feature names when you move your pointer over them.

File Structure

MapCreate stores all waypoints, routes, and tracks in .usr files. All of these items go into a single file. By default, data is stored in the MapCreate data folder, located at C:\Program Files\LEI\MapCreate\Data.

 Map border files define the boundaries of maps to be transferred to your GPS. You can save these .lmp files to your hard disk for future use with **Save Map Border File**. This may come in handy if you are constructing a series of complex maps that you will use again.

Maps are transferred to your GPS as .lcm files.

Waypoints and Waypoint Management

Most users will find it easier to create and manage waypoints and routes using buttons found on the **GPS Data** toolbar. To display these buttons, select **View**, point to **Toolbars**, and choose **GPS Data**.

 Click **Create Waypoint**, then click anywhere on the map to place a waypoint. A numerical name, such as Wpt 001, will be assigned automatically. To modify the name, right-click it and then select **Edit Waypoint** to open the dialog box shown in Figure 19D. To modify the waypoint symbol, select **Change Symbol**, then double-click the symbol of your choice.

To display a list of waypoints, press F2, or select **View**, then select **Waypoint List**. Double-click any waypoint in the list to open the **Insert/Edit Waypoint** dialog box shown in Figure 19D. Click **Center Waypoint** to center the map at the location of the waypoint.

Figure 19D

> **TIP: CUT, COPY, AND PASTE** You can use **Cut**, **Copy** and **Paste** just like you would in any Windows-compatible software. Let's say you have several hundred waypoints in one .usr file, and you want to work only with those starting with a certain prefix. Select them, click **Copy**, then **New**, to open a blank .usr file, then click **Paste**. You can use these commands in the waypoint, route, or track lists. While you can use the CTRL key to highlight multiple items, you cannot use SHIFT.

To move a waypoint:

 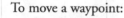

1. Click **Center Map** or **Zoom Area**.

2. Move the pointer over the waypoint and right-click it.

3. Select **Move Waypoint**.

4. Move the waypoint to the desired location and click there to place it.

To delete a waypoint:

1. Click **Center Map** or **Zoom Area**.

2. Move the pointer over the waypoint and right-click it.

3. Select **Delete Waypoint**.

Routes

 To create a route, click **Create Route**, then click anywhere on the map to place the first waypoint. Continue clicking to place waypoints, then either right-click or press ESC when finished.

To insert a waypoint into a route:

1. Right-click the waypoint immediately before the desired insertion point.

2. Select **Insert Waypoints into Rte (route number)***. Right-clicking at this point will cancel the operation.

3. Click at the location for the new route waypoint, then right-click or press the ESC key to finish.

To create a route from existing waypoints:

 1. Click **Insert Route**.

 2. Click **Insert Route Waypoints**.

3. Click any waypoint on the map to start the route. Continue clicking waypoints in sequence to add them to the route.

  4. If you use a different tool, such as the **Center Map** or **Zoom Area** tool, you must click **Insert Route Waypoints** again before selecting additional waypoints for the route.

5. Right-click or press ESC to complete the route.

Undo/Redo
Use the **Undo** and **Redo** buttons throughout operations in MapCreate to correct errors. These buttons are rare in mapping programs, but are a great help, especially when it comes to working with routes.

Press F3, or select **View**, then **Route List**, to display a list of routes. Routes are numbered in consecutive order (e.g., Rte 001*). Unfortunately, there is no way to change their names to something more meaningful.

 Double-click a route in the list to open the **Route Waypoint List**. In this list you can drag waypoints to a new location in the route or select one and click **Delete**. You can also move or delete a route waypoint using the techniques for deleting any waypoint.

TIP: You can drag the edge of the **Route List** window to increase its size so you can see additional columns.

Tracks

Tracks, referred to as trails by MapCreate, can be transferred between the program and your GPS unit. Tracks downloaded from your GPS are displayed as green lines. To view the track list, press F5, or select **View**, then **Trail List**.

You cannot draw tracks freehand on the map, nor can you alter the display of tracks on the map screen. This limits your ability to customize the display on your GPS. If you know of trails that are not shown in MapCreate, you could use a program such as USA PhotoMaps to create a track, move it to your GPS, and display it on the map. This is also what the programs in Section Six are designed to do—allow you to customize your maps, though the one for MapCreate (OziMC) works only with Version 4 and earlier. Chapter 25 explores alternatives for owners of later versions.

The rudimentary track display and lack of ability to draw tracks is one reason MapCreate is not the best program for printing maps for field use. Many of the programs covered in previous sections of this book are much better suited for this task.

Converting Tracks to Routes
To convert a track to a route made up of 25 waypoints:

1. Open the data file containing the track.

2. Open the Trail and Route Lists.

3. Select the track you wish to convert and right-click it.

4. Select **Create Route From Trail**. The route name will be the same as the trail name (e.g., Trail 1).

GPS Interface

To transfer data (waypoints, routes, and tracks) to your GPS, connect your memory card reader to your computer and insert the MMC/SD card. Select **File**, point to **Save**, then choose **Save GPS Data File As**. Navigate to the MMC/SD card and save the data.

To transfer data from your GPS to MapCreate, use **My Computer** or **Windows Explorer** to copy data files from your MMC/SD card to the MapCreate data folder on your hard disk, at Program Files\LEI\MapCreate\Data. You can also transfer data to your GPS this way.

Be sure to use Windows' Safely Remove Hardware feature before you remove the MMC/SD card and reader.

> **TIP:** Once you transfer data to the card and insert it in your GPS, you will still need to load the data files. Maps are loaded automatically.

Transferring Maps to Your GPS

1. Place your MMC/SD card in the card reader and connect it to a USB port on your computer.

2. Now zoom the map to show the entire area you wish to transfer.

3. Click **Draw Map Border** and, starting in the upper left corner, drag a rectangle to define the area to be exported to your GPS.

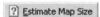

4. You can also click **Estimate Map Size** to estimate the size of the map file to be transferred.

5. Click **Create Map**. If you haven't registered your SD/MMC card yet, you will be prompted to do so now. See Five-Card Limit, below, for more information.

Five-Card Limit

No, I'm not talking about a card game. The five-card limit refers to MMC/SD cards. MapCreate 6.3 requires that you register any cards you transfer data to and limits you to five cards. A reasonably sized card can hold a large number of maps, and the cards can be erased over and over. Still, think twice before registering five 16MB cards. You never know when the urge will hit to do a cross-country trip and, if you don't have a laptop along, you could be severely limited.

When you use a new card for the first time, a copyright warning screen will appear. You will be given the option to label the card and have the label appended to maps you create.

Creating Corridor Maps from Routes

In addition to rectangular maps, MapCreate can create corridor maps. An easy way to do this is to create one from a route. Before getting started, select **View**, then **Map Display Options**. Now choose the **Map Borders** tab shown in Figure 19E. The **Corridor Width** slider bar allows you to control the width of corridors. For many purposes, the low end of the scale will be fine. Let's try it out:

1. Create or open a route.

2. Press the F3 key to open the **Route List**.

3. Right-click the route and select **Draw Borders Around Route**.

> **TIP:** Want to start over? Click **New Map Border File** to erase all map borders from the screen.

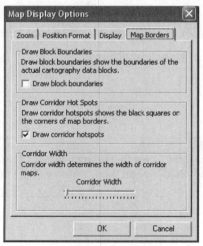

Figure 19E

Creating Corridor Maps Manually

1. Position the map so that you can see the entire area for which you wish to create a corridor.

2. Click **Draw Corridor Map Borders**. If you cannot see this option, select **View**, point to **Toolbars**, and choose **Create Map (Advanced)**.

aw Corridor Map Borders

3. Click along the center of the corridor, clicking at bends. Press the ESC key or right-click when finished.

Printing

MapCreate has very limited print capabilities. To print the map shown on the screen, click **Print Master Map**, or select **File**, point to **Print**, and choose **Print Map**.

Moving Map/3-D

MapCreate has no moving map or 3-D display capabilities.

Working With Other Programs

In addition to its native .usr format, MapCreate can open .low files from MapCreate 4 or 5. **Click Open GPS Data File**, and choose the appropriate category in the **Files of Type** box.

Select **File**, then **Import** to import waypoints or routes from a comma-delimited ASCII text file. You can also **Export** waypoints and routes to a text file from the **File** menu.

More Tips

• The **Map Use** box (see Figure 19F), affects which **Map Category Options** are available.

• You can use **Insert Icon** to place symbols on the map.

Figure 19F

Updates to this book will be posted at www.MakeYourOwnMaps.com.
Bookmark and visit often to see what's new in the world of digital mapping.

Section Six Power Mapping

f you've made it this far, you're definitely ready for power mapping! In this section we'll explore the world of aerial photos, satellite imagery, and three-dimensional perspectives. We'll also look at ways to take your maps with you, whether on a Palm, a Pocket PC, or the screen of your GPS. And no discussion of digital mapping would be complete without exploring geographic information systems (GIS) and the tons of amazing data available for free online. Finally, every power user is bound to run into roadblocks when trying to transfer data from one program to another. We'll close the book by looking at data compatibility among programs, and how you can surmount compatibility problems with various utilities.

Chapter 20
Aerial Photos and Satellite Imagery

Aerial imagery, including aerial photos, adds an entirely new dimension to mapping. Can't find that four-wheel-drive track on a map? Has the newest USGS quad for an area not been updated in twenty years? Not to worry. Aerial photos, typically updated much more frequently than maps, are a great tool for digital cartographers.

The programs in this book use USGS DOQQ (digital orthophoto quarter quadrangles) aerial photos. Because the resulting image files are large, they are broken down into four files per 7.5' quad. Each DOQQ covers 3.75' of longitude by 3.75' of latitude. DOQQs use NAD83 datum and UTM projection, and their image resolution is approximately 1 meter per pixel. Most DOQQs are black and white, and color imagery is beginning to appear for some urban areas, offering resolution down to .25 meters per pixel!

Before we go any further, let's define aerial photos. They're not satellite images. (We'll discuss those a little later in this chapter.) The type of aerial photos we're talking about are images shot from aircraft flying at 20,000 feet.

All of the programs covered in this book that offer aerial photos require them to be downloaded in some manner. The programs fall into one of three categories, defined below and summarized in Table 1:

- **TerraServer.** These are programs that use Microsoft's TerraServer online images. These programs are very easy to use, and they offer aerial photos of nearly the entire U.S. Some of these programs allow you to toggle back and forth between aerial images and topographic maps. Because the DOQQs have been converted to .jpg images, the resolution is not as good as it is on the original images.

- **Proprietary.** With proprietary images, your options are limited to the images provided by the software company. While introductory offers including image access are common, ultimately you must pay for additional downloads. Topo USA is the only product in this category that offers access to maps of the entire U.S. with the purchase of a single software title.

- **Download.** With these programs, you can download USGS images, often for free, but you must then import them into the software and make sure they are properly georeferenced. It's not that complicated, but it's nowhere near as simple as using TerraServer-based programs.

Table 1. Programs that offer aerial photo capability.

Chapter	Program	Type	Cost of Images	Cost of Program
5	USA PhotoMaps	TerraServer	Free	Free
9	Terrain Navigator Pro	Proprietary	Free in year one; $99.95 annually thereafter	$99.95
10	3-D TopoQuads	Proprietary (satellite only)	$99.00 (satellite only)	$99.95
11	Topo USA	Proprietary	$1.00/square kilometer	$99.95
12	TopoFusion	TerraServer	Free	$40.00
13	ExpertGPS	TerraServer	Free	$59.95
15	OziExplorer	Download	Free	$85.00
16	Fugawi	Download	Free	$99.00

Sources of DOQQs

A good place to start looking for aerial photos is **home.pacbell.net/lgalvin/drgnotes.htm**. While the site primarily focuses on DRGs, free sources of DOQQs are included for many states. The new color urban imagery for the U.S. is available at **seamless.usgs.gov**. It is also worth doing a Web search with the name of your state and "DOQQ."

GIS Data Depot sells DOQQs on CD at **data.geocomm.com**.

Satellite Imagery

Landsat 7 false-color satellite imagery for much of the world is available at **https://zulu.ssc.nasa.gov/mrsid/mrsid.pl**. 1990 and 2000 datasets are available; 2000 images have a resolution of 14.25 meters per pixel, while images from 1990 are 28.5 meters per pixel. Note, though, that the accuracy of these images is only around 50 meters. These are downloaded as MrSID images, which you can import into OziExplorer. The images are in WGS84 datum and UTM projection. The file names begin with the UTM hemisphere and zone.

See **www.vterrain.org/Imagery/satellite.html** for more information on satellite imagery.

Tips

• The National Agricultural Imagery Program (**www.apfo.usda.gov/naip.html**) has recently shot one- and two-meter true-color aerial photos of much of the U.S. They're not free, but the prices are very reasonable.

• You'll find an interesting Web site devoted to using aerial photos for hunting at **www.jesseshuntingpage.com/site/aerial.html**.

• It's very cool to be able to download aerial photos and locate roads and even trails. But wait until you convert what you find to a three-dimensional image! Read on for more fun.

Chapter 21
Viewing Maps and Aerial Imagery in 3-D

3-D mapping is the next best thing to being there, especially when you combine it with aerial photos. Digital elevation models (DEMs) and other elevation datasets make 3-D mapping possible by creating a grid of elevation points upon which a map or aerial photo is superimposed.

The programs in this book that support 3-D mapping can be categorized in one of two ways. One type has elevation data built in to the program. In these you basically click a button and the 3-D model appears. The other type requires you to download elevation data for a given area. Table 1 shows a summary of the programs offering 3-D capabilities, and the categories in which they fit.

Table 1. Programs offering 3-D capabilities.

Chapter	Program	Type	Cost of Program
8	Terrain Navigator	Built-in	$99.95
9	Terrain Navigator Pro	Built-in	$299.95
10	3-D TopoQuads	Built-in	$99.95
11	Topo USA	Built-in	$99.95
12	TopoFusion	Download	$40.00
15	OziExplorer	Download	$85.00

Since the programs with built-in 3-D modeling are so easy to use, most of this chapter will focus on downloading elevation data. It is surprisingly easy to generate a 3-D image of a map or aerial photo. If you have successfully downloaded DRG or DOQQ files, this should be a breeze.

Types and Sources of Elevation Data

There are many types of elevation data that you may come across online:

Digital Elevation Model (DEM)

This is a format used by both OziExplorer and TopoFusion. 1:24K data is available from **data.geocomm.com**, while 1:250K data is available from **edc.usgs.gov/geodata**. Another good source of free elevation data is **www.mapmart.com**, which allows you to zoom in and see quad names and boundaries in the selection process.

Another Web site, **http://64.83.8.153/SDTS_DL_b.htm**, provides a simple and fast way to download a DEM for a 7.5' USGS quad. Enter the coordinates for any point on a 7.5' quad to download the DEM. Be sure to use the correct format, which may appear similar to decimal degrees, but is asking for degrees.minutes. Under this format, 123° 30' W is entered as -123.30

National Elevation Dataset (NED)

This format carries a resolution of one arc second (approximately 30 meters) for most of the U.S. and two arc seconds for Alaska. This data is available from **seamless.usgs.gov.** A download example is given in the 3-D section of Chapter 12.

Shuttle Radar Topography Mission (SRTM)

SRTM features one arc second (30 meter) coverage of the continental U.S. and three arc second (90 meter) coverage of much of the planet. The area covered is between 60° N latitude and 56° S latitude, encompassing 80 percent of the earth's surface. You can download data from **ftp://e0mss21u.ecs.nasa.gov/srtm**. File names carry an .hgt extension and are based on the latitude and longitude of the southwest corner of the map. A download example is given in the Tracks section of Chapter 16.

Internet Resources

Sources of information about elevation data and three-dimensional mapping:

• **www.vterrain.org**

• **www.terrainmap.com**

• **members.shaw.ca/davepatton/demcompare.html**

• **http://216.218.220.254/ozi3d/height_data.html**

Video Drivers

Your computer can have two types of video drivers. One is software for your video card. The other is a hardware driver, which can provide faster display. This is known as hardware acceleration; not all video cards have this additional driver.

Check at regular intervals to be sure that you are using the most current driver for your video card. You first need to know the make and model of your video card. Right-click on the Windows desktop, then select **Properties.** Choose the **Settings** tab and select **Advanced.** Now choose the **Adapter** tab and record your make, model, and software version. Go the manufacturer's Web site and check for an updated driver.

More Tips

• For fast rendering and rotation of 3-D images, it is best to have a graphics card with as much RAM as possible. I suggest at least 32 MB; 64 MB is even better.

• 3DEM, discussed briefly in the 3-D section of Chapter 12, is an excellent program in itself. With it you can make use of a wide range of elevation data types, overlay aerial photos and DRGs, and even generate animated fly-bys. It is available as a free download from **www.visualizationsoftware.com/3dem.html**.

Chapter 22
Moving Maps for PDAs

Moving maps are becoming commonplace, with GPS tracking devices showing up in automobiles as factory-installed equipment. Automotive navigation systems tend to be expensive, and some can't accommodate topo maps that show details such as the location of a specific trailhead. Fortunately, there are other reasonably priced ways to take mapping fun to your vehicle.

First, a definition: A moving map tracks your position in real time, updating it every few seconds. If you have a GPS that can show detailed maps, that may be all you need. If you don't, or you want a larger screen, multiple options are available.

But why would you want a moving map? They're great in the city, when you're trying to find that cool restaurant you just read about. But this book is aimed at outdoors enthusiasts. How will moving maps help you find that favorite fishing spot or summit that peak you've been dreaming of? Sure, moving maps are cool, but for many of us they mean lugging along a laptop or PDA. You wouldn't want to have to carry that baggage around in the woods, right? You're absolutely correct, yet moving maps can still be a great help in getting there.

From finding that obscure trailhead to navigating a half dozen turns on poorly signed Forest Service roads, a moving map can make all the difference in the world.

Maybe you tend to do solo trips. You can't watch the screen and drive at the same time (a really bad idea). No problem—many of these programs call out your turns ("Turn left, 400 feet") and let you know when you have arrived at the trailhead.

My favorite approach to moving maps is to use a PDA rather than a laptop. The screen may be small, but I don't want to take my laptop on a dusty washboard road. Leaving such a valuable piece of equipment in the car while I'm miles away, or in a trendy but somewhat seedy part of the city, doesn't seem like a good idea, either. A PDA solves this. It will get you where you want to go, but it's compact enough to throw in the glove compartment.

I've already covered moving map capabilities of the software we've reviewed in the prior chapters. In this chapter, we'll look only at PDA applications for the backcountry, for finding those remote trailheads. I won't cover the numerous software packages designed for city navigation, though some of the software in this chapter can do that as well.

Finally, remember our previous caveats about safety. A passenger should serve as navigator; the driver should never be distracted by the moving map.

Cables

If you want your GPS to talk to your PDA, you'll have to get special cables to connect them. Two popular sources are **www.pc-mobile.net** and **www.pfranc.com**. You might want to consider getting an adapter that allows you to power your PDA or GPS via your cigarette lighter. Remember, PDAs tend to go through batteries a lot faster than your GPS will. If your PDA has a proprietary battery that must go in a charger, a car charger is almost a necessity.

> ### Cable-Free
> You don't need a cable if you have a PDA with an integrated or add-on receiver. In addition, Bluetooth (wireless) PDAs and GPS units can send a signal up to 30 feet or so. (See Chapter 2 for more on these options.)

Mounting Systems

In a collision, your GPS and PDA could become lethal missiles, so you'll need a mounting system for both. Your GPS and PDA units should never be placed on top of the air bag or in its zone of deployment; you should never mount them in an area that blocks any of your field of vision; nor should you leave them loose on the dashboard.

A good starting point for finding GPS mounts is at **www.pocketgpsworld.com/ menu_gpsmounts.php**. You might also check **www.gpsinformation.net**. Look under "Links to Accessories." RAM (**www.ram-mount.com**) is a popular supplier of mounts for both PDAs and GPS units.

Message boards focusing on PDA and GPS units, especially those for specific brands, are a good place to look for sources of cables, mounts, and other gear. Some places to start are listed in the next section.

> ### NMEA Protocol
> Check your software manual, but in most cases you'll need to switch your GPS communications protocol to NMEA (for more on NMEA, see Chapter 2). If you can't establish communication between your GPS and PDA, check your communication protocol. Remember, though, to switch back from NMEA to your usual interface when you reconnect your GPS to your computer, otherwise you'll get connection error messages. Any time this happens, check whether the interface protocol is set correctly.

Internet Resources

- **www.gpspassion.com/forumsen**

- **groups.yahoo.com/group/Pocket_PC_Community**

- **groups.yahoo.com/group/palm-soft**

- The Dell Axim Site (**www.aximsite.com/boards/forumdisplay.php?s=&forumid=34**) is a great example of a message board devoted to the happy marriage of PDAs and GPS units.

- Search at Yahoo groups (**groups.yahoo.com**) for groups that focus on your brand of PDA and GPS.

Communication Problems

In addition to being sure you are using the NMEA communications protocol, you should be aware of a few other common problems. One is that synchronization software, such as ActiveSync, can interfere with GPS communications—so dive into your PDA's menus and disable this software before connecting it your GPS. If your PDA still can't communicate with your GPS, try this: Start your PDA first, then your mapping software. Have the software start looking for your GPS. At that point, and not before, connect your GPS cable to the PDA.

PDA/Moving Map Software

Table 1 shows various PDA software programs with real-time tracking capabilities.

An exhaustive treatment of such programs could fill a book in itself, so we'll look only at the highlights of each.

Table 1. PDA programs that offer real-time tracking.

PDA Software	Compatible With	Palm	Pocket PC	Cost
Pocket TOPO!	TOPO!	Yes	Yes	$24.95
Outdoor Navigator	N/A	Yes	Yes	$19.95
Pocket Navigator	Terrain Navigator	No	Yes	$99.95
Street Atlas USA 2005 Handheld	Topo USA 5.0	Yes	Yes	$39.95
OziExplorerCE	OziExplorer	No	Yes	$30.00
Fugawi 3	Fugawi 3	Yes	Yes	Included with Fugawi 3

Pocket TOPO!

National Geographic's entry in this field allows you to transfer maps from its TOPO! state packages to a Palm- or Pocket PC-based PDA. In addition to real-time tracking, Pocket TOPO! allows you to add notes, symbols, and routes to the map for transfer back to your PC.

Outdoor Navigator

This Maptech product allows you to download online U.S. topo maps to your PDA.

• For $19.95, you get access to multiple scales of USGS topo maps for the continental U.S., along with more than 2,000 NOAA nautical charts.

• A free trial is available at **www.maptech.com**.

Pocket Navigator

Another Maptech product; this one allows you transfer maps from Terrain Navigator, Terrain Navigator Pro, Digital Charts (nautical), and Aeronautical Charts to your PDA. (Of course, you have to own those products to do so.)

> ### Memory
> Most of these programs rely on raster maps (images), and so act as memory hogs. This makes memory cards very important for PDA-based mapping, as they let you carry a greater number of maps.

Street Atlas USA 2005 Handheld

This DeLorme product has some interesting advantages:

• Unlike the other software in this chapter, this product offers autorouting. Enter a start address and a destination, and Street Atlas will calculate your route.

• It includes street-level maps for the entire U.S., along with primary and secondary roads for Canada.

• A desktop version is included.

• Street Atlas supports Topo USA 5.0 maps and aerial data packets, allowing you to import vector topo maps and aerial photos.

• It also offers voice prompts.

> **TIP:** G7toWin, discussed in Chapter 26, is a data conversion utility with extensive support for Street Atlas files.

OziExplorerCE

OziExplorerCE uses maps you create in OziExplorer.

• A free demo version is available with only slight restrictions. A "Demo Version" watermark appears on the screen; GPS communication is interrupted with a nag screen after twenty minutes and every ten minutes thereafter.

• You can use virtually any map created in OziExplorer, including aerial photos.

• While autorouting is not supported, it is possible to create routes with voice prompts in OziExplorerCE.

Fugawi 3

Fugawi 3 GPS Mapping Software includes Palm and Pocket PC versions at no extra charge.

• Just as with OziExplorer, you can use almost any map you use in Fugawi, allowing you to use aerial photos.

• Map transfer is very simple.

• Fugawi 3 comes packaged with street maps for the entire U.S.

> Updates to this book will be posted at www.MakeYourOwnMaps.com.
> Bookmark and visit often to see what's new in the world of digital mapping.

Chapter 23 Geographic Information System (GIS) and Vector Maps

Geographic information system (GIS) data formats are used by governments and businesses across the globe, and an incredible amount of governmental GIS data is available for free online. The ability to incorporate GIS data into your maps can make a dramatic difference in the type of information you are able to display and use.

Let's look at an example. Much of my outdoor recreation time is spent mountain biking. I live in an area with a fair amount of public land, but it is dwarfed by the hundreds of thousands of acres of commercial timberland. One of the local timber companies has graciously opened its land to non-motorized access, and my wife and I spend most weekends exploring remote sections of our county. These massive land holdings have became something of a private mountain bike park for us.

Once I got into computerized mapping, I have to admit it became a bit of an obsession to create detailed maps for our weekend playground. While surfing the Web, I came across a local watershed protection site that offered free disks of GIS data. I ordered the disks and found that they contained topographic maps, aerial photos, layers of road information, and much more. Perhaps most interesting was the inclusion of private timber company ownership boundaries. To say the least, it was a major boon to get hold of these files.

Following this, I was able to add additional layers of GIS data. I found boundary files for the Bureau of Land Management and state parks, and general public land boundary files that included university holdings of natural areas. I even discovered boundary files for a Department of Fish and Game series of ecological reserves. I soon had one of the most complete maps for my area.

Vector vs. Raster

Vector maps are discussed at the beginning of Chapter 11, but let's have a brief review: Almost all of the programs we've looked at so far are raster-based. Raster maps are basically scanned images. They take up a lot of room on storage media. That's why it can take ten CDs to cover all of California. Each point on these maps is represented by a single pixel of a certain color. If you try zooming in on an image of, say, a 1:24,000 scale map, you quickly lose resolution.

GIS applications, in addition to allowing you to use raster images, can also make use of vector data. Vector data files are composed of lines and points; there are no image files. There are also polygons, though these are just closed loops of lines. The only vector programs we've looked at so far are DeLorme's TopoUSA (Chapter 11) and the GPS-based mapping programs in Section Five. Because vector programs use data files and not images, vector maps take up a lot less room than raster maps. For example, Magellan's MapSend Topo for the United States (Chapter 18) takes up only one CD. This is possible because lines and points require less storage space than pixel-based images. Remember, raster images must assign a color to every pixel.

> ### Raster + Vector = Power Mapping
> One key point here: you can combine these formats, layering vector data on top of raster images. That's how I produced my boundary maps.

GIS as Database

What has made GIS so popular among land managers is not the space-saving qualities of vector files. Rather, it's the ability to combine maps and databases in one software program. For example, if you are looking at a road on a GIS system, you might be able to click on it and get a wide range of "attributes": name, year built, category of road, and so on. Because of this, GIS programs are powerful analytic, interpretive, and research tools—the reason corporations and government agencies favor them.

File Formats

GIS data comes in two common file formats:

Shapefiles. These come in sets composed of at least three different file types:

• **.shp** The actual line or point files.

• **.shx** The georeference files that store the coordinates of the lines or points.

• **.dbf** dBASE files that store the attribute information of features.

You may also see other files such as spatial index files (.sbn and .sbx) and the all-important projection files (.prj).

.e00 files. This is a data exchange format. It contains all spatial feature information and associated attribute data. Should you run across a situation where you need to convert .e00 files to .shp, I suggest OziExplorer. Another option is the Import 71 utility, which will convert .e00 to .adf or .shp, though it is a little more complicated than conversion with Ozi. It's available at **ftp://download1.geocomm.com/sd2/IMPORT71.EXE**.

GIS Software

The following programs allow you to make use of GIS data:

- **OziExplorer**. This software, covered in Chapter 15, is the only major program in this book that allows the import of shapefiles and .e00 files. Ozi is available from **www.oziexplorer.com**.

- **Global Mapper**. This program, discussed briefly in Chapter 24 and available from **www.globalmapper.com**, has extensive capabilities. The demo version has some limitations on data use, though.

- **ArcExplorer**. This free GIS data viewer is available from Environmental Systems Research Institute (ESRI) at **www.esri.com/software/arcexplorer**. While its functionality is limited, it works well for simple data viewing. *GIS for Everyone*, a book published by ESRI, is a good introduction to GIS that comes with a copy of ArcExplorer.

- **ArcView**. This expensive, full-function GIS software from ESRI costs $1,500, but a 30-day free evaluation disk is available. (For details, see **www.esri.com/software/ arcview/eval**.) I mention this because you may find data in an unfamiliar format. At one point I came across data that I desperately wanted to use, but it was in an .adf format. I was only able to convert the data using the ArcView demo. (By the way, the name ESRI has become synonymous with GIS, but ESRI is not the only player in the game. Read on for other options.)

Many free GIS programs are available. You might want to investigate these resources:

- **www.freegis.org**
- **www.gislounge.com/ll/freegis.shtml**
- **www.digitalgrove.net/fgis.htm**

Data Sources

One of the best ways to find GIS data sources is to conduct an Internet search using "GIS" and the name of a county, state, national park, government agency, etc. Apart from that, here are few sources of free data to get you started.

- **libinfo.uark.edu/GIS/us.asp**
- **data.geocomm.com/catalog**. This is a great place to go for international data. Normal downloads are free, but you'll need to set up a password.
- **www.doylesdartden.com/gis**. Even with all the out-of-date links, this site remains a useful resource.

- www.cgrer.uiowa.edu/servers/servers_geodata.html

- www.gisuser.com/content/view/607/28/. Use the clickable U.S. map.

- www.gisuser.com/content/section/10/41

Internet Resources

Listed below are some GIS discussion groups that may be helpful:

- The newsgroup Comp.infosystems.gis
  (**groups.google.com/groups?hl=en&lr=&group=comp.infosystems.gis**)

- Yahoo ESRI GIS group (**groups.yahoo.com/group/esri_gis**)

- Yahoo Global Mapper group (**groups.yahoo.com/group/global_mapper**)

It's also worth searching **groups.yahoo.com** for GIS groups focused on the area where you live.

Updates to this book will be posted at www.MakeYourOwnMaps.com.
Bookmark and visit often to see what's new in the world of digital mapping.

Chapter 24 Make Your Own Maps: Creating Custom Vector Maps for Your GPS

For the more adventurous souls out there, we're about to really have some fun. We're going to build on the last chapter and learn how to acquire vector data and convert it into formats that can be used in custom GPS-based maps.

Our primary goal in this chapter is converting other data formats to shapefiles. We'll also look at how to convert shapefiles to tracks, for those readers whose GPS units lack the ability to display detailed maps. If you already have shapefiles, Chapter 25 looks at how to transfer them to your GPS.

You might want to create custom maps for your GPS for a number of reasons—from creating up-to-date maps to showing trails you have previously traveled to creating maps for international locales.

This can be a simple process or a fairly complex one. If all you need to do is convert shapefiles to tracks, or tracks to shapefiles, it will be easy. A more complicated process involves acquiring and converting USGS digital line graphs (DLGs). Let's start with the simpler approach.

Using OziExplorer to Convert Shapefiles and Tracks

For this you'll need OziExplorer, covered in detail in Chapter 15. The conversions below can be done in the shareware demonstration version of OziExplorer. Though this version has limitations on the types of maps that can be used, you do not have to have a map image loaded to convert these file types. Simply click **Map** and then **Blank Map (Auto Scale)**.

Converting Tracks to Shapefiles

This operation could come in handy for owners of Magellan and Garmin units, or for Lowrance owners using MapCreate 4, who want to add an extensive collection of tracks to their GPS maps.

1. Start OziExplorer and load the blank map or a map of the area for the track you wish to convert.

2. In OziExplorer, select **Load**, then **Load Track from File (Multi)**. Open the desired track.

3. Choose **Save**, point to **Export to ESRI Shape File**, and then select **Tracks to Polylines**.

4. Name the shapefile and click **Save**.

5. In the **Shape File Import/Export Options** dialog box, choose the correct **Datum** and **Position Format**. Unless you have reason to choose otherwise, I suggest using **WGS84** as the **Datum**, the standard for data transfer, and **Lat/Lon** as the **Position Format**. This is the most common datum/projection for shapefiles. These settings are required if you're going to use MobileMapper Office 1.0 to transfer shapefiles to your Magellan.

Converting Shapefiles to Tracks

This technique is useful for owners of GPS units that are not capable of displaying detailed maps. In terms of creating custom maps for more sophisticated GPS units, this technique is perhaps most useful to those using Lowrance MapCreate versions 5 or 6, which cannot accommodate shapefiles.

1. Start OziExplorer and load the blank map or a map of the area for the shapefile you wish to convert.

2. Choose **Load, Import ESRI Shape File**, then select **Polylines and Polygons**.

3. In the **Shape File Import** dialog box, choose **Import**.

4. In the **Import Shape File** dialog box, select a .shp file and click **Open**.

5. In the **Shape File Import/Export Options** dialog box, enter the correct **Datum** and **Position Format**, and click **OK**.

6. In the **Shape File Attributes** dialog box, click **Continue**.

> **TIP:** If you choose a .dbf file as the **Type Field**, a new track will be created each time the **Type Field** comments change.

7. **Close** the **Shape File Import** dialog box.

8. Click **Save**, then **Save Track to File**.

9. **Name** the track file and click **Save**.

Acquiring and Converting Digital Line Graph Files

As noted previously, Garmin's MapSource United States Topo contour lines are based on 1:100K data, meaning that the contour lines are 130 to 140 feet apart. The remainder of this chapter will be devoted to creating a map that displays 40-foot contour intervals, based on USGS 1:24K DLG files. Now before users of other products move on to another chapter, I want to note that there are many uses for DLG files and other useful techniques covered in this chapter, such as how to convert .mif files to shapefiles. Also discussed is the use of an incredibly powerful program called GlobalMapper.

Making your own maps often involves juggling a handful of programs and utilities. Though you won't need them all, in this chapter we'll discuss the following software:

• Global Mapper

• MapScan

• SDTS2MIF

• WinRAR

• OziExplorer

• DEM2TOPO

Map Authoring Resources

The science, art, and sport of creating your own maps has been dubbed "map authoring" by some enthusiasts. An excellent discussion board focusing on this topic can be found at **groups.yahoo.com/group/map_authors**.

Step 1: Acquiring the Data

A wonderful source of DLG and DEM information is available at **edc.usgs.gov/geodata**. Along the top, select the type of data set that you wish to download, such as **1:24K DLG**. On the next screen, choose **FTP via Graphics,** then select the appropriate index map.

At some levels, notably 1:100K DLG files, you will have the option of downloading SDTS or the older DLG-O (.opt) format. Note that each SDTS file comes in four pieces when you choose the .opt format. We'll focus on SDTS files in our examples here. (In case you're wondering, SDTS stands for spatial data transfer standard.)

> **TIP: DLG-O, THE .OPT FORMAT** If, instead of SDTS, you are using the older DLG-O, or .opt, format, you'll find helpful information on the nuances of this file type and an alternative format converter, DLG2MIFX, at **www.gpsnuts .com/Ozi/OziMCJohnG/vector.html**. The original DLG2MIF program was written by Sol Katz of the Bureau of Land Management. John Galvin, author of the Web page cited in the lower box on page 308, modified it to create DLG2MIFX, which automatically removes neatlines (see Step 4, later in this chapter). Unfortunately though, DLG-O files, while more common for 1:100K data, are rarely available for 1:24K data.

Let's get started. Years ago, I was fortunate to live near Pisgah National Forest, a beautiful part of the Southern Appalachians. This area, which is bisected by the Blue Ridge Parkway, seems to have something for everyone—rock climbers, mountain bikers, fishermen, and just about any other lover of the outdoors. We'll use the area's Shining Rock quad for our 1:24K tutorial, so let's start by downloading the appropriate DLG files. Go to **edc.usgs.gov/geodata**. Click on **1:24K DLG**, then **FTP via State**, then select **North Carolina**, scroll all the way down to **Shining Rock**, and click the link.

> **NOTE: USGS DLG ACRONYMS**
> You'll see the following categories and subcategories in USGS DLG files:
> • **BD.** Boundaries
> • **HY.** Hydrography (water features)
> • **HP.** Hypsography (contour lines)
> • **PL.** Public lands
> • **TR.** Transportation, with the following subcategories:
>   – **RD.** Roads
>   – **RR.** Railroads
>   – **MT.** Mass transit

Select **Boundaries**, then **1175992.BD.sdts.tar.gz**. Click **Save** and, using the **Save As** dialog box, create a new folder on your desktop named **DLG Files**. Now click **Save**. Go back and download the files in the **Hydrography**, **Hypsography**, and **Transportation** folders. When you download the latter, you'll actually end up with three files, as noted in the box "USGS DLG Acronyms." Note that there are no Public Lands files available for this quad. Not all quads will have all files. This "missing" information is often available in the 1:100K DLG files. But what happens if your favorite 1:24K quad is missing hypsography (contour) data? See "Contour Lines From DEM Files," below, for some great solutions.

> **WARNING:** Downloading SDTS.TAR.GZ files using Internet Explorer versions 5.0 or older, or Netscape Navigator, may change the dots (.) within a filename to underscores (_). If you use either of these browsers, be sure to change filenames back to the original format. You can do this at the beginning of the download process using the **Save As** option.

Contour Lines From DEM Files

Hypsography (contour) files are not available for many 1:24K quads. Fortunately, it's possible to convert digital elevation model (DEM) files to contour lines using a program called DEM2TOPO, available from **people.uleth.ca/~brad.gom/dem2topo**. You'll have to download and install IDL Virtual Machine, available from the same site, to run DEM2TOPO. A tutorial can be found at **people.uleth.ca/~brad.gom/dem2topo/ howto. htm#process_mp**. Fortunately, you can generate .shp and .mp files directly from DEM2TOPO. You can also generate contour lines from DEMs in GlobalMapper.

Step 2: Data Extraction

I'll present two approaches for data extraction and conversion. The first can be done with free software or shareware, but it is a multistep process and you lose the shape-file attributes, which limits your ability to customize what appears on your GPS screen at various zoom levels. I don't see this as a serious drawback, and it can actually save you some time.

The second approach is made with a program that allows you to convert the data in the demo version. You must pay for the program if you wish to export it, although you can apparently request temporary permission to use the export feature. See "Using Global Mapper for Steps 2 through 4" for information on this alternative approach.

WinZip File Corruption

WinZip's default setup enables **TAR file smart CR/LF conversion**, which will mangle your data when you use it to decompress .gz files. One option is to disable this feature. Another is to use an alternative program for decompressing files. I prefer WinRAR, a trial version of which is available at **www.rarlab.com/download.htm.com**.

WARNING: Take a look at your **DLG Files** folder. It should have six folders with the following abbreviations we discussed earlier—**HY, BD, HP, RD, RR, MT**. As mentioned previously, the last three are all transportation files. Transportation data sets for some 24K maps can be quite large, so they are broken down into these three files. Unfortunately, if you try to extract all of these from a common folder, there will be naming conflicts in the converted files. So... go into your DLG Files folder and select **File**, point to **New**, and choose **Folder** to create a new folder. Name it **RD**. Now do this twice more, creating new folders named **RR** and **MT**.

Assuming you are using WinRAR, you'll need to do one of two things, depending upon whether or not it is the default handler for .gz files:

1. If WinRAR is the default handler for .gz files, you can simply double-click one of the .gz files you just downloaded to open WinRAR. You'll see a screen similar to the one in Figure 24A. It shows you the contents of the .gz file. The .DDF extension stands for Data Descriptive File, an extension used for the multiple files stored in a single USGS SDTS file. Click **Extract** to open the **Extraction Path and Options** dialog box. For the HY, BD, and HP layers, navigate to the **DLG Files** folder, select it, and click **OK**. Extract the .gz file to the **RD**, **MT**, and **RR** folders, to keep each of these transportation layers separate.

TIP: To set WinRAR as the default handler for various file types, use Windows' **Program** menu to open WinRAR. Select **Options**, then **Settings**. Choose the **Integration** tab and select **GZip** as shown in Figure 24B. I suggest selecting **TAR** as well. Now click **OK**.

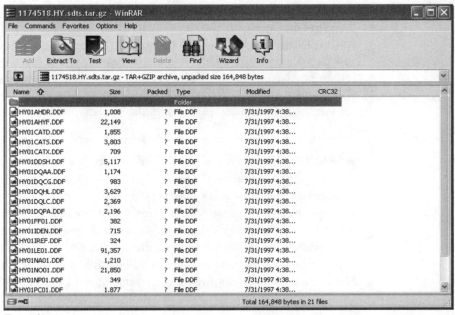

Figure 24A

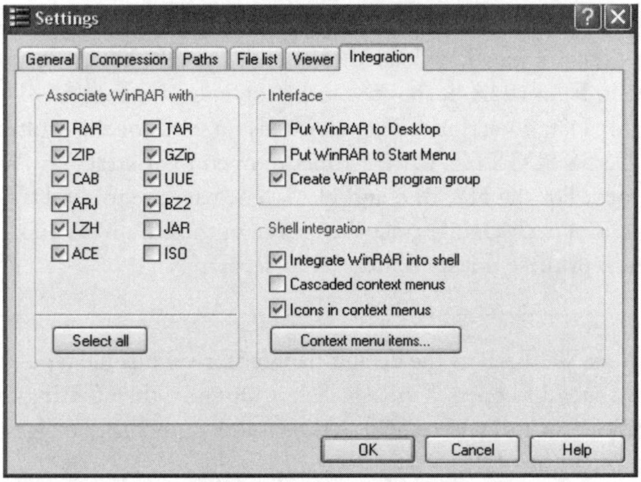

Figure 24B

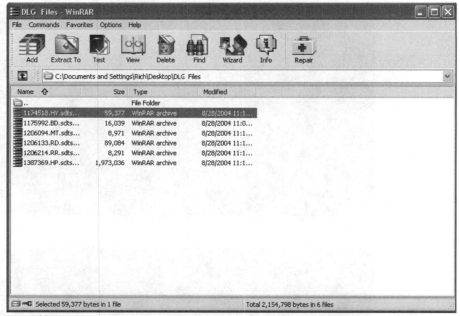

Figure 24C

2. If WinRAR is not the default handler, click Windows' **Start** button, point to **All Programs**, point to **WinRAR**, and select **WinRAR** to start. Navigate to the **DLG Files** folder, select a .gz file, and click **Extract To**, as shown in Figure 24C. This will open an **Extraction Path and Options** dialog box. Navigate to the **DLG Files** folder, select it, then click **OK**. Repeat the process until all .gz files have been extracted, making sure that you extract each of the three transportation layers to its own folder.

Step 3: Data Conversion (SDTS to MIF)

In this step, we will convert the SDTS files into the MapInfo format .mif.

First, download the free program SDTS2MIF from **ftp://ftp.blm.gov/pub/gis/sdts/dlg/ sdts2mif.exe** and place the program in your DLG Files folder. This is important because the program must be in the same directory as the SDTS files that will be converted.

1. Open the **DLG Files** folder and click **SDTS2MIF**.

2. A DOS window (Figure 24D) will open, asking you to enter a four-character SDTS base filename. Type **HP01** and press ENTER.

3. You'll be asked to enter a base output file name. Use the same name: type **HP01** again and press ENTER.

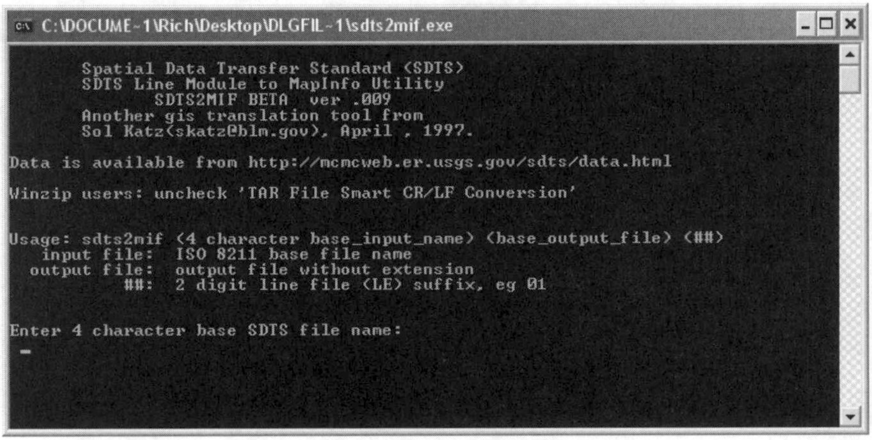

Figure 24D

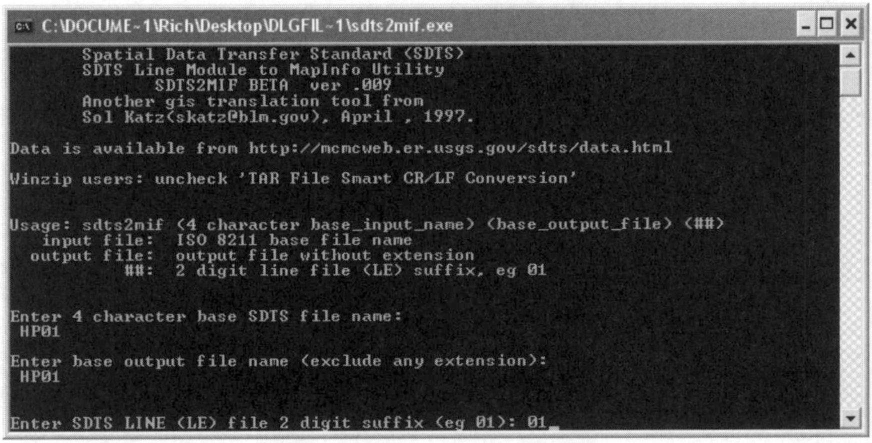

Figure 24E

4. Next you will be asked to enter a two-digit suffix. Type **01**. At this point the DOS window should look like Figure 24E.

5. Press ENTER and, in a few seconds, the DOS window will disappear. An HP01.MIF file will have been created in the DLG folder.

6. Start SDTS2MIF again and repeat the process for the HY and BD layers, using the appropriate two-letter prefix—for example, HY01.

7. Now do the same thing in each of the transportation folders. Remember that SDTS2MIF has to be in the same folder as the data to be converted. Find **sdts2mif.exe** in the **DLG Files** folder, right-click it, and then click **Copy**. Go to your **RD**, **RR**, and **MT** folders, click each one to select it, right-click, and select **Paste**.

8. Now we're going to repeat Steps 1 through 5 in each of these folders, except that we're going to use **TR01**, **TR01**, and **01** at the three prompts for each one. Do not use RD, RR, or MT as suffixes!

> **NOTE: 1:100K CONVERSIONS** 1:100K DLG files are a little more complicated, with each map type broken down into four sections, each of which represents a quarter of the map. For information on how to structure SDTS2MIF commands for these files, I'm going to once again refer you to John Galvin's excellent Web page Go to **www.gpsnuts.com/Ozi/OziMCJohnG/vector.html** and look under "Convert to mif format."

Step 4: Data Conversion (MIF to SHP)

For this step, I'm going to give you two options, one for perfectionists and one for folks who just want a functional map as quickly as possible.

The decision point has to do with neatlines. Neatlines are rectangular boxes that surround quads, like the borders on a map. Figure 24F is a screen shot of our Shining Rock quad road (RD) layer, showing neatlines. The shot is from MapScan, a program you can use to remove neatlines.

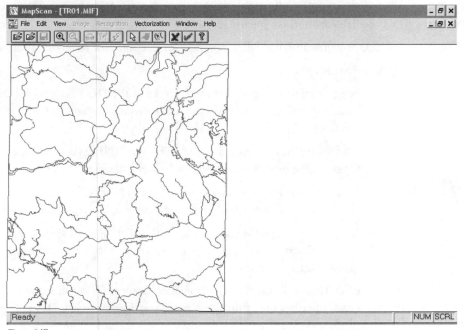

Figure 24F

Removing neatlines is a major pain, a tedious task best suited for those aspiring to develop carpal tunnel syndrome. This is a tutorial, so by all means try it out, but you may want to save this tool for those areas you visit frequently. It may take twenty-five to thirty minutes to do a quad with this much local relief. And there are alternatives:

- First of all, you can leave neatlines in place, even if you're creating maps from multiple quads—but you'll see the neatlines at the boundary of each quad.

- DLG2MIFX will automatically remove neatlines on DLG-O files. Unfortunately, DLG-O files are much more commonly available for 1:100K maps, and are rarely available at the 1:24K scale.

- Another option is to convert DEM files to contour lines, with a program like DEM2TOPO, discussed earlier in this chapter.

- Or you can spring for Global Mapper, which also removes neatlines. It will be discussed later in this chapter.

If neatlines don't bother you, skip ahead to "Option B: Using OziExplorer to Convert MIF Files to Shapefiles."

Option A: Using MapScan to Remove Neatlines and Convert MIF Files to Shapefiles.
MapScan, a free program developed by the United Nations, can be used to remove neatlines. It is available from **netgis.geo.uw.edu.pl/free/mapscan**. A .pdf help file is available from the same site.

Once you've installed MapScan, here are the steps for removing neatlines:

1. Start **MapScan**.

2. Select **File**, then **Open Vector**. Navigate to the **DLG Files** folder. Note that MapScan will truncate folder names, so your Documents folder may appear as DOCUM~1.

3. Under **List files of type**, choose ***.mif – MAPINFO files**. Select **HP01.MIF**. The **Open** dialog box should appear as it does in Figure 24G. Click **OK**.

 4. Maximize the map window so that you have the full screen to work with. Use the **Zoom In** and **Zoom Out** buttons and the scroll bars to move around the screen.

5. You'll see a floating **Vector** tool bar, shown in Figure 24H, which can be dragged to a new location on the screen as necessary. If it doesn't appear, select **View**, point to **Toolbox**, and choose **Vector**.

 6. Click **Delete Segment** and start clicking away at the neatlines on the perimeter of the quad. After any use of the zoom tools, you'll need to click **Delete Segment** again.

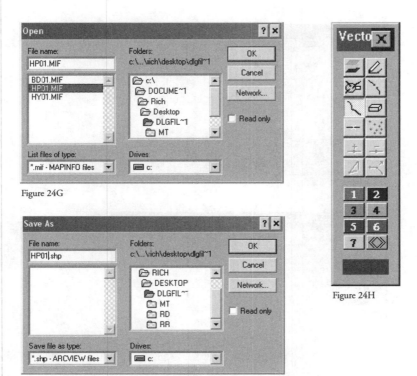

Figure 24G

Figure 24H

Figure 24I

7. After going through this laborious process, shake out your hands and select **File**, then **Export Vector**. In the **Save file as type** box, select ***.shp - ARCVIEW files**. Save this file as **HP01.shp,** as shown in Figure 24I. Click **OK**.

8. In the **Select Layer** box, click **Select All**, moving the **5** to the right, as shown in Figure 24J. (The 5 shown in the image is the code for the color, red, which is unimportant.) Click **OK**.

9. Repeat Steps 2 through 7 for the **BD, HY, RD**, and **MT** layers. (You will not be able to save a file for RR, since there is no data there to be saved.) Select **View**, then **Full View** to see the entire map. Removing neatlines on these remaining files will go much more quickly. Save all files to the **DLG Files** directory. Use the file names RD01.shp and MT01.shp when saving the transportation layers.

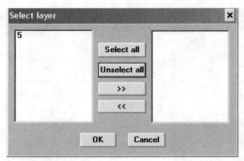

Figure 24J

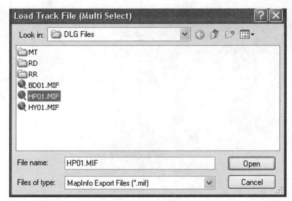

Figure 24K

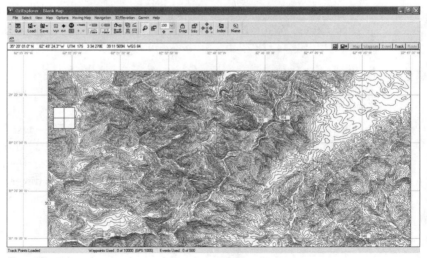

Figure 24L

> ## MapScan Tips
> • If you make an error, select **Edit**, then **Undo**.
>
> • If you find that using the scroll arrows is slow, try grabbing the scroll box and dragging it to a new position. After a while you'll get the hang of just how far to drag it.
>
> • The **Zoom** tools are perhaps the quickest way to move around the map.
>
> • Select **View**, then **Full View** to see the entire quad.

Option B: Using OziExplorer to Convert MIF Files to Shapefiles

If you haven't purchased OziExplorer, you'll need the free demonstration version for this step. For full information on OziExplorer, see Chapter 15.

1. Start OziExplorer.

2. Select **Map**, then **Blank Map (Auto Scale)**.

3. Click **Load**, point to **Import**, and select **From MapInfo MIF** files. Navigate to your **DLG Files** folder and select **HP01.MIF**, as shown in Figure 24K. Click **Open**. This is a big file, so be patient. Within a minute or so, you should see the screen shown in Figure 24L, with neatlines intact. Congratulations! You just imported your contour lines.

4. Click **Save**, point to **Export to ESRI Shape File**, and choose **Tracks to Polylines**. Save this file in your **DLG Files** folder as **HP01.SHP**.

5. In the **Shapefile Import/Export Options** dialog box, shown in Figure 24M, select **NAD27 CONUS** as the **Datum** and **UTM** as the **Position Format**. Enter **17** as the **Grid Zone** and click **OK**.

Figure 24M

> **TIP:** Shapefiles that have been converted from SDTS or DLG-O data will always have a UTM position format and a NAD27 CONUS datum. If you don't know the **Grid Zone,** a good resource is available at **www.dmap.co.uk/utmworld.htm.** If you have USAPhotoMaps (see Chapter 5), all downloads are saved by default in folders based on UTM zone, so this is another good way to ascertain this information.

6. Now select **Maps,** then **Clear All Tracks from Map** and click **Yes** in the **Confirm** dialog box.

7. Notice the points left on the map. These are spot elevations on summits. Click **Save,** then point to Export to **ESRI Shape File** — but this time select **Point Set 1 to Points.** Let's save this file as **HPPOINTS.SHP.** Repeat Step 5 and choose **Maps,** then **Clear All Points from Map.**

8. Now repeat Steps 1 through 6 for the **HY, BD, RD,** and **MT** layers, making sure that you save the latter two as **RD01.SHP** and **MT01.SHP.** Don't use the TR prefix because they both carry it.

Steps 2 through 4: The Global Mapper Alternative

If you chose to use SDTS2MIF and either MapScan or OziExplorer to convert your MIF files to shapefiles, you can skip ahead to Step 5.

Global Mapper is a nice alternative to Steps 2 through 4 above. A free demo is available at **www.globalmapper.com.** To export the converted data, though, you need the registered version ($219). Global Mapper's Web site states, however, "If you are interested in the export functionality of Global Mapper, but would like to test drive the features before you make a purchase, we can provide you with a demo that does just that. Just contact us and we'll do our best to accommodate you." For the purpose of this tutorial, we'll assume that you have the fully functional version, allowing export.

1. Start Global Mapper and select **File,** then **Open Data File(s).**

2. Find the **DLG Files** folder; click the HY layer **1174518.HY.sdts.tar.gz.** and **Open.** Streams, springs, and waterfalls will appear on the map as shown in Figure 24N. If you were trying to construct a map from multiple quads, you could select all HY layers for the various quads, extracting and converting them all in one operation.

3. Select **Tools,** then **Configure** to open the **Configuration** dialog box.

4. Choose the **Vector Display** tab. As shown in Figure 24O, in the **Render** section, select **Lines,** making sure that the check boxes for **Area** and **Points** are cleared. This is because streams are shown as lines, and are not represented by areas or points.

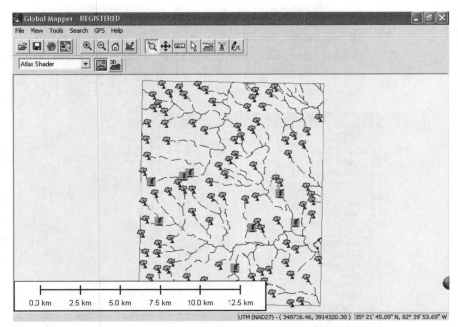

Figure 24N

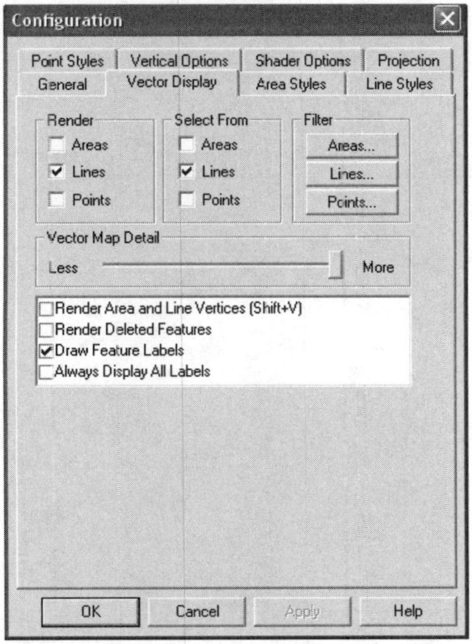

Figure 24O

5. In the **Filter** section, select **Lines** to open the **Feature Filter** dialog box. Click **Clear All**, then select **Stream**, as shown in Figure 24P. Now click **OK** to close the **Feature Filter** dialog box. Click **OK** to close the **Configuration** dialog box. The intermittent streams, waterfalls, and springs will all disappear from the screen, leaving only the year-round streams, as shown in Figure 24Q.

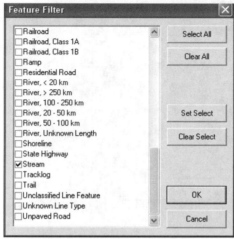

Figure 24P

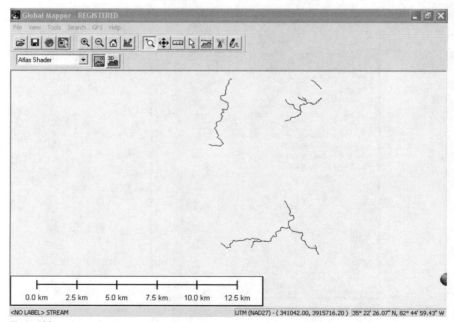

Figure 24Q

6. Now select **File**, then **Export Vector Data**, and choose **Export Shapefile.** (If this is the first time you've used Global Mapper, a **Tip** dialog box may appear with information about changing projections. Don't make any changes to your projection at this point.) This will open the **Shapefile Export Options** dialog box shown in Figure 24R. On the **File Selection** tab, click **Export Lines.**

7. Let's find a good place to store the generated data, separate from our DLG files. Create a project folder on the desktop named **Shining Rock.** Save the file using the name **Water–Streams**, and click **Save**, then click **OK** to close the **Shapefile Export Options** dialog box.

8. Now we just do the above for different types of features:

• Repeat Steps 3 through 7. When you get to Step 5, though, this time select **Intermittent Stream or River.** Export the shapefile as lines, and save it as **Water– Intermittent.** Your map should now look like the screen in Figure 24S.

• Try it again, with Steps 3 through 7, but this time select all the **River** types. When you get to the end of the process, you'll see the dialog box shown in Figure 24T, letting you know there are no features of that type in the dataset.

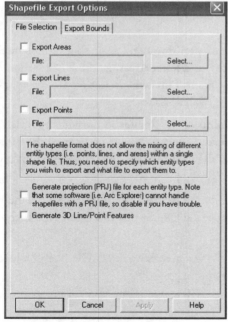

Figure 24R

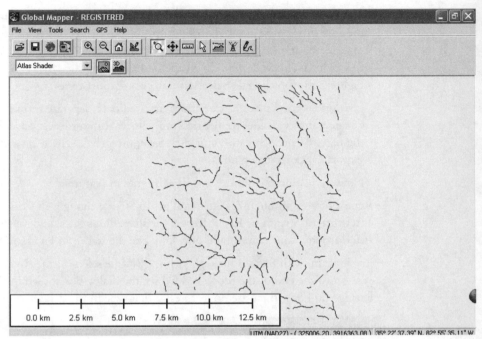

Figure 24S

- You aren't done yet. Repeat Steps 3 through 7 again, but in Step 4, change the **Render** section to clear **Lines**, and select **Areas**. In the **Filter** section click **Areas**, and check all the **Lakes** options. A small line will appear on the screen; export it as an **Area** type with the file name **Water–Lakes**.

- Now let's switch and use **Points** in the **Render** section in Step 4. In the **Filter** section click **Points**, and check **Stream Origins**. (Whoa! Look at all the springs! Don't worry; they won't look like that on the final map.) Export this as a **Point** type with the file name **Water–Springs**.

- One more time: Use **Points** in the **Render** section in Step 4. In the **Filter** section click **Points**, and check **Waterfalls**. Export this as a **Point** type with the file name **Water–Waterfalls**.

9. We're finally done with the water layer, so select **File**, then **Unload All**.

> **TIP:** Now you might ask, how did I know what those BD line types were? I didn't. I just tried different line types that might represent boundaries until something appeared on the screen. I compared those to a quad map of the area (easily done with many of the mapping programs discussed in earlier chapters), and figured out what those lines represent.

10. Repeat Steps 1 through 9 with the boundaries (BD), hypsography (HP), and transportation (RD, MT, and RR) layers. Let's look at each of these layers:

• BD–**Filter Lines** and choose **Unclassified Line Feature**. Export as a **Line** file named **Boundaries–National Park**. Now **Filter Lines** again and select **Unknown Line Type**. Export this as a **Line** file named **Boundaries–Wilderness**. Don't forget to click **File** and **Unload All** when finished with the BD layer and each of the following ones.

• HP–**Filter Lines** and choose **Contour Line, Minor**. **Export** as a **Line** file named **Topo–Contours Minor**. Do the same for **Intermediate** and **Major Contours**. Now switch to **Points** in the **Render** section and **Filter Points**. Choose **Spot Elevations** and export this as a **Point** file named **Topo – Summits**.

• RD – Filter **Lines** and choose **Major/US Highway**. Export as a **Line** file named **Roads –US Highway**. Save **Arterial Roads** as **Roads–BRPkwy** (Blue Ridge Parkway). Continue with **Collector Roads**, **Residential Roads**, and **Trails**. Save each of them with the Roads prefix.

• RR– There are no railroads features, so you can skip this.

• MT– Filter **Lines** and choose **Powerlines**. Export it as a **Line** file named **Misc–Power Lines**.

11. Before leaving this layer, let's go back and take a quick look at the projection information. Select **File**, then **Open Data File(s)**, and load any of the .gz files we've been working with. Now select **Tools**, then **Configure**, and choose the **Projection** tab. As seen in Figure 24U, the data we have been working with is in **UTM** projection (**Zone** 17) and **NAD27 CONUS** datum.

Congratulations! You are now ready to move your shapefiles into your GPS.

Figure 24T

NOTE: Shapefiles that have been converted from SDTS or DLG-O data will always have a UTM position format and a NAD27 CONUS datum. If you don't know the Grid Zone, a good resource is available at **www.dmap.co.uk/utmworld.htm**.

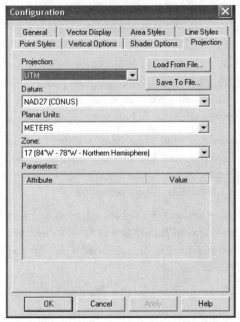

Figure 24U

Updates to this book will be posted at www.MakeYourOwnMaps.com. Bookmark and visit often to see what's new in the world of digital mapping.

Chapter 25 Make Your Own Maps: Transferring Custom Vector Maps to Your GPS

In the last chapter we looked at how to acquire map data, and how to extract and convert it into a format we can use. Now that you have the data, we're going to look at how to transfer it to your GPS. Different approaches are required, depending upon your GPS make and model. I'll show you how to use this data in Garmin, Magellan, and Lowrance receivers, three major brands of GPS receivers in the U.S.

> **DISCLAIMER** Some of what we'll be looking at is reverse-engineered software that could theoretically kill your GPS. Having said that, a lot of people are using it without problems. If you have qualms, check out the appropriate Yahoo discussion groups. You may feel more comfortable once you see the discussions taking place there.

Internet Resources
As we go along in this chapter, I'll list specific resources for each of the major brands of GPS. While it tends to focus a little more on Garmin, a good general resource and excellent discussion board is found at **groups.yahoo.com/group/map_authors**.

Transferring Custom Maps to Lowrance Receivers
There is no way to transfer shapefiles directly to the current version of MapCreate, or more recent GPS units such as the iFinder series, but we'll look at a good alternative shortly. Readers with compatible units and the earlier Lowrance MapCreate version 4 have the option of using OziMC to create their own maps. (OziMC is an OziExplorer add-on found at **www.oziexplorer.com**. Click the **Utilities** link, where OziMC is listed.)

Internet Resources
Here are some additional Web sites to help you get started with OziMC:

• **www.gpsnuts.com/Ozi/OziMCJohnG/vector.html**

• **www.gpsnuts.com/myGPS/GPS/Software%20reviews/OziMC/ozimc.htm**

For those working with later versions of MapCreate, the Yahoo iFinder group is one of the best resources available: **groups.yahoo.com/group/ifinder_gps**.

Customizing Lowrance with Tracks

You can't import vector data directly into the newer versions of MapCreate, but you can convert it to tracks (see Using OziExplorer to Convert Shapefiles and Tracks in Chapter 24) and import those tracks into your GPS map.

Consider, for example, the Lowrance iFinder. Maps for the iFinder can be customized extensively, since it is capable of holding 100 tracks and 10,000 points per track. The iFinder can hold approximately 53,000 track points, depending upon how much memory waypoints, routes, and icons consume. Once you move the tracks into your GPS, you can customize the display style of individual tracks. Furthermore, each of the 100 tracks can have its own custom style when displayed in your GPS. (John Galvin deserves credit for this excellent tip.)

I find OziExplorer to be a convenient vehicle for preparing maps for Lowrance products. As discussed in the previous chapter, it can import shapefiles and .mif files and convert them to tracks. It also has extensive track editing capabilities. Once the data is converted, Ozi can export it as Lowrance .usr files.

Transferring Custom Maps to Magellan Receivers

Magellan owners are fortunate to have a free Magellan product designed to accommodate shapefiles and .mif files. Thales Navigation, the parent company of Magellan, has a professional product called MobileMapper Office (MMO). Some curious Magellan users have discovered that MMO, which was designed for the company's high-end survey-grade GPS units, also works on Meridian and SporTrack receivers.

Internet Resources

Here are some good resources for Magellan owners:

- **groups.yahoo.com/group/mobilemapper2**. This group has excellent information in its Links and Files sections.

- **www.msh-tools.com**. This site has a number of utilities you might find helpful, including the converter for versions of MMO beyond 1.0 (MMOconverter).

> Updates to this book will be posted at www.MakeYourOwnMaps.com.
> Bookmark and visit often to see what's new in the world of digital mapping.

The original Yahoo MobileMapper group disappeared from the Internet on February 8, 2005, and was replaced with the MobileMapper2 group a few days later. This may have been due to issues associated with copyright infringement, but it does not seem to be due to the use of MMO.

In the course of researching this book, a Magellan staff person told me that "the Mobile Mapper license is for single end use—which means the buyer can use it to make maps for themselves (or to use in their business) but not to make maps for redistribution to the public. It's also important for people to understand that it's a potential copyright infringement on our map data suppliers if people use our MapSend products in Mobile Mapper in such as way as to derive map content from the MapSend product—e.g., tracing the roads, duplicating the points of interest, etc."

At press time, MMO version 2.6 was available on the Thales Navigation ftp site. This is a fluid situation and updates regarding MMO will be posted at www.MakeYourOwnMaps.com.

Though the directions in the Magellan section of this chapter focus on MMO 1.0, users of later versions must go through an additional conversion step in order to upload maps to their GPS units. A utility to do this is available at **http://www.msh-tools.com/mmoconverter.html**.

Using MobileMapper Office

While several different versions of MMO are available, we'll focus on version 1.0 because later versions require an additional conversion step using another utility. Be aware, though, that version 1.0 accepts data only in WGS84 datum and latitude/longitude projection.

If your data is not in WGS84 and lat/lon, you can use OziExplorer (see Chapter 15) to convert shapefiles or .mif files to the correct format:

1. Start OziExplorer and select **Map**, then **Blank map (Auto Scale)**.

2. Select **Load**. At this point you can do one of two things—(a) point to **Import** and then click from **MapInfo MIF Files** or (b) point to **Import ESRI Shape File** and choose the type of file to import.

3. Click **Save**, point to **Export to ESRI Shape File**, and choose the type of file to export.

4. Name the file and a **Shape File Import/Export Options** dialog box will open. Select WGS84 for **Datum** and Lat/Lon for **Position Format** and click **OK**.

Now that your data is in the proper format, let's get started with MobileMapper Office. To start, download and install a copy of MMO version 1.0. (At publication time, a link was posted at **groups.yahoo.com/group/mobilemapper/links**.)

Once you do that, we're ready to start.

TIP: MMO version 2.6 is available at **ftp://ftp.thalesnavigation.com/software**. To download, drag the MMO folder to your desktop.

Use the procedure below to create a base map of your own and transfer it to your GPS.

1. Start MobileMapper Office.

2. Select **Tools**, then **Background Maps** to open the dialog box shown in Figure 25A.

Figure 25A

3. Select **Create New** to open the dialog box shown in Figure 25B. To make a later exercise a little clearer, leave the **Map Name** field as it is, showing "NewMap." Typically, you would enter a name for your map here.

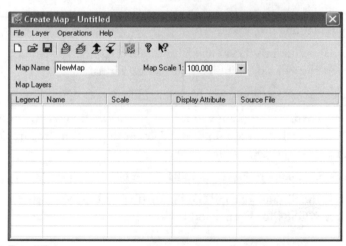

Figure 25B

4. In the **Map Scale** field, enter a scale above which the map will not be shown on the GPS or on your computer screen.

5. Click **Add layers.** In the **Files of Type** area, notice that you can import shapefiles (.shp), MapInfo files (.mif), or AutoCAD files (.dxf). As you do more mapping, you'll appreciate this flexibility. Continue adding as many layers as you wish.

6. Select **File**, then **Save**, using the default name NewMap once again.

7. Click **Create Map**. Close the dialog box.

8. This will open the dialog box shown in Figure 25C. Click **Close**.

Figure 25C

Uploading MMO Maps to Your GPS
Uploading MMO maps works very much like it does in MapSend:

• Click **Create Map Region** and drag a rectangle around the area to be exported. Right-click when you're finished.

• Click the drop-down arrow beside **Upload Job**.

• Now select **Upload Background Map.** This will open a dialog box in which you will be given a choice of sending the map to your GPS, an SD card, or your hard disk.

Transferring Custom Maps to Garmin Receivers
The following process works with Garmin receivers capable of loading MapSource maps.

Making your own maps often involves juggling a handful of programs and utilities. We'll discuss the following software in this section:

• cGPSmapper

• GPSMapEdit

• SendMap

• GPS Map Manager

Internet Resources

Here are a few links to Web sites that focus on this exciting topic:

• The excellent discussion board at **groups.yahoo.com/group/map_authors**

• **www.travelbygps.com/authoring.php**

• **www.keenpeople.com** (check out the GPS and Cartography section)

• **rwsmaps.griffel.se**

Step 1: Converting to the Polish Format with GPSMapEdit and cGPSMapper

A few years ago, an enterprising Polish gentleman named Stanislaw Kozicki managed to "reverse engineer" Garmin's MapSource product, making it possible to make your own maps for a compatible Garmin GPS. Without his efforts and those of many others, we would not be discussing this topic.

Let's get started:

1. First, download MapEdit from **www.geopainting.com/en**.

2. Now you are going to need something called a blank base map. I got my first one from Richard Smith's Web site, **rwsmaps.griffel.se**. Near the bottom of the page is a link to a tutorial on making 1:24K maps for compatible Garmin GPS receivers. If you download the .zip file, you'll find a text file named "How to Create 24K Topo Maps." This contains a sample blank base map file. The file below looks similar but has been modified somewhat. In the interest of saving you from retyping, the text below will be posted on this book's companion Web site, **www.MakeYourOwnMaps.com**. (If you want to delve deeper, the syntax for this file is discussed at **plrecgps.pp.org.pl/bin/view/GPS/PFMsyntaxDescr**.)

```
[IMG ID]
ID=12345678
Name=Shining Rock
Preprocess=F
TreSize=2000
```

```
TreMargin=0.02000
RgnLimit=1024
POIIndex=N
Levels=4
Level0=23
Level1=21
Level2=20
Level3=18
Zoom0=0
Zoom1=1
Zoom2=2
Zoom3=3
[END-IMG ID]

[RGN10]
Type=0x660e
Label=Place Holder
Levels=3
Origin0=(35.37000,-82.88000)
[END-RGN10]

[RGN10]
Type=0x660e
Label=Place Holder
Levels=3
Origin0=(35.24700,-82.74500)
[END-RGN10]
```

Start a text editor such as WordPad or NotePad. These are often found in the Windows Accessories folder. Paste the text of the template into a blank document and save it as **Blank Base Map Shining Rock.txt.**

3. Start MapEdit, select **File**, choose **Open**, and load the blank base map you just created. We need this to start with since MapEdit will not allow us to work with a completely blank map.

Here the steps diverge, with the path you take depending on whether you used Global Mapper or SDTS2MIF and OziExplorer. If you used the latter process, skip ahead to "Converting Shapefiles Derived from SDTS2MIF and OziExplorer." Global Mapper users, read on.

Step 1A: Converting Shapefiles Derived from Global Mapper

1. Choose **File**, point to **Import**, and select **ESRI Shape (*.shp)**. Find your **Shining Rock** folder, and load **Topo–Contours Major.shp**.

2. In the **Import** dialog box, scroll down and select **Major land contour**, as shown in Figure 25D. Click **Next**.

3. Select the header labeled **Elevation**, as shown in Figure 25E. Click **Next**.

Feature Labels

Figure 25E shows us selecting a column, which will determine which labels are placed on the map. We selected a label header here for major elevation contours, because we want those contours labeled. Not all items require or deserve a label; too many clutter the map.

---

4. Remember our last step in Global Mapper? On the next screen, change the **Coordinate system** to UTM, the **Zone** to 17, and the **Datum** to NAD27 CONUS. Click **Next**.

5. On the next screen, check all three levels and click **Finish**.

Zoom Levels

Maps for Garmin GPS units have several zoom levels. Three visible levels (one additional level is blank) is a good choice for most maps. At Level 0, the most detailed, you might want 40-foot contour intervals. Level 1 is intermediate; Level 2 has the least detail. Major features, such as major contour lines and highways, are typically shown at all levels.

---

6. Your screen should now look like the one in Figure 25F. See the placeholders near the northwest and southeast corners of the map? These artifacts from the blank map are placed just outside the image, at the longitude and latitude specified near the end of your blank base map text file as Origin0.

7. Click **Select Objects**, then select a placeholder. Press the DELETE key. Repeat to delete the other placeholder.

8. Now repeat Steps 1 through 5, importing **Topo–Contours Intermediate**. Select **Intermediate land contour** but, this time, don't click on a column header for labeling. Choose levels 0 and 1. If you get a warning message like the one shown in Figure 25G, select **Yes** to apply the action.

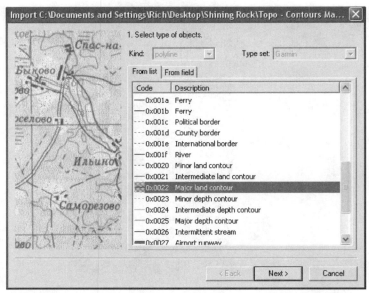

Figure 25D

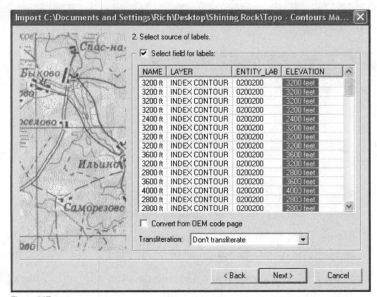

Figure 25E

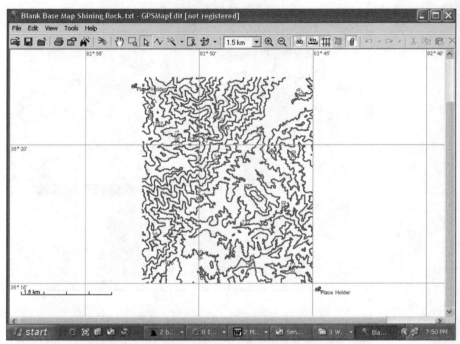

Figure 25F

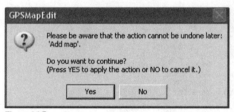

Figure 25G

9. Repeat Steps 1 through 5 again for the minor contours, choosing the appropriate category. Don't click a label column header, and choose level 0.

10. Repeat Steps 1 through 5 once more for **Summits** and choose the appropriate category. Select the **Elevation** label header and choose levels 0 and 1.

11. Select **File**, then **Save As** and save the document in your **Shining Rock** folder as **Topo.mp**. Then select **File** and **Close**.

Repeat this process with the other layers:

- Load the blank base map, import both **Boundaries** files, and (for lack of a better choice) use **Political border.** Don't use a label, and choose all three levels. Let's import **Misc–Powerlines** too, placing it at levels 0 and 1. Remember to delete the placeholders. Save this file as **Misc.mp** and then close the file.

- Do it again, this time with the **Roads** layer. **US Highways** are obviously major highways. Let's label it with ROUTE_NUMB and put it in all three levels. For **Roads– BRPkwy**, choose **Other Highway**. Note that there is no appropriate label. Put it in all three levels. For **Roads–Collector** choose **Arterial thin**, no labels, and all three levels. For **Roads–Residential**, use no labels and place only on level 0. Place **Trails** on level 0. Save the layer as **Roads.mp**.

- Finally, do the hydrology layer. Import **Streams** without labels and place on all three levels. Import **Lakes** as **Small lake** and place on all three levels. Import **Springs** and **Intermittent Streams** into layer 0 only. Import **Waterfalls** into levels 1 and 0. Save the layer as **Water.mp**.

- Select **File**, then **Open**, and select all four files—**Topo**, **Water**, **Roads**, and **Misc**. Now select **File**, then **Save As**, and save the file as **Shining Rock.mp**.

Step 1B: Converting Shapefiles Derived from SDTS2MIF and OziExplorer
This is where life becomes a little simpler. While you won't have quite the degree of control available to those using Global Mapper, the following steps definitely take less time.

1. Select **File**, point to **Import**, and choose **ESRI Shape (*.shp)**. Find your **DLG Files** folder and load **HP01.shp**.

2. In the **Import** dialog box, scroll down and select **Intermediate land contour**. Click **Next**, then click **Next** again.

3. On the next screen, make sure the **Coordinate system** is UTM, the **Zone 17**, and the **Datum** is **NAD27 CONUS**. Click **Next**.

4. On the next screen, check levels 0 and 1 and click **Finish**. For more information on this step, read "Zoom Levels" earlier in this section.

5. Your screen should now look like the one shown in Figure 25H. See the placeholders near the northwest and southeast corners of the map? These artifacts from the blank map are placed just outside the image, at the longitude and latitude specified near the end of your blank base map text file as Origin0.

6. Click **Select Objects**, then select a placeholder. Now press your DELETE key. Repeat to delete the other placeholder.

7. Click **File**, point to **Import**, and click **ESRI Shape (*.shp)**. Find your **DLG Files** folder, and load **HPPOINTS.shp**.

8. In the **Import** dialog box, scroll down and select **Summit**. Click **Next**, then **Next** again.

9. Repeat Steps 6 and 7. If you get a warning message like the one shown in Figure 25G, click **Yes** to apply the action.

10. Select **File**, then **Save As** and save the document in your **DLG Files** folder as **Topo.mp**. Then select **File** and **Close**.

Repeat this process with the other layers:

- Load the blank base map, import **BD01.shp,** and (for lack of a better choice) use **Political border**. Choose all three levels. Remember to delete the placeholders. Save this file as **Boundaries.mp** and then close the file.

- Do it again, this time with the hydrology layer. Import **HY01** as **Streams** and place on all three levels. Save the layer as **Water.mp**.

- Import **MT01** as **Power line** and place on levels 0 and 1. Save as **Misc.mp**.

- Finally, do the **RD01** layer as **Arterial roads, thin** and place them on all three levels. Save the layer as **Roads.mp**.

- Select **File**, then **Open**, and select all five files—**Misc**, **Topo**, **Water**, **Roads**, and **Boundaries**. Now select **File**, then **Save As,** and save the file as **Shining Rock.mp**.

Step 2: Compile the MapSource .img file

1. Download cGPSmapper from **gps.chrisb.org/en/download.htm**. (You'll sometimes see this program listed as GPSmapper without the c as a prefix.)

2. Create a folder in your Program Files directory called **GPSmapper** and unzip the downloaded GPSmapper zip file to it.

3. Now go back to GPSMapEdit and make sure that the composite file **ShiningRock.mp** is loaded. Select **File**, point to **Export**, and choose **Garmin IMG/cgpsmapper.exe**. Navigate to the **GPSmapper** directory and save the file as **12345678.img**. This is the ID number from our blank base map file. Each map you produce must have a unique eight-number ID associated with it. If you go on to make your own maps, be sure to change this when you put in coordinates for new placeholders.

4. In the **Export to cGPSmapper.exe** dialog box, click **GPSmapper Browse** and select **cGPSmapper.exe** in the **GPSmapper** directory, as shown in Figure 25I. Click **Open**, then click **Run**. This may take several minutes. When it's done, you'll see a dialog box like the one in Figure 25J. Click **OK**, then **Close**. The new **12345678.img** is found in the GPSmapper directory.

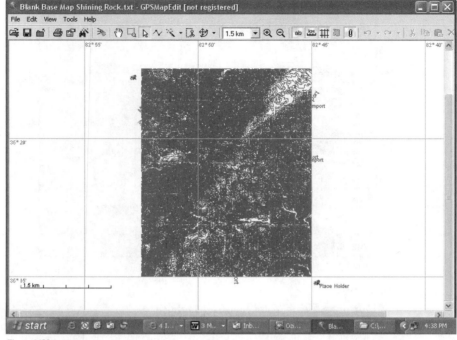

Figure 25H

Figure 25I

Step 3: Transferring the Map to Your Garmin GPS

The free program SendMap makes it incredibly simple to send maps to your Garmin GPS. Download version 2.0 from **gps.chrisb.org/en/download.htm** and install it directly to you desktop. Connect your GPS to your computer, turn it on, and drag any .img file (or copy of an .img file) you create onto the SendMap icon. That's it— a refreshingly simple step to end a complex process.

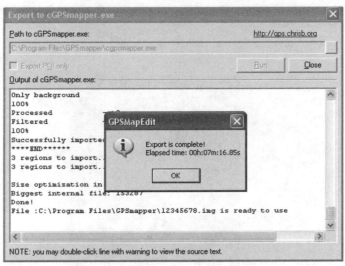

Figure 25J

Optional: Using Your Map in MapSource

Though you can easily load your map into your GPS now, we're going to look at how to get it into MapSource. This procedure will allow you to load multiple maps into your GPS.

To view and use your maps within MapSource, we're going to trick it into thinking you have a new MapSource product called My Maps. We'll have to use another text file to do this. Once again, I'm using a modified version of one posted on Richard Smith's Web site (**rwsmaps.griffel.se**) as part of his "How to Create 24K Topo Maps" tutorial—also known as the Crater Lake tutorial. To save you from retyping the file, it will be posted at this book's companion Web site, **www.makeyourownmaps.com**.

```
;Sample file accepted by cGPSmap to create new map data-set
;
;In order to create new TDB and preview map file run cGPSmap :
;cGPSmap pv test_pr.txt
;
;
;FileName      = file name for new IMG and TDB files, no more than 8
;                characters must be without extension!
;
;MapVersion    = map version, must be between 100 and 999
;
;ProductCode   = unique product ID, each GARMIN product has its ID number
```

```
;                   I suggest to use values above 40, but I cannot
;                   guarantee that those values are not used!
;                   You can check products id in windows registry
;                   under path:
;
HKEY_LOCAL_MACHINE\Software\Garmin\MapSource\Products
;
;MapSetName      = map name in GPS
;
;Copy1,Copy2     = copyrights info
;
;MapsourceName = map name in MapSource programm
;
;CDSetName       = CD set name - visible in MapSource menu
;
;
;After you create new MapSet, you can install it into MapSource
adding new entry into
;HKEY_LOCAL_MACHINE\Software\Garmin\MapSource\Products
;with your product ID
;then create 3 strings:
;
;Loc    path to your IMG files
;Bmap   file name with full path to the preview IMG created by cGPSmap
;Tdb    file name with full path to the TDB file created by cGPSmap

[Map]
FileName=BaseMap

MapVersion=100

ProductCode=900

Levels=2
Level0=18
Level1=17

Zoom0=6
Zoom1=7

MapsourceName=My Maps
MapSetName=My Maps
CDSetName=My Maps
Copy1=Compiled from data provided by the USGS
[End-Map]


;
;IMG files to be included in new map-set
;!!REMEMBER to fix the path to IMG file!!
;
[Files]
img=12345678.img
[END-Files]
```

Figure 25K

1. Using a text editor, save the above file to the **GPSmapper** directory as **MyMaps_pv.txt**.

2. Make sure that the file, **12345678.img**, is in the GPSmapper directory.

3. Open a command prompt window. This option is typically found in Windows'
   Accessories menu.

   • Type **cd..** and press ENTER to move up in the directory structure. Repeat as
   necessary until you are in the directory that contains your **Program Files**. For
   most people this is the C: directory.

   • Once you get to the C: directory, type **dir/w**. Your command prompt window
   should look something like the one shown in Figure 25K. Press ENTER.

   • You will now see a list of the folders in your C: directory. Type **cd Program Files**,
   assuming that is the name of the programs folder shown in the directory. Press
   ENTER. Now type **dir/w** again and press ENTER.

   • Type **cd GPSmapper** and press ENTER.

   • Type **cgpsmapper pvx MyMaps_pv.txt** and press ENTER.

   • You should now have two new files in your GPSmapper directory, **BaseMap.img**
   and **BaseMap.tdb**.

4. Download GPS Map Manager, available from **vip.hyperusa.com/~dougs/GPSSM**,
   to your desktop.

5. Unzip the downloaded files to a folder on your desktop.

6. Create a folder in your **Program Files** named **GPS Map Manager**.

Figure 25L

7. Run the **setup.exe** file from your desktop. When prompted, have it installed to the **GPS Map Manager** folder in your **Program Files** directory.

8. Start **GPS Map Manager** and click **Create**. Use the **Browse** buttons to locate the new **BaseMap.img** and **BaseMap.tdb** files. The UGPID is 900, the product code in the MyMaps_pv.txt file.

9. Select **Create Installable Map**, and the **GPS Map Creator** dialog box should appear as the one in Figure 25L.

10. Now click **Import Maps** and, in the **Import Complete** box, click **OK**, then **Close**.

11. In the **GPS Map Manager** dialog box, select **900** and then click **Export**, as shown in Figure 25M.

12. Select **900** by placing a check mark next to it, as shown in Figure 25N. Click **Export**.

13. In the **Export Complete** dialog box, click **OK**.

14. Finally, using **Windows Explorer** or **My Computer**, go to the **GPSmapper** directory and right-click **12345678.img**, then click **Copy**. Locate the **GPS Map Manager** directory and right-click it, then choose **Paste** to send the copy of **12345678.img** to the directory.

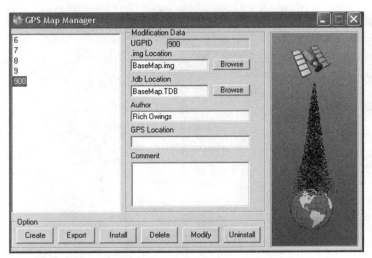

Figure 25M

Figure 25N

Now open **MapSource** and, in the **Product List**, select **My Maps**. The **Shining Rock** quad will appear ready for export.

Figure 25O shows a "preview" MapSource map created using Global Mapper, while Figure 25P shows a preview map of the same area created using SDTS2MIF and OziExplorer.

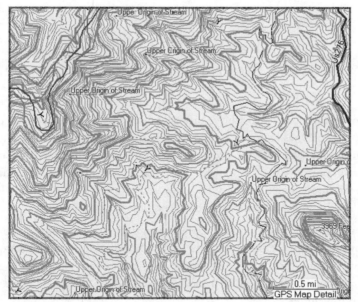

Figure 25O

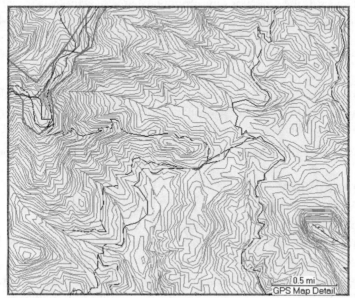

Figure 25P

Chapter 26 Transferring Data
Between Programs: Utilities and Compatibility

If you've made it this far, you've probably discovered that no program does everything and that each has its strengths and weaknesses. For these reasons, many mappers end up using multiple software programs. Unfortunately, this means that at some point you will probably need to transfer data between programs. Complicating matters is the fact that most programs and GPS units use proprietary file formats. There are four major ways to get around this and successfully transfer your data:

- Transfer data through a GPS. Upload data from one program to your GPS and then download it to the other program. The only major problems here are that (1) you can run into limits on the amount of data that can be transferred (e.g., the number of waypoints, tracks getting truncated, etc.) and (2) you have to deal with cables and desktop clutter.

- Transfer data directly between programs that allow the import or export of various file types. If the programs can accommodate the file types you're working with, the only hassle is navigating program folders to find the data. The File Management section of most chapters describes the file formats and where data is stored. This all-too-infrequent option is great when available.

- Export data to a text file (.txt), a comma-separated value file (.csv) or an Excel spreadsheet (.xls). The idea is to manipulate the data in such a way that it can be read by another program. If you're comfortable doing this, it lets you move data that could not otherwise be transferred between certain programs.

- Use a utility that converts the data for you. We'll look at two free ones shortly.

Compatibility
At the end of this chapter, tables 1 and 2 show what types of files can be imported and exported by the major programs discussed in this book. Below each program name are the file types that program can import and export. The tables are divided into sections for waypoints, tracks, routes, maps/images, and other.

Please note that some formats used by multiple manufacturers (including .txt, .wpt, .trk, and .rte) tend to be proprietary; the data usually cannot be shared directly between programs.

G7toWin

This utility, created by Ron Henderson, is available free from **www.gpsinformation. org/ronh**. The site offers an interesting story about how the software got its cumbersome name.

Figure 26A shows the main window for the program. To import a file for conversion, select **File**, then **Open**. Use the **Files of type** drop-down menu to select the type of file to import. To convert and export, select **File**, then **Save As**. Use the **Save as type** drop-down menu to select the file type for export. Don't forget to name the file.

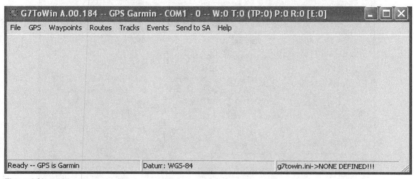

Figure 26A

In addition to converting data, G7ToWin can transfer data to and from your GPS, and perform a number of valuable functions. Let's look at some options you should be aware of:

• Select **File**, then **Configuration**. There are six tabs but, unless you use DeLorme's Street Atlas, you'll need to concern yourself with only two. The contents of the **General** tab are shown in Figure 26B. Click **Help** at the bottom of this tab, opening the help screen that shows the **Configuration** dialog box. Click anywhere in this help screen for context-sensitive help.

• Select **Waypoints** to display the menu shown in Figure 26C. Anyone moving waypoints between programs will eventually run into duplicate waypoints. This menu offers some excellent tools for cleaning up waypoint files.

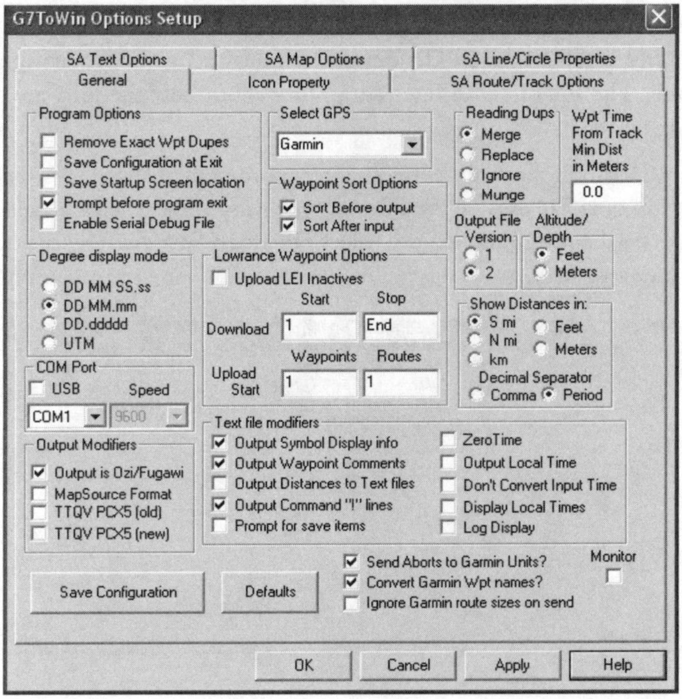

G7ToWin Options Setup

SA Text Options | SA Map Options | SA Line/Circle Properties

General | Icon Property | SA Route/Track Options

Program Options
- ☐ Remove Exact Wpt Dupes
- ☐ Save Configuration at Exit
- ☐ Save Startup Screen location
- ☑ Prompt before program exit
- ☐ Enable Serial Debug File

Select GPS
Garmin

Waypoint Sort Options
- ☑ Sort Before output
- ☑ Sort After input

Reading Dups
- ⦿ Merge
- ○ Replace
- ○ Ignore
- ○ Munge

Wpt Time From Track Min Dist in Meters
0.0

Output File Version
- ○ 1
- ⦿ 2

Altitude/Depth
- ⦿ Feet
- ○ Meters

Degree display mode
- ○ DD MM SS.ss
- ⦿ DD MM.mm
- ○ DD.ddddd
- ○ UTM

Lowrance Waypoint Options
- ☐ Upload LEI Inactives

| | Start | Stop |
| Download | 1 | End |

| | Waypoints | Routes |
| Upload Start | 1 | 1 |

Show Distances in:
- ⦿ S mi   ○ Feet
- ○ N mi   ○ Meters
- ○ km

Decimal Separator
- ○ Comma   ⦿ Period

COM Port
- ☐ USB   Speed
- COM1   9600

Output Modifiers
- ☑ Output is Ozi/Fugawi
- ☐ MapSource Format
- ☐ TTQV PCX5 (old)
- ☐ TTQV PCX5 (new)

Text file modifiers
- ☑ Output Symbol Display info
- ☑ Output Waypoint Comments
- ☐ Output Distances to Text files
- ☑ Output Command "l" lines
- ☐ Prompt for save items

- ☐ ZeroTime
- ☐ Output Local Time
- ☐ Don't Convert Input Time
- ☐ Display Local Times
- ☐ Log Display

[Save Configuration] [Defaults]

- ☑ Send Aborts to Garmin Units?
- ☑ Convert Garmin Wpt names?
- ☐ Ignore Garmin route sizes on send

Monitor ☐

[OK] [Cancel] [Apply] [Help]

Figure 26B

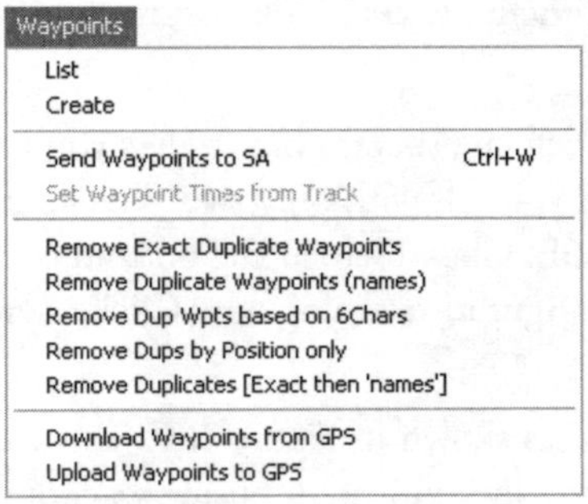

Waypoints

List
Create

Send Waypoints to SA   Ctrl+W
Set Waypoint Times from Track

Remove Exact Duplicate Waypoints
Remove Duplicate Waypoints (names)
Remove Dup Wpts based on 6Chars
Remove Dups by Position only
Remove Duplicates [Exact then 'names']

Download Waypoints from GPS
Upload Waypoints to GPS

Figure 26C

GPSBabel

GPSBabel, developed by Robert Lipe, can be downloaded at **gpsbabel.sourceforge.net**. While it's not quite as user-friendly as G7toWin, it does have some strong points. GPSBabel works on a variety of operating systems and can be run from a command prompt or through a Windows interface. The **Documentation** link on the Web site has useful information on file formats. The **Mailing Lists** link gives access to the archives of an active discussion board.

> **TIP:** Both utilities can upload data to, and download data from, your GPS. G7toWin is compatible with Garmin, Magellan, and older Lowrance/Eagle units. GPSBabel can transfer Garmin and Magellan data, including data stored on Magellan SD cards. It can also transfer data to and from MapSend and MapSource.

Other Utilities

There are many other utilities available for more specialized purposes. Check the discussion boards for your software or GPS. In Yahoo groups, check the links and files sections.

Table 1. The following programs can import the types of files listed below them.

Waypoints / Format	3-D Topo Quads	Easy GPS	Expert GPS	Fugawi GPS Mapping Software	G7to Win	GPS Babel	Map Create	Map Send Topo in the US
Proprietary				.wpt (Fugawi)	.wpt (Ozi)			.wpt (MapSend)
Garmin PCX				.wpt (pcx)		.pcx		
Text	.txt			.txt		.txt (Fugawi)		
WP+								
Excel								.xls
TopoGrafix		.gpx	.gpx		.gpx	.gpx		
Geocaching.com		.loc	.loc		.loc	.loc		
Terrain Navigator			.mxf		.mxf			
TOPO!						.tpg		
Fugawi					.fwp			
MapSource								
Holux						.wpo		
MS Streets & Trips								

Table 1, continued. The following programs can import the types of files listed below them.

Waypoints / Format	Map Source US Topo	Ozi Explorer	Terrain Navigator	Terrain Navigator Pro	TOPO!	Topo Fusion	Topo USA	USA Photo Maps
Proprietary	.wpt (Ozi and MapSend)							
Garmin PCX	.wpt (pcx)							
Text		.txt			.txt	.txt (DeLorme)	.txt	
WP+		.txt						
Excel								
TopoGrafix						.gpx		.gpx
Geocaching.com								
Terrain Navigator				.mxf, .mtf	.mxf, .mtf		.mxf	
TOPO!								
Fugawi								
MapSource		.mps						
Holux	.wrt							
MS Streets & Trips								.psp

Tracks	Format	3-D Topo Quads	Easy GPS	Expert GPS	Fugawi GPS Mapping Software	G7to Win	GPS Babel	Map Create	Map Send Topo in the US
	Text				.txt				
	Proprietary				.trk Fugawi (2 or 3)	.trk (Fugawi)			.trk
	Garmin pcx						.pcx		
	Excel								.xls
	TopoGrafix			.gpx		.gpx	.gpx		
	OziExplorer					.plt			
	Terrain Navigator			.txf		.txf			
	MapSource								
	IGC					.igc	.igc		

Tracks	Format	Map Source US Topo	Ozi Explorer	Terrain Navigator	Terrain Navigator Pro	TOPO!	Topo Fusion	Topo USA	USA Photo Maps
	Text		.txt						
	Proprietary	.trk	.trk (Map Send & Compe GPS)						
	Garmin pcx								
	Excel								
	TopoGrafix						.gpx		.gpx
	OziExplorer		.plt						
	Terrain Navigator				.txf	.txf		.txf	
	MapSource								
	IGC		.igc						

Table 1, continued. The following programs can import the types of files listed below them.

Routes Format	3-D Topo Quads	Easy GPS	Expert GPS	Fugawi GPS Mapping Software	G7to Win	GPS Babel	Map Create	Map Send Topo in the US
Text				.txt				
Excel								.xls
TopoGrafix		.gpx	.gpx		.gpx	.gpx		
Geocaching.com		.loc	.loc					
Ozi					.rte			
Garmin pcx								
Terrain Navigator			.rxf		.rxf			
Fugawi				.rte (Fugawi 2 or 3)				
DeLorme								
OziCE					.rt2			
IGC						.igc		

Table 1, continued. The following programs can import the types of files listed below them.

Routes Format	Map Source US Topo	Ozi Explorer	Terrain Navigator	Terrain Navigator Pro	TOPO!	Topo Fusion	Topo USA	USA Photo Maps
Text								
Excel	.xls							
TopoGrafix								
Geocaching.com								
Ozi			.rte					
Garmin pcx		.rte						
Terrain Navigator				.rxf, .mtx	.rxf, .mtx			
Fugawi								
DeLorme							.ant	
OziCE								
IGC								

Table 1, continued. The following programs can import the types of files listed below them.

Maps/Images Format	3-D Topo Quads	Easy GPS	Expert GPS	Fugawi GPS Mapping Software	G7to Win	GPS Babel	Map Create	Map Send Topo in the US
Tagged Image File Format			.tif/tfw	.tif				
NOAA				.bsb				
ChartTiff				.jpr				
SoftChart				.nos/.geo				
Maptech				.rml				
Maptech PCX				.hdr				
Maptech				.024				
Maptech				.aer				
Enhanced Compressed Wavlet				.ecw				
OziExplorer			.map					
LizardTech								
Bitmap			.bmp	.bmp	.bmp			
Joint Photographic Experts Group			.jpg/ .jpw	.jpg				
Portable Network Graphics			.png	.png				
Graphic Interchange Format				.gif				
Fugawi				.fxf, fx3, .fx4				
Military				.toc				
(CIB /CADRG)				.thf				
Military (ADRG)				.gmf				
Fugawi			GeoGrid					
World file			.pgw					
World file			.bpw					

Table 1, continued. The following programs can import the types of files listed below them.

Maps/Images	Format	Map Source US Topo	Ozi Explorer	Terrain Navigator	Terrain Navigator Pro	TOPO!	Topo Fusion	Topo USA	USA Photo Maps
	Tagged Image File Format		.tif						
	NOAA		.bsb						
	ChartTiff								
	SoftChart		.nos/.geo						
	Maptech		.rml						
	Maptech PCX		.hdr						
	Maptech		.024						
	Maptech		.aer						
	Enhanced Compressed Wavlet		.ecw						
	OziExplorer		.map						
	LizardTech		.sid						
	Bitmap		.bmp						
	Joint Photographic Experts Group		.jpg						
	Portable Network Graphics		.png						
	Graphic Interchange Format		.gif						
	Fugawi								
	Military (CIB /CADRG)								
	Military (ADRG)								
	Fugawi								
	World file								
	World file								

Table 1, continued. The following programs can import the types of files listed below them.

Other/Multiple								
Format	3-D Topo Quads	Easy GPS	Expert GPS	Fugawi GPS Mapping Software	G7to Win	GPS Babel	Map Create	Map Send Topo in the US
MapInfo								
MapGen								
ArcInfo								
GIS								
Garmin								
Garmin Forerunner Logbook					.xml			
Garmin							.usr	
Garmin			.mps					
Lowrance			.usr	.usr				
DeLorme	.ano							
DeLorme	.sa*				.sa*			
AAA	.mn*							
DeLorme	.gpl				.gpl			
DeLorme	.dmt							
DeLorme								
.csv			.csv		.csv			
TOPO!			.tpg					
TOPO!								
G7toWin					.g7t			
Ozi Event					.evt			
Gardown					.gdn			

Table 1, continued. The following programs can import the types of files listed below them.

Other/Multiple	Format	Map Source US Topo	Ozi Explorer	Terrain Navigator	Terrain Navigator Pro	TOPO!	Topo Fusion	Topo USA	USA Photo Maps
	MapInfo	.mif							
	MapGen	.dat							
	ArcInfo	.e00							
	GIS	.shp							
	Garmin	.grm	.grm						
	Garmin Forerunner Logbook								.xml
	Garmin		.gdb						
	Garmin		.mps						
	Lowrance		.usr						
	DeLorme							.ano	
	DeLorme							.sa*	
	AAA							.mn*	
	DeLorme							.gpl	
	DeLorme							.dmt	
	DeLorme							.an1	
	.csv			.csv	.csv				
	TOPO!					.tpg			
	TOPO!					.tpo			
	G7toWin					.g7t			
	Ozi Event								
	Gardown								

Waypoints

Format	3-D Topo Quads	Easy GPS	Expert GPS	Fugawi GPS Mapping Software	G7to Win	GPS Babel	Map Create	Map Send Topo in the US
Proprietary								.wpt
Text	.txt			.txt	.wpt (Ozi)	.txt (Fug)		.txt
Waypoint+								
Excel				.xls				.xls
TopoGrafix		.gpx	.gpx		.gpx	.gpx		
Geocaching.com		.loc	.loc		.loc	.loc		
Garmin Forerunner Logbook					.xml			
Garmin						.pcx		
Terrain Navigator			.mxf		.mxf	.mxf		
TOPO!						.tpg		
Lowrance				.lwr	.fwp			
Fugawi								
Holux						.wpo		
Holux								

Table 2, continued. The following programs can export the types of files listed below them.

Waypoints

Format	Map Source US Topo	Ozi Explorer	Terrain Navigator	Terrain Navigator Pro	TOPO!	Topo Fusion	Topo USA	USA Photo Maps
Proprietary			.wpt (Ozi)					
Text	txt	.txt					.txt	
Waypoint+		.txt						
Excel								
TopoGrafix								
Geocaching.com								
Garmin Forerunner Logbook								.xml
Garmin						.pcx		
Terrain Navigator				.mxf	.mxf			
TOPO!						.tpg		
Lowrance								
Fugawi								
Holux		.wrt						
Holux								

Table 2, continued. The following programs can export the types of files listed below them.

Tracks	Format	3-D Topo Quads	Easy GPS	Expert GPS	Fugawi GPS Mapping Software	G7to Win	GPS Babel	Map Create	Map Send Topo in the US
	Proprietary				.trk (Fugawi)	.trk (Fugawi)			.trk
	Text				.txt				
	Comma Separated Values					.csv			
	TopoGrafix			.txf			.gpx		
	Terrain Navigator					.txf			
	Ozi Plot					.plt			
	Holux								
	Garmin						.pcx		
	IGC								

Table 2, continued. The following programs can export the types of files listed below them.

Tracks	Format	Map Source US Topo	Ozi Explorer	Terrain Navigator	Terrain Navigator Pro	TOPO!	Topo Fusion	Topo USA	USA Photo Maps
	Proprietary		trk (Ozi)						
	Text								.csv
	Comma Separated Values								
	TopoGrafix								
	Terrain Navigator			.txf	.txf				
	Ozi Plot		.plt						
	Holux		.tlg						
	Garmin								
	IGC		.igc						

Table 2, continued. The following programs can export the types of files listed below them.

Routes	Format	3-D Topo Quads	Easy GPS	Expert GPS	Fugawi GPS Mapping Software	G7toWin	GPS Babel	Map Create	Map Send Topo in the US
	Text				.txt				
	Proprietary				.rte (Fugawi)	.rte (Ozi)			
	TopoGrafix		.gpx	.gpx		.gpx	.gpx		
	Geocaching.com		.loc	.loc		.loc			
	Terrain Navigator			.rxf		.rxf			
	DeLorme								
	Magellan								.wpt
	OziCE					.rt2			

Table 2, continued. The following programs can export the types of files listed below them.

Routes	Format	Map Source US Topo	Ozi Explorer	Terrain Navigator	Terrain Navigator Pro	TOPO!	Topo Fusion	Topo USA	USA Photo Maps
	Text								.txt
	Proprietary		.rte (Ozi)						
	TopoGrafix								
	Geocaching.com								
	Terrain Navigator			.rxf	.rxf				
	DeLorme							.anr	
	Magellan								
	OziCE								

Table 2, continued. The following programs can export the types of files listed below them.

Maps/Images Format	3-D Topo Quads	Easy GPS	Expert GPS	Fugawi GPS Mapping Software	G7to Win	GPS Babel	Map Create	Map Send Topo in the US
Joint Photographic Experts Group								
Bitmap (Garmin)					.bmp (LEI)			
Portable Network Graphics								
Tagged Image File Format								
TIF World Files								
MapInfo								
USGS								
ESRI								
CompuServe								
Adobe								
PC Paintbrush								
Garmin			.mps					
Magellan								.rgn

Table 2, continued. The following programs can export the types of files listed below them.

Maps/Images Format	Map Source US Topo	Ozi Explorer	Terrain Navigator	Terrain Navigator Pro	TOPO!	Topo Fusion	Topo USA	USA Photo Maps
Joint Photographic Experts Group			.jpg	.jpg	.jpg	.jpg		.jpg
Bitmap (Garmin)		.bmp	.bmp	.bmp	.bmp	.bmp		
Portable Network Graphics		.png						
Tagged Image File Format			.tif	.tif	.tif			
TIF World Files				.tif / .tfw				
MapInfo				.tif / .tab				
USGS				.tif / .fgd				
ESRI				.jpg / .jgw				
CompuServe					.gif			
Adobe					eps			
PC Paintbrush					.pcx			
Garmin			.mps					
Magellan		.shp						.rgn

Table 2, continued. The following programs can export the types of files listed below them.

Other/ Multiple	Format	3-D Topo Quads	Easy GPS	Expert GPS	Fugawi GPS Mapping Software	G7to Win	GPS Babel	Map Create	Map Send Topo in the US
	ESRI				.shp				
	Lowrance			.usr	.usr			.usr	
	DeLorme	.dmt							
	DeLorme								
	DeLorme					.gpl			
	AutoCAD								
	Comma Separated Values		.csv						
	TOPO!			.tpg					
	TOPO!								
	G7toWin					.g7t			
	Ozi Event					.evt			
	DeLorme					.sa*			
	Gardown					.gdn			

Table 2, continued. The following programs can export the types of files listed below them.

Other/ Multiple	Format	Map Source US Topo	Ozi Explorer	Terrain Navigator	Terrain Navigator Pro	TOPO!	Topo Fusion	Topo USA	USA Photo Maps
	ESRI								
	Lowrance		.usr						
	DeLorme							.dmt	
	DeLorme							.an1	
	DeLorme					.gpl		.gpl	
	AutoCAD	.dxf							
	Comma Separated Values								
	TOPO!					.tpg			
	TOPO!					.tpo			
	G7toWin								
	Ozi Event								
	DeLorme								
	Gardown								

Concluding Notes

Technology changes so fast; it's hard to say where digital mapping will lead in the future. Miniaturization, cheaper memory, and new battery technologies will undoubtedly expand what can be done in the field with a GPS unit.

I am committed to updating the material in this book regularly, bringing you news of technological change and improvements to both hardware and software. I see this first edition as a prototype likely to go through significant changes in the future. Many decisions will be based on reader feedback. What have you found useful and what was superfluous? What's missing? Please send any comments, suggestions, or corrections to **updates@makeyourownmaps.com**. And please visit our Web site (**www.makeyourownmaps.com**) frequently, to check for updated information on this exciting topic.

Finally, remember what all of this is for—to make your outdoor trips more enjoyable, help you to explore, and help you take your adventures to the next level. Digital mapping is a great tool, but time at the computer is best reserved for rainy days and dark nights. If the sun is out, grab the maps you've created and your GPS and hit the trail!

Rich Owings
March 2005

Bibliography

Egbert, R.I. and King, J.E. *The GPS Handbook: A Guide for the Outdoors.*
Burford Books, Springfield, NJ, 2003.

Hinch, S.W. *Outdoor Navigation with GPS.*
Annadel Press, Santa Rosa, CA, 2004.

Letham, L. *GPS Made Easy: Using Global Positioning Systems in the Outdoors.*
Third edition. Mountaineers Books, Seattle, WA, 2003.

Resources

Top Web Sites

www.MakeYourOwnMaps.com
The companion website to this book will be continuously updated to keep all links in the book current.

http://gpsinformation.net
The top U.S. site for GPS, put together by Jack Yeazel, Dale DePriest, and Joe Mehaffey.

www.geocaching.com
The top geocaching site in the U.S.

http://home.pacbell.net/lgalvin/drgnotes.htm
John Galvin's list of sites for downloading digital raster graphic (DRG) maps for every state in the U.S.

http://libre.redjar.org/maps
The Libre Map project, another great source for DRG maps.

http://www.dragonbbs.com/members/1117/drg.html
The "Mostly Free DRG Page," yet another source of U.S. DRG maps.

http://data.geocomm.com
The GIS Data Depot, a great source for Digital Line Graphic (DLG) and Digital Elevation Model (DEM) files.

http://mapy.mk.cvut.cz/index_e.html
A good source for scanned international maps.

https://zulu.ssc.nasa.gov/mrsid/mrsid.pl
Landsat 7 false-color satellite imagery is a lot of fun, though it doesn't offer much detail.

http://64.83.8.153/SDTS_DL_b.htm
The easiest site for downloading DEMs.

ftp://e0mss21u.ecs.nasa.gov/srtm/
This Shuttle Radar Topography Mission site offers elevation data for 80% of the earth's surface. A great starting point for constructing international topo maps.

http://edc.usgs.gov/geodata
Another source of DLG files.

Best Free Software

USAPhotoMaps
www.jdmcox.com

OziExplorer
www.oziexplorer.com

TopoFusion
www.topofusion.com

EasyGPS
www.easygps.com

Best Discussion Boards

Yahoo Map Authors
http://groups.yahoo.com/group/map_authors

Yahoo OziUsers
http://groups.yahoo.com/group/OziUsers-L

Yahoo MobileMapper
http://groups.yahoo.com/group/mobilemapper2

Yahoo MacMap (Macintosh-based GPS applications)
http://groups.yahoo.com/group/macmap

Google Groups: Sci.geo.satellite-nav
http://groups.google.com/groups?group=sci.geo.satellite-nav

Index